The Origins of Music

The Origins of Music

Carl Stumpf

Edited and Translated by

David Trippett

OXFORD
UNIVERSITY PRESS

**European
Society for the
Cognitive Sciences
Of
Music**

OXFORD

UNIVERSITY PRESS

Great Clarendon Street, Oxford, OX2 6DP,
United Kingdom

Oxford University Press is a department of the University of Oxford.
It furthers the University's objective of excellence in research, scholarship,
and education by publishing worldwide. Oxford is a registered trade mark of
Oxford University Press in the UK and in certain other countries

First Edition published in 2012

Impression: 1

British Library Cataloguing in Publication Data

Data available

Library of Congress Cataloging in Publication Data
Library of Congress Control Number: 2012939883

ISBN 978–0–19–969573–7

Printed in Great Britain on acid-free paper by
CPI Group (UK) Ltd, Croydon, CR0 4YY

Whilst every effort has been made to ensure that the contents of this work
are as complete, accurate and-up-to-date as possible at the date of writing,
Oxford University Press is not able to give any guarantee or assurance that
such is the case. Readers are urged to take appropriately qualified medical
advice to all cases. The information in this work is intended to be useful to the
general reader, but should not be used as a means of self-diagnosis or for the
prescription of medication.

Links to third party websites are provided by Oxford in good faith and
for information only. Oxford disclaims any responsibility for the materials
contained in any third party website referenced in this work.

Contents

Editorial preface

It is something of a paradox that language excludes even as it communicates. The European Society for the Cognitive Sciences of Music (ESCOM) project to translate seminal European literature on psychology and music is based on the belief that only with a translation into English, the lingua franca of scientific discourse, will these texts reach the widest readership at first hand.

Historical distance has proven the value of Carl Stumpf's writings and their enduring relevance. The two texts included in this inaugural volume, *The Origins of Music* (1911) and *Self-Portrait* (1924), are both summary texts of a kind, and bear upon a variety of academic and intellectual circles, from the various brands of the study of music, including the cultural anthropology of music, to the cognitive sciences, psychoacoustics, and the history of philosophy. With his research into sound perception, Stumpf became a pioneer in experimental psychology and effectively detached the discipline from its close traditional relationship to philosophy (though Stumpf's lifelong interest in epistemology underscores the fact that he did not identify himself as an experimental psychologist). He was convinced that psychophysics and physiology are fundamental methods of psychology, but he was equally convinced that they were unable to answer the fundamental question: 'How do we perceive the world?'

Against this background of psychological investigation, *The Origins of Music* presents the reader with a path-breaking hypothesis about the prehistory of music. It is based on Stumpf's research with Erich von Hornbostel at the Berlin Phonogram Archive, and establishes a template for the methods of comparative musicology (the elder sibling of modern ethnomusicology), while interpreting the development of music through the twin lenses of (pre-Husserlian) phenomenology and evolutionary biology. Indeed, psychological functions remain the focus of his theory of sound perception. Part I explores the topic of music's origination, while part II consists of analyses of melodies from non-European cultures to demonstrate the psychological principles of tonal organization. Along the way, the text develops the concept of fusion or *Verschmelzung*, which was first introduced in his *Psychology of Tone* (2 vols.; 1883, 1890a), and its concomitant theory of consonance, both of which have remained central topics in the scientific study of music. In seeking to identify universal structures in music, Stumpf's text exemplifies the European discourse on music and evolution around the turn of the twentieth century. Published shortly before the First World War, this work predates the current subdivisions within the field of Anglophone musicology—now very much under critique—and offers a generous vision of how a more integrated discipline may look.

To contextualize this text, and to offer the reader a sense of the breadth of Stumpf's academic purview, *Self-Portrait* presents an autobiographical survey of his life and work. It was written shortly after he retired from all lecturing at Berlin University in 1923. The first part is autobiographical, the second is a summary of the different threads—from academic philosophy to mathematics and the natural sciences—that are interwoven in his various publications to form the dense woof of his interdisciplinary legacy. The text is given here in a new translation as a short introduction to the author's scientific convictions, and to his motivation for investigating music as a means of understanding the psychological functions of our intellect.

* * *

This volume is the inaugural publication in a new series, 'Classic European Music Science Monographs', which is a project to publish English translations of seminal historic European treatises on systematic and scientific musicology from the twentieth century and earlier. The project is an initiative of ESCOM, made possible by an endowment entitled the Irène Deliège Translation Fund, which is held and administered by the King Baudouin Foundation of Belgium, and which is earmarked to support translation and related expenses for the series.

The main criterion for inclusion in the series is that the work concerned should have made a major and historically significant contribution to the theory or method of analysing and understanding the structure, organization, and underlying psychological mechanisms of music; and it should not have been previously published in high-quality English translation.

ESCOM has appointed an editorial committee to select volumes for the series and oversee their production, including the commissioning of translations and contemporary commentaries. This committee is chaired by John Sloboda (UK), and its membership, with dates of service to 2012, has been Irène Deliège (Belgium, 2010–12), Reinhard Kopiez (Germany, 2012) John Rink (UK, 2011–12), Jaan Ross (Estonia, 2010–11), and Geraint Wiggins (UK, 2010). A special responsibility for this particular volume has been taken by Reinhard Kopiez.

The team at OUP led by Martin Baum and Charlotte Green has also played an invaluable part in the realization of this text, and we are particularly grateful to Kathleen Lyle and Jane May, our indefatigable copy editors, and to Abigail Stanley for deftly steering the work through to final production. We are also grateful to Bev Wilson for the musical examples. Finally, the committee would especially like to thank Martin Ebeling (University of Dortmund, Germany), Margret Kaiser-El-Safti (Carl Stumpf Society, Germany), Lars-Christian Koch (Berlin Ethnological Museum, Germany), Karola Obermüller (University of New Mexico, USA), Albrecht Wiedmann (Berlin Ethnological Museum, Germany), and Uwe Wolfradt (University of Halle, Germany) for their help and support in realizing this project.

David Trippett (editor and translator) and
John Sloboda (Chair of Editorial Board)

Sound examples

All sound examples (found online at: http://www.oup.co.uk/companion/ stumpf and denoted in the text by ♩) are taken from the collection of about 30,000 wax cylinders of the Berlin Museum of Ethnology/Berlin Phonogram Archive. The Phonogram Archive was founded in 1900 by Carl Stumpf and Erich Moritz von Hornbostel.[1] We are indebted to Prof. Lars-Christian Koch for giving permission to use the archive and to Albrecht Wiedmann for the identification of cylinders and digital transfers. We would also like to thank the Hermann von Helmholtz-Zentrum für Kulturtechnik (Humboldt-University of Berlin) for giving permission to publish the voice sample of Carl Stumpf.

All recordings that could be identified as being part of Stumpf's book have been included. Due to the loss of cylinders during the Second World War, however, not all recordings mentioned in the book were available. The recordings have been left unrestored; editing was limited to adding fade-in and fade-out. The quality of recordings varies due to the difficulty of keeping the physical distance constant between the phonograph and the sound source in field research. More information on the technical aspects of wax cylinders can be obtained from http://www.cylinder.de.

The track listing is as follows:

---

[1] For a history of the Archive, see Lars-Christian Koch, Albrecht Wiedmann, and Susanne Ziegler, 'The Berlin Phonogramm-Archiv: A treasury of sound recordings', *Acoustical Science and Technology* 25 (2004): 227-231; Susanne Ziegler, *Die Wachszylinder des Berliner Phonogramm-Archivs* (Berlin: Staatliche Museen zu Berlin, 2002); and Ziegler, 'Erich M. von Hornbostel und das Berliner Phonogramm-Archiv', in Sebastian Klotz (ed.), *"Vom tönenden Wirbel menschlichen Tuns". Erich M. von Hornbostel als Gestaltpsychologe, Archivar und Musikwissenschaftler: Studien und Dokumente* (Berlin: Schibri, 1998), 146–168.

Track no.	Berlin Museum of Ethnology classification	Musical example	Page number	Duration
1	VII W 5243 Selenka Vedda SEL W 1	4.1a	111	2:08
2	VII W 5244 Selenka Vedda SEL W 2	4.1b	112	2:08
3	VII W 5260 Hagen Kubu 18	4.5	118	1:37
4	VII W 5252 Hagen Kubu 10	4.6	118	1:16
5	VII W 5267 Hagen Kubu 25	4.7	118	1:45
6	VII W 5420 Stephan Ozeanien 12	4.11	123	2:51
7	VII W 5412 Stephan Ozeanien 3	4.12	123–4	2:17
8	VII W 4368 Lehmann-Nitsche Patagonien 31	4.14	126	2:43
9	VII W 4341 Lehmann-Nitsche Patagonien 8	4.16	127–8	2:40
10	VII W 4383 Lehmann-Nitsche Patagonien LN 46	4.17	128	3:26
11	VII W 1357 Boas Thompson River Indianer 143	4.42	157	2:15
12	VII W 1371 Boas Thompson River Indianer PR 158	4.43	158	1:35
13	VII W 1388 Boas Thompson River Indianer PR 177	4.44	158	1:38
14	VII W 1389 Boas Thompson River Indianer PR 178	4.45	158	1:27
15	VII W 1374 Boas Thompson River Indianer PR 162	4.46	159	1:21
16	VII W 1387 Boas Thompson River Indianer PR 176	4.47	159	2:05
17	VII W 6395 Weule Ostafrika 42	4.57	171	1:42
18	VII W 6395 Weule Ostafrika 45	4.58	171	1:15
19	VII W 1642 Czekanowski Ruanda 83	4.59	172	1:58
20	"On ethical scepticism"	–	xii–xiii	3:24

Transcriptions of the recordings were typically made by von Hornbostel and proof-read by Erich Fischer as well as Stumpf, who emphasized the advantages of this collaborative effort. In some cases the resulting notation does not transcribe the beginning of a recording but begins with a section in the middle. It seems this was determined by von Hornbostel on a case-by-case basis, who occasionally chose to focus on different sections of the recordings in his transcriptions. Close listening to the recordings will make clear which sections have been transcribed and which left out.

The voice sample of Carl Stumpf (Track 20) was recorded shortly before his death in 1936, when he was 88 years old. Stumpf is reading the beginning of "On ethical scepticism", a speech first given to students on 3 August 1908, when he was president of the Humboldt University of Berlin. This recording was transferred from a gramophone disc, and a translation is given immediately below.

Further material about Stumpf, including his writings and sound examples for other publications, can be obtained from the continuously updated Virtual Laboratory of the Max Planck Institute for the History of Science, Berlin (http://vlp.mpiwg-berlin.mpg.de).

❶ *Track 20*

From my commemoration speech 'On ethical scepticism', August 1908

Vitality and lineament occur only in a life imbued with objective goals. Indeed, they say if a rose adorns itself it also adorns the garden, though that is not the right analogy for humanity. And if Nietzsche, the offspring of an odd marriage between Romanticism and Darwinism, dreams of superior human beings [*Herrenmenschen*] who savour their lonely greatness high above the mundane crowd, like Alpine peaks, then this is conceived more poetically than psychologically. By shifting all aims of the will into the subject, only superior human beings in the sense of Cesare Borgia emerge, caricatures of true human greatness. All of Nietzsche's verbal dexterity cannot compensate for the simple sentence that contains the true basic formula for our era as well as the secret of all greatness: only he who loses his soul is able to gain it.

It is this formula that finds expression in the tremendous movement towards a social ethics, a movement that sweeps over all the still brilliantly formulated subjectivism like a storm tide, because it is rooted far deeper in human nature.

Whoever does not live according to objective values has his reward (while condemned in this way) in sharing his own miserable company throughout his life, which he has voided of all content, and which he is able to doll up only artificially. How else does one open up an artwork, problems of science, of technology, of national welfare: what richness in life, in true reality he suckles without wanting to engage it!

In this way an ethical attitude shows itself to be identical with an *objective* attitude. The quintessence of deontology [*Pflichtenlehre*] is resolved herein.

One of the main demands of such an ethics emerges—when it seeks to penetrate life—as the most comprehensive knowledge possible of the relationships of reality. For the best will can achieve the worst if it is not accompanied by knowledge of the real conditions for the entry of Good into this world. A force that always seeks the Good but achieves evil is even less welcome than one constituted the other way around.

* * *

An extract modified by Stumpf from his published text, 'Vom ethischen Skeptizismus', in *Philosophische Reden und Vorträge* (Leipzig: J. A. Barth, 1910), 197–224, here 216–219.

Section I

Introductory essays

Chapter 1

Carl Stumpf: Impulses towards a cognitive theory of musical evolution

Helga de la Motte-Haber

Even in a science as vigorously progressive as psychology, some historical knowledge cannot do any harm.
(Carl Stumpf)[1]

The translation of a text from 1911 in the year 2011 is indicative of the historical significance that befits the author who, for his part, made his mark with seminal writings on music psychology, even if he is not really the founder of the discipline of psychology. Can we still regard Stumpf's consideration of *The Origins of Music* as timely, or is this merely an interesting historical document? At any rate, this translation of Stumpf's text appears at a time when whole issues of prestigious scholarly journals such as *Cognition* (100/1, 2006) and *Musicae Scientiae* (Special Issue 2009–2010) are dedicated to this subject. A review of differing theoretical concepts shall answer the above questions and clarify the significance of Stumpf's text within the framework of an intensive, fifteen-year discussion on the evolutionary origins of music.

---

[1] Carl Stumpf, 'Zum Gedächtnis Lotzes', *Kantstudien* 22 (1917): 1–16, here 3.

1.1. Self-contradictory concepts of the evolution of music

These concepts can be divided very roughly in terms of their approaches to music: whether they seek the origins of music in an adaptive function, or whether they pursue a non-adaptive approach. There is considerable differentiation within both of these groups, but also points of overlap in the research.

Although adaptive theories are favoured today, they belong at the same time to the early history of research into the evolution of music that arose in the Enlightenment, when the divine origins of music were no longer considered reputable. In his *Essai sur l'origine des langues* (1755), Jean-Jacques Rousseau had considered vocalizations of passion as the foundation of music as well as language, i.e. both originated in vocal utterances such as cries, shouts of joy or pain, sighs, blustering, or cheering, and both granted a communicative function to these emotional vocal utterances. This thesis of a proto-language has been very persuasive down to the present day. It served a communicative purpose for 'singing Neanderthals'—as Mithen put it—whose vocal organs were still underdeveloped.[2] Brown reinvented the thesis of a proto-language, coining the neologism 'Musilanguage' for it.[3] Rousseau, whose essay had arisen in the context of an outline for a new social order, had already gone one step further. He believed that understanding through vocalization of passion equates with a community-building function. This means that for Rousseau 'sing-song speech' [*singendes Sprechen*], as Stumpf formulated it, has an important adaptive function, useful for survival because a community can defy hardship better than an individual. Dunbar and Oerter established this theory of social cohesion afresh without making reference to the history of the idea.[4] It was

---

[2] Steven J. Mithen, *The Singing Neanderthals: The Origin of Music, Language, Mind and Body* (London: Phoenix, 2005).

[3] Steven Brown, 'The "Musilanguage" Model of Music Evolution', in N. L. Wallin, B. Merker and S. Brown (eds.), *The Origins of Music* (Cambridge, MA.: MIT Press, 2000), 271–300.

[4] Robin I. M. Dunbar, 'Language, Music, and Laughter in Evolutionary Perspective', in D. Kimbrough Oller and U. Griebel (eds.), *Evolution of Communication Systems:*

embedded in the new context of brain physiology by Livingstone and Thompson: in the mirror neuron system of empathy and imitation. They too speculated that 'affective engagement provides the foundation of the emergence of music'.[5]

The adaptive functions of primordial music were emphasized particularly strongly after the appearance of Charles Darwin's book *The Descent of Man, and Selection in Relation to Sex*.[6] Comparable to the behaviour of animals, human vocal communication—as one assumed—is supposed to have served sexual selection as well as the demarcation of territory. This thesis has been advocated up to the present day, typically by appealing to Darwin.[7] It is problematic to draw analogies between animal and human behaviour from certain Darwinian positions—even if well intentioned—in order to be able to derive from biological explanations potential universals for all musical cultures. Moreover, we rarely discuss the fact that the so-called 'biogenetic law' resonates in the process, namely Ernst Haeckel's 'theory of recapitulation' (the assumption that ontogeny recapitulates phylogeny) from his *General Morphology*.[8] Haeckel's theory has been considered archaic for fifty years, and—on account of its creationist implications—politically incorrect as well.

Adaptive perception has not been unopposed, as Fitch sceptically remarked.[9] Nevertheless, explanations seemed to be lacking when similarities were found in the audible utterances of animals and humans. Besides, the experiments carried out by McDermott and Hauser

---

A Comparative Approach (Cambridge, MA.: MIT Press, 2004), 257–274; Rolf Oerter, 'Musik—Einheit und Vielfalt ihrer kultureller Ausprägung', *Erwägen—Wissen—Ethik* 18 (2007): 521–532.

[5] Steven R. Livingstone and William F. Thompson, 'The Emergence of Music from the Theory of Mind', *Musicae Scientiae* (Special Issue 2009–10): 83–118, here 83.

[6] Charles Darwin, *The Descent of Man, and Selection in Relation to Sex* (London: John Murray, 1871).

[7] See, for instance, Geoffrey F. Miller, *The Mating Mind: How Sexual Choice Shaped the Evolution of Human Nature* (New York: Doubleday, 2001), 329–360.

[8] Ernst Haeckel, *Generelle Morphologie der Organismen* (Berlin: Georg Reimer, 1866).

[9] William Tecumseh Fitch, 'The Biology and Evolution of Music: A Comparative Perspective', *Cognition* 100 (2006): 173–215.

adduced that, given free choice, non-human primates (cotton-top tamarins) prefer silence to music.[10]

In order to be able to classify Stumpf's position and appreciate its timeliness, we must take a brief look at a second group of theories: basic non-adaptionist approaches. Pinker, above all, has put forward the idea that music is a useless by-product of human cognitive faculties, which triggers pleasure and hence has become a kind of recreational drug.[11] The animal kingdom too is familiar with evolutionary by-products: the waving of a peacock's tail, for instance. Yet nine times out of ten they are tied to sexual courtship, where music—in spite of the beautiful love songs that are only rarely performed by males as a serenade—has no human equivalent. At least with regard to literature, Pinker revised his idea of the arts' redundancy—which was damaging for cultural policy— in a review of Gorrschall and Wilson's *The Literary Animal*: 'The arts could be evolutionary by-products, and be among the most valuable human activities for all that'.[12]

But why, in this non-adaptionist discourse, is there no mention of anything pertaining to the evolution of music, which concerns cultural achievement and factors in specific human cognitive faculties? One of Stumpf's fundamental ideas would be outlined by his enquiries into the prehistory of music. Moreover, he raises a question lacking in today's discussion, the answer to which would be a logical requirement of evolutionary theory: what is music? Stumpf's conception of music is thus shaped by his psychological research. This is evident above all in his use of particular key words. In *The Origins of Music* he does not refer directly to this research. In what follows I shall try nevertheless to shed light on these concepts, which is to say, unfurl a piece of the history of psychology. Stumpf's cognitive conception will be partially clarified

---

[10] Josh McDermott and Marc D. Hauser, 'Nonhuman Primates Prefer Slow Tempos but Dislike Music Overall', *Cognition* 104 (2007): 654–668

[11] Steven Pinker, *How the Mind Works* (New York: Norton, 1997).

[12] Steven Pinker, 'Toward a Consilient Study of Literature', *Philosophy and Literature* 31 (2007): 162–178, here 170; Jonathan Gotschall and David S. Wilson, *The Literary Animal* (Evanston: Northwestern Univ. Press, 2005).

in this way, though there are also obvious limitations in its possible significance for the present discussion.

1.2. A brief summary of significant aspects of the 1911 text

At the turn of the twentieth century, Stumpf was—along with Wilhelm Wundt (1832–1920)—the most famous German psychologist alive. Like all psychologists of the period, he had taken philosophy as his starting point. In 1893 Stumpf founded the Department of Psychology at Berlin University. Important works, such as *On the Psychological Origin of Spatial Conception* [*Über den psychologischen Ursprung der Raumvorstellung*, 1873] or the two-volume *Psychology of Tone* [*Tonpsychologie*, 1883, 1890a] had been completed. Thereafter came *Speech Sounds* [*Die Sprachlaute*, 1926], *Feeling and Sensation of Feeling* [*Gefühl und Gefühlsempfindung*, 1928], and, posthumously, the two-volume *Epistemology* [*Erkenntnislehre*, 1939, 1940].[13] Stumpf may be regarded as the founder of music psychology even if this term was first used by Ernst Kurth in place of 'psychology of tone'.[14]

The small book *The Origins of Music* is based on a lecture, to which Stumpf added extensive footnotes. He later added a second part which included a wealth of musical examples pertaining to the songs of indigenous peoples. Before proceeding to evolutionary theory, let me first offer some explanatory words about this latter part.

Stumpf was firmly of the view that psychology is a science based on empiricism. This attitude is still to be gleaned from the official speech at his eighty-fifth birthday in 1933.[15] Extensive experimental papers also exist. He regarded the songs of indigenous people transcribed in the text of 1911 almost as a survey of empirical psychological data. Thus he could, in part, have recourse to his own research since he had founded the Berlin Phonogram Archive in 1900, analogous to the

---

[13] Carl Stumpf's complete publications are given in the bibliography on pages 253–259 of this volume.

[14] Ernst Kurth, *Musikpsychologie* (Berlin: M. Hesse, 1931).

[15] See Helga Sprung and Lothar Sprung, *Carl Stumpf—Eine Biographie: Von der Philosophie zur Experimentellen Psychologie* (Munich and Vienna: Profil, 2006), 334ff.

Viennese archive of 1899;[16] one inducement for his doing so was biographical in nature, namely, the impression of a guest performance of Thai theatre music that he had recorded with the help of an Edison phonograph. For Stumpf, who was a very talented violinist (and in his youth had considered becoming a musician), music retained a great, lifelong significance. Music ethnology, which has since developed a momentum of its own, was regarded by him—like other researchers of the time—as an ancillary discipline to study the fundamental mental state of affairs. Stumpf attributed this kind of psychological significance to his musical examples. Recourse to ethnological evidence is common in evolutionary studies down to the present day.

At the beginning of the twentieth century ethnological data were frequently used to support psychological theorizing. The development of psychology as an independent discipline is reflected therein. Its point of departure had been the demarcation of speculative philosophy in the second half of the nineteenth century. There followed a dependence on the experimental procedures of the natural sciences. Psychology was initially committed, therefore, to the idea of looking for the cause of human sensation in external conditions. Its research paradigm rests on the schema of stimulus and response in order to specify feelings by causes, wherein feelings counted as the foundation of human consciousness. This concept had led to the establishment of psychophysics by Erich Heinrich Weber and Gustav Fechner. Around 1900, though, the practices of psychophysics were felt to be restrictive. Stumpf expressed some discomfort about them in the preface to the second volume of his *Psychology of Tone*. Moritz Lazarus and Haijm Steinthal, whose purpose was to research higher mental processes, demonstrated a dependence on ethnologically active folk psychology.[17] An obvious example of this is the ten-volume *Folk Psychology* [*Völkerpsychologie*] by Wilhelm Wundt, who in 1879 had established the first experimental

---

[16] See http://www.phonogrammarchiv.at/wwwnew/ [accessed 8 May 2012].

[17] Moritz Lazarus and Haijm Steinthal edited the *Zeitschrift für Völkerpsychologie und Sprachwissenschaft* 1–20 (1860–1890).

laboratory for psychology in Leipzig.[18] From a present-day perspective, this orientation towards folk psychology seems a precursor to social psychology. Stumpf used the songs of indigenous peoples not in their cultural context, but rather as evidence of musical circumstances that he regarded as fundamental.

Stumpf's theory of evolution belongs to the non-adaptive theories. He felt himself to be in keeping with William James, who said of music: 'It has no zoological utility . . . It is a pure incident of having a hearing organ'.[19] The two scientists were very close friends, even after James had turned to pragmatism, which Stumpf could not support for ethical reasons. In addition, an extensive correspondence testifies to their internationality, for Stumpf spoke good English and James good German.[20]

Stumpf had great admiration for Charles Darwin and Herbert Spencer, to whom we owe the formula 'survival of the fittest'. Darwin was the intellectual father for studies on animal psychology at Stumpf's institute. In the matter of music, however, Stumpf regarded Darwin's notion of evolution as false. He represents Darwin's ideas somewhat ironically with the words: 'In the beginning was love' (an allusion to the formulation at the beginning of Goethe's *Faust* and, more distantly, the New Testament). Stumpf counters the idea of gorgeous, song-loving male animals in courtship with the argument—used to the present day—that there is hardly a comparable gender-specific differentiation among humans;[21] and music only serves the struggle for existence with well-trained piano fingers, which could help to earn lots of money. He can definitely take something from 'spoken singing', Rousseau's 'musi-language', but he assesses it as something independent, something that has retained its religious, ceremonial significance. It is not about

---

[18] Wilhelm Wundt, *Völkerpsychologie*, 10 vols. (Leipzig: Kröner, 1900–1920).

[19] William James, *Principles of Psychology*, 2 vols. (New York: Holt, 1890), 2: 627.

[20] Henry James (ed.), *The Letters of William James,* 2 vols. (London: Longman & Green, 1920).

[21] Gunter Kreutz and Helga de la Motte-Haber, 'Evolution', in Helga de la Motte-Haber, Heinz von Loesch, Günther Rötter, Christian Utz (eds.), *Lexikon der Systematischen Musikwissenschaft* (Laaber: Laaber Verlag, 2010), 114–115, here 114.

a preliminary stage of music. Regarding the comparison of language and music, Stumpf counters that language uses different narrowly gliding levels of intonation, and thereby gains its special expressive content. He invokes as evidence the investigations into experimental phonetics by Edward Wheeler Scripture, a pioneer of American experimental psychology who had studied with Wundt.[22] Scripture made enlargements of the waveforms of speech recordings on a gramophone record.

These and other objections to an adaptive explanation of the emergence of music occur, however, as a sideshow to Stumpf's thoughts, for he won the principal argument by answering the question of what music is: 'We do not call music the mere production of tones, rather the production of certain arrangements of tones, however simple they may be'. With this, he touched upon relationships between tones that allow melodic successions to be transposed. And he invoked the experiments carried out by Otto Abraham. Abraham was a colleague of Stumpf's who, in 1903, wrote a book on Japanese music with Erich von Hornbostel, the head of the Phonogram Archive from 1905 until his emigration in 1933.[23] Abraham was also entrusted with research into the potential ability of birds to transpose melodies. His findings admitted the conclusion that such transposition is a case of a congenital faculty approaching that of humans, which is already verifiable among indigenous peoples. Incidentally, using fixed tonal steps means creating relationships between notes, i.e. thinking in intervals. Such 'correlative thinking' [*beziehendes Denken*]—a phrase often used by Stumpf—also applies to singers, despite their use of portamento and vibrato. Stumpf explained thinking in tonal steps and intervals as a general cognitive achievement. By this he meant comprehension through comparison, allowing assessment of equality, similarity, and difference, which again is the basis of abstract thought. The recognition and sameness of a 'form' [*Gestalt*] under completely different stimulus conditions, the

---

[22] Edward W. Scripture, 'How the voice looks', *Century Magazine* 64 (1902): 148–154; and *Research in Experimental Phonetics: the Study of Speech Curves* (Washington: Carnegie Institute, 1906).

[23] Otto Abraham and Erich von Hornbostel, *Studien über das Tonsystem und die Musik der Japaner* (Leipzig: Breitkopf & Härtel, 1903).

identification of similar relationships in dissimilar material, constitutes the first stage of music's development.

Within the scope of non-adaptive theories, Stumpf introduces a new approach, which one wishes he had taken further. He defines his principal item, namely music, by mental operations that imply comparative, analytical, and abstractive processes. From a present-day perspective, this raises the problem of what the significance may be of including pre-linguistic and pre-musical material (among them noises of the urban and natural environment) in popular and new music. Such practices do not concern Stumpf's idea of a cognitive theory of evolution, however. It is the development of the brain that is responsible for the differences between animals and humans. This idea is also discussed very carefully within non-adaptive theories of brain psychology. According to Stumpf, the brain's higher development is responsible for the usage of intervals, the fusion of consonant intervals and chords, and the divergence of dissonant ones, just as it is responsible for a precisely regulated rhythm in polyphony. Development, in the present book, means higher development vis-à-vis indigenous peoples as well.

In this context we ought to be mindful of the footnotes that Stumpf later added to the lecture notes; see, for instance, endnote xxviii (pp. 98–99) with its reference to François-Joseph Fétis, whose *Traité* of 1844 was fundamental for the theory of tonal music. But Fétis also numbers among the founders of music ethnology, and hence postulates that no tonal 'fundamental structure' can claim universality. He was a pronounced opponent of the belief in progress. To be sure, Stumpf had quickly tempered any such belief in progress in the context of his ethnological studies. This became apparent in the dispute with Hugo Riemann over the latter's theory of harmonic function.[24] And his revision of notions of progressiveness does not relate to the significance he attributed to the idea that psychological research must maintain a dual path alongside studies into brain psychology.

---

[24] See Helga de la Motte-Haber, *Psychologie und Musiktheorie* (Frankfurt: Diesterweg, 1976).

But Stumpf's 1911 text also has a historical dimension. It stands on the same intellectual ground as his *Psychology of Tone*. Details attest this, such as the significance he ascribes to the impression of fusion, one of his central research topics. But it is attested above all in the earlier mentioned concepts of relationship formation, perception of form, and speculations about brain physiology. *Psychology of Tone* was committed to research on cognition. The same goes for his *Origins* book. The emotional component of music is neglected entirely. It should also be noted that even Stumpf's essay on emotion constitutes a cognitive theory.[25] Tracing the ideas in *Psychology of Tone* in light of a smaller text like *The Origins of Music* is justified by the fact that the former points to more comprehensive studies.

1.3. Psychology of tone instead of psychophysics

How do we perceive the world? Stumpf shared this question, which sits at the centre of his thinking, with his contemporaries. Psychology was extensively conceived as a theory of cognition whereby important stimuli came from the separation of the cognitive subject from that of the content given in consciousness, a position shared with British empiricists, who for their part had postulated that nothing is given in the imagination that does not rest on sensory information. Psychophysics, with its study into the connection between stimulus and response, rests on this paradigm. Particular significance was assigned to Hermann von Helmholtz's acoustic research, which had explained the impression of consonance and dissonance by a theory of coincidence, i.e. by the coincidence or separation of harmonics.[26] Non-coincident harmonics cause beats and unevenness through the mixture of difference tones that occur. Helmholtz did not assume that the perception of the world would be clarified only by investigating its external conditions, however; in fact he granted independent significance to the achievements of consciousness. He thereby developed a model that has been valid to the

---

[25] Carl Stumpf, *Gefühl und Gefühlsempfindung* (Leipzig: Barth, 1928).

[26] Hermann von Helmholtz, *Die Lehre von den Tonempfindungen als physiologische Grundlage für die Theorie der Musik* (Braunschweig: Vieweg, 1863).

present day as so-called 'correlative psychophysics', and is expressed in the description of information processing by an interplay of bottom-up and top-down processes. Stumpf dealt intensively with Helmholtz's acoustic research, even though he initially rejected the model of consciousness. The research of both authors on the perception of simultaneous pitches cannot be compared anyway, for Helmholtz, like Bregman later on,[27] had not advanced a theory of consonance, as Stumpf had, but a theory of dissonance in which consonance is explained negatively from the absence of dissonant features.

During Stumpf's studies for *Psychology of Tone*, his teacher Rudolph Hermann Lotze and his mentor Franz Brentano provided crucial intellectual stimuli. Lotze is experiencing a rediscovery at the moment. As the founder of phenomenology, Brentano's reputation has continued uninterrupted, not least because of the further development of phenomenology by his student Edmund Husserl. Furthermore, Brentano had recommended to Husserl that he study for his Habilitation with Stumpf, who, for his part, was so fascinated by Brentano that he dedicated the second volume of *Psychology of Tone* to him as well as *Epistemology*, which appeared posthumously.

Brentano had in fact developed a radical new perspective while focusing exclusively on mental processes, i.e. on what is phenomenologically given.[28] Here, the external thing is given immanently. There is no consciousness without a content of consciousness. Mental phenomena as such, and not potential underlying stimuli, were thereby granted central importance. Imagination and thought could become the focus of research. No longer did the discussion take place solely in the context of stimulus and response. Nowadays, imagination, motivation, emotion, etc. belong so unquestionably to the central objects of study in psychology that the innovations which resulted from phenomenology can hardly be retraced. So-called 'qualia', e.g. the white colour of snow, the fusion of pitches into an octave, or the impression of a dissonance that

---

[27] Albert Bregman, *Auditory Scene Analysis* (Cambridge, MA: MIT Press, 1990).

[28] Franz Brentano, *Psychologie vom empirischen Standpunkt*, 2 vols. (Leipzig: Duncker & Humblot, 1874).

can arise without difference tones, can be explained neither physically nor physiologically. They are achievements of consciousness. Before Brentano, Lotze had already advocated this view and moved 'qualia' to the centre of his thoughts.

According to Lotze, one of the most important processes of consciousness is comparison (of similitude and dissimilitude), through which the impression of correlative knowledge is added; these together can lead to abstraction, and involve attention and analysis.[29] Herein lay the roots of later cognitive psychology: the idea of 'analysis by synthesis'. Stumpf adopted these thoughts of comparison and forming of relationships, both mental processes, which he also led back to the origin of music. The process of evolution cannot occur without music's tonal steps and intervals. Stumpf spoke of mental functions or correlative thought. It should be noted in passing that Husserl's phenomenological method of eidetic vision [*Wesenschau*] harnesses comparison and abstraction, and, incidentally, he took the term 'fusion' [*Verschmelzung*] from Stumpf. He also grappled intensively with Lotze's *Theory of local signs* [*Theorie der Lokalzeichen*]. Local signs are mental physiological innervations that accompany perception. They are necessary concomitant circumstances that ought to be researched but which neither explain nor materialize the content of consciousness. Recalling these considerations of local signs had an impact on Stumpf's later thought.

In his *Psychology of Tone*, Stumpf introduced fundamental observations that are cited today under different names. Virtual melodic formation numbers among these, and was later dubbed the streaming effect; spatial characteristics of volume also belong here, however, as do density and its dependency on pitch and intensity, and descriptions of the dimensions of timbre through features like sharpness, roughness, and brightness. But the importance he attributed to the impression of consonance—evident in the number of pages in the second volume of *Psychology of Tone*—witnesses a decisive turn in his thinking. In *The Origins of Music* he uses the concept of gestalt quite self-evidently. But

[29] Rudolph H. Lotze, *Medicinische Psychologie oder Physiologie der Seele* (Leipzig: Weidmann, 1852).

through his studies of consonance he became the father of gestalt theory. He wrestled with such concepts. Once he discussed the impression of supersummativity [*Übersummativität*], i.e. the impossibility of fragmentation into component parts, by using the example of pitches fused into the octave. It concerns entirely independent 'perceptual content' that 'forms not a mere sum but a whole'.[30] To this he adds that 'both simultaneous notes do not just gradually fuse into a certain unity in one's consciousness. Fusion signifies to us not a process, but an existing relationship'.[31] To describe this phenomenon was not new in any case: Johann Friedrich Herbart, Ernst Heinrich Weber, Theodor Lipps (and others)—with whom Stumpf engaged extensively—had done this before him. What was new, though, was the interpretation of an easily observable phenomenon—an interpretation that led to the idea of 'whole perception' and thereby to a new doctrine of perception, to integral psychology [*Ganzheitspsychologie*] and gestalt theory. Similar views were held elsewhere too, above all in Graz. But neither the thoughts of Alexius Meinong nor those of Christian von Ehrenfels—both influenced by Brentano—were granted comparable effect.[32] Stumpf laid a foundation. His students or colleagues were major gestalt theorists, among them Max Wertheimer, Kurt Koffka, Wolfgang Köhler, and Kurt Lewin.

But Stumpf did not let go of the old questions about a material basis, or that of potential 'local signs', which admittedly did not seem to bring clarity to mental phenomena but could vouch for a unity of body and soul in human consciousness. Between the years 1883 and 1890 a development took place in his thinking. In the first volume of *Psychology of Tone* he remarked that 'a physiological explanation [for fusion] cannot be devised, much less proven'.[33] In the second volume, by contrast, he referred to 'brain structure' and a 'collaboration of two

---

[30] Carl Stumpf, *Tonpsychologie*, 2 vols. (Leipzig: Hirzel, 1883, 1890) 2: 128.

[31] Ibid., 2: 184–218.

[32] Christian von Ehrenfels, 'Über Gestaltqualitäten', *Vierteljahresschrift für wissenschaftliche Philosophie* 14 (1890): 249–292; Alexius Meinong, *Abhandlungen zur Psychologie* (Leipzig: Barth, 1914).

[33] Carl Stumpf, *Tonpsychologie*, 1: 101.

nervous systems'.[34] To this he linked the conjecture that 'evolution must have taken place over an immense stretch of time, and even during prehistoric times'. He justified this in 1911 by using the songs of indigenous peoples as evidence. With his speculation about brain physiology, Stumpf came close to Helmholtz's cognitive model, as he was well aware. He increasingly advocated the view that forms [*Gestalten*] had to have a foundation: 'forms can never be perceived in themselves, but rather always only on and in a given material. They must cling to a support'.[35] In 1890 he had called fusion an 'existing relationship'.[36] In contrast to the gestalt theorists, forms were not primarily an actuality for him. The notion of relationships, which preoccupied him throughout his scientific career, points to an intellectual activity, namely to a recognition of abstract characteristics. These could, for their part, have a physical as well as a physiological material equivalent. Protracted studies would be required in order to ascertain the extent to which Wolfgang Köhler's systems-theoretical consideration of an isomorphism between psychophysical processes and mental things is based on Stumpf's idea of an abstract totality of relations. In place of the unsatisfactory causal nexus of physiological and psychological findings much publicized today, the idea of isomorphisms could yet lead to further meaningful hypotheses.

Acknowledgement

A sincere debt of gratitude is owed to Reinhard Kopiez for adjustments to this text, and to David Trippett for his translation of it.

---

[34] Ibid., 2: 214.

[35] Carl Stumpf, *Erkenntnislehre*, 2 vols. (Leipzig: Barth, 1939–1940), 1: 232.

[36] Ibid., 1: 231.

Chapter 2

Carl Stumpf: A reluctant revolutionary

David Trippett

If historical events are to mark the boundaries of a life lived, one could be forgiven for suspecting that Carl Stumpf (1848–1936) might have been a political revolutionary: born during the months of revolutionary uprisings across Europe, he died a few months after Hitler's troops occupied the Rhineland in violation of the Treaty of Versailles. Yet, as a scientist, his convictions carried no muscular force; still less any political conviction. His sphere was intellectual. Though, as we shall see, this would prove no less influential in charting the course of the disciplines of psychology and (ethno)musicology, than the events that framed his life would serve to alter the course of European history.

Stumpf came from a family of doctors and acknowledged in 1924 that a central portion of his professional life was devoted to bridging his early love of music and his familial inclination towards the natural sciences. Between 1875 (with his work on the *Psychology of Tone*) and 1911 (when he published *The Origins of Music*) he investigated the phenomenon of sound as a stimulus at once physical, physiological, and psychological, i.e. something following the laws of Newtonian physics, operative within the functions of the brain, and hence traceable within the more opaque realm of the mind. Music, as the perception of sound configurations cultivated by people, thereby effected Stumpf's theories of sensation, perception, and cognition. With his 1911 hypothesis about the prehistory of music, Stumpf added a historical dimension to this study, one that is influenced by, though also differentiated from, Charles Darwin's evolutionary theory first documented in *On the Origin of Species* (1859). This had been on the shelves for more than sixteen years when Stumpf first began his studies into acoustics, and had already proven itself more than faddish, having gone through six editions by 1872.

Yet within this nexus of music and psychology—for which Stumpf is predominantly remembered today—it is easy to overlook his grounding in Plato and Aristotle, which, for William James, made him one of 'the most philosophical and profound of all ... writers'.[1] Indeed, it is arguably the recursive inclination towards philosophical reasoning in Stumpf's thought that first drew him to Franz Brentano, who had argued that 'true philosophical methods are none other than those of the natural sciences', as Stumpf once put it.[2] By collapsing the distinction between disciplines on the basis of their shared methodology, this stance rested on the foundation of an enduring epistemology that governed the humanities as much as the hard sciences. This, for Stumpf, 'was and remains a guiding star for me'.

Inevitably, the degree of abstraction occasioned by this philosophical foundation had certain consequences. In 1911, Stumpf's argument about the historical development of music can seem dislocated from the modernism of his age. That very year saw the premiere in Paris of Stravinsky's ballet *Petrushka*, whose polyrhythmic textures and irregular, changing metres capture the cardinal elements that Stumpf diagnosed in indigenous musical cultures less developed than that of the musical West. The year 1911 also witnessed the premiere of Richard Strauss' opera *Der Rosenkavalier*, whose equally complex tonality borders on the polytonality that Stumpf ascribes to an underdeveloped appreciation of harmonic function. To say that influence works both ways (from indigenous musics to Western classical music, as well as vice versa) would be unduly simplistic here; it is rather the artistic diversity within modernism, and its experiments in exceeding the limits of traditional art music, that highlight the strictness of the criteria Stumpf uses to determine musical elements in other cultures: pitch, interval, metre, patterning, and form.

---

[1] William James, *The Principles of Psychology* [1890], rpt. (Cambridge, MA.: Harvard Univ. Press, 1983), 911.

[2] See this volume, 192.

As Stumpf's careful comments in Part II of *The Origins of Music* show, the distinctions between detuned pitches and non-diatonic pitches, between stable rhythmic patterning and disorganized ensemble playing, rely on the musicians' intent as determined by consistency across multiple performances. A case in point is the use of quarter tones. Alois Hába's quarter tone suite for string orchestra would appear barely six years after *The Origins* differentiated between the wavering of pitch and what in 1911 was still the 'theoretical' concept of microtones, albeit one with a number of historical anticipations in the nineteenth century. In tandem with Hába's suite, Willi von Möllendorf's *Music with Quartertones* (1917) would argue that the expressive potential of diatonic and chromatic harmony had been exhausted, and that in order to continue towards ever richer means of expression the number of scale steps must be doubled by using quarter tones.[3] Of course, Stumpf was speaking about music from a conservative late Romantic epoch, not the experimental avant-garde, but the context of his study indicates that his criteria for tracking music's origination were Janus-faced. Some non-tempered pitching in indigenous musics is precise, just like the ancient Greek theory of an enharmonic genus of tetrachord or Hába's suite, but some pitching is imprecise, accidental, and hence indicative for Stumpf of a 'primitive' or intermediate stage in the development of music. The question is: which is which?

2.1. Legacy

The technology available to Stumpf to help in making such judgements was itself 'primitive' by modern standards. The rotation speed of Edison phonographs was variable, often driven unevenly by a crank handle, and before the use of copper negatives, the runic grooves written into the wax cylinders steadily degraded with multiple playing. (This was the Heisenberg problem of the earliest recordings: the more one listens to a cylinder, the less what is heard can be taken to be accurate.) It meant

---

[3] Willi von Möllendorf, *Musik mit Vierteltönen. Erfahrungen am Bichromatischen Harmonium* (Leipzig: F. E. C. Leuckart, 1917). Eng. trans. Klaus Schmirler, *Music with Quartertones*, see: http://tonalsoft.com/monzo/moellendorf/book/contents.htm [accessed 16 September 2011].

that even where original recordings were available to Stumpf, their condition and absolute pitch (coupled to tempo) remained in doubt except—putatively—in cases where an identifiable pitch pipe was used. Yet the legacy of the Berlin Phonogram Archive, which Stumpf tasked Otto Abraham with running within the larger Psychological Institute he officially founded at Berlin University in 1900, has endured and is now part of UNESCO's Memory of the World Register. It was this collection of recordings that provided an institutional basis on which to develop comparative methods in the study of music. And it was Stumpf who ensured that comparative musicology received certification as a legitimate discipline within the university. Following the flowering of comparative studies of music during the 1930s under Erich von Hornbostel,[4] systematic approaches to music have survived to this day. Their practitioners have also retained the optimism attendant on new technologies. As recently as 2004 the editors of a broad study of empirical methods in music issued the rallying cry that 'musicology is or could be, in many instances, a significantly "data richer" field than we generally give credit for'.[5] While this may seem a long way from the philosophy of origins or *Ursprungsphilosophie* that preoccupied so many late nineteenth-century writers wherein 'the origin . . . is a past moment that bestows truth on the present',[6] the rationale of providing a justification (*auctoritas*) for our current understanding of our own culture remains the same, where empirical, comparative studies and the search for cultural origins become two sides of the same coin.

2.2. Contemporary discourse

To be sure, Stumpf was not alone in contributing to the growth and formation of comparative musicology. And given the weave of ideas

---

[4] Dieter Christensen, 'Erich M. von Hornbostel, Carl Stumpf, and the institutionalization of comparative musicology', in Bruno Nettl and Phillip Bohlman (eds.), *Comparative Musicology and Anthropology of Music* (Chicago and London: Univ. of Chicago Press, 1991), 201–209.

[5] Eric F. Clarke and Nicholas Cook (eds.), *Empirical Musicology: Aims, Methods, Prospects* (Oxford and New York: Oxford Univ. Press, 2004), 4.

[6] Alexander Rehding, 'The quest for the origins of music in Germany circa 1900', *Journal of the American Musicological Society* 22 (2002): 345–385, here 347.

binding leading experimental researchers together, it is not surprising that the ideas of others are traceable in Stumpf's own text. To take one example, Graf views the appointment of Richard Wallaschek (1860–1917) as an associate lecturer at Vienna University in 1896 as the official inauguration of comparative musicology.[7] Wallaschek, a contemporary of Guido Adler, made extensive comparisons between ethnic instruments in *Primitive Music* (1893), yet Stumpf remained sceptical of his search for the beginnings of music in the need for rhythmic forms within communal singing and dancing. Nevertheless Stumpf's admission in Part II of *The Origins* that metrical groupings can legitimately be conceived (and transcribed) differently indicates a certain point of agreement with Wallaschek, who argued that 'time-sense is . . . a mental work of grouping the sensations, and this takes place not in the senses themselves but in the cortex'. Hence the process of rhythmic grouping becomes a 'cortical process of group perception'.[8] Because our sense of time is cognitive rather than sensory—i.e. not inherent in the music as such—different individuals can hear different metrical groupings while listening to the same metre. This is a problem for putatively objective transcriptions, particularly when migrating non-Western music into Western notation. Stumpf's rationale for selecting changing metres (where necessary) is that 'it is better to use this aid where it works: the division of accents given by the bar structure makes an overview of the whole structure easier, extraordinarily so'.[9] Thus his decisions about metre ultimately relate to pattern recognition as a prerequisite for the perception of a synoptic structure in indigenous musics.

Another influential figure for Stumpf is the psychologist and philosopher Christian von Ehrenfels (1859–1932), whose early writings on 'gestalt qualities' found music to be a particularly good example; while Stumpf never saw himself as a gestalt psychologist and even criticized Ehrenfels for his terminology in this field, some of their ideas

---

[7] Walter Graf, 'Die vergleichende Musikwissenschaft in Österreich seit 1896', *Yearbook of the International Folk Music Council* 6 (1974): 15–43.

[8] Richard Wallaschek, 'On the difference of time and rhythm in music', *Mind* 4 (1895): 28–35, here 29.

[9] See this volume, 109.

overlapped. Ehrenfels pointed out that when a melody is transposed to a different key, it is heard as being identical to the original melody, even though the two have an entirely different set of pitches. Thus, the perception of a melody is more than the perception of its individual parts, he proposed. A melody is, therefore, a gestalt quality.[10] For Stumpf, the ability to transpose a melody distinguishes human from animal musical faculties, underscoring his argument that it is the relationship between pitches (intervals) as such, and not the melody as defined by its absolute pitches, that signals the richer human appreciation of sonic forms.

For Stumpf, of course, these intervals were predominantly the perfect consonances (octave, fifth, and fourth), whose transposition indicated an appreciation of consonance *sui generis* among humans. But thirty years before Stumpf's lecture on *The Origins*, at least one writer investigating 'animal music' had already suggested that the overtone series played a determining role in 'primitive' musical forms. Whereas Stumpf extracted consonant dyads from the overtone series, the American philosopher Xenos Clark had argued in 1879 that the intervals of linear melodic structures are determined by the harmonic structure of overtones, which has 'in some way impressed itself upon the auditory mechanism' over time. As a result, Clark summarizes, the 'physical peculiarities of vibrating bodies [that existed] long before any living being came upon the earth, are also the basis of human and . . . extra-human melody'.[11] While Stumpf was sceptical, disbelieving even, of Clark's transcriptions of diatonic bird scales, sparks had been flying for some time—so to speak—between overtones and musical forms in the discourse of musical origination. Hence this linkage could support increasingly bold claims, the most long-standing of which arguably

---

[10] Christian Ehrenfels, 'Über Gestaltqualitäten', *Vierteljahrsschrift für Wissenschaftliche Philosophie* 14 (1890): 249–292. See also Mitchell G. Ash, *Gestalt Psychology in German Culture 1890–1967: Holism and the Quest for Objectivity* (Cambridge: Cambridge Univ. Press, 1995); Robert Gjerdingen, 'The psychology of music', in *The Cambridge History of Western Music Theory*, ed. Thomas Christensen (Cambridge: Cambridge Univ. Press, 2002); Duane P. Schultz and Sydney E. Schlutz *A History of Modern Psychology*, 7th ed. (Belmont, CA.: Wadsworth, Thomson Learning, 2000).

[11] Xenos Clark, 'Animal music, its nature and origin', *The American Naturalist* 24 (1879): 209–223, here 211.

belongs to Stumpf with the concept of *Verschmelzung* (translated throughout this book as 'fusion').

2.3. Fusion

The concept of fusion is first advanced as a hypothesis in the second volume of *Psychology of Tone* (1890): two tones are perceived as a single entity; their degree of consonance, by Stumpf's definition, depends on the integer ratios of their frequencies. In descending order, these intervals are: the octave (1:2), fifth (2:3), fourth (3:4), major third (4:5), and minor third (5:6), though it is only the first three, the so-called perfect consonances, with the simplest frequency ratios, that Stumpf looks for within his transcriptions of non-Western musics. He broached the concept in the first volume of *Psychology of Tone* (1883) with the notion that our initial judgement or analysis of an interval is not an analysis of the two constituent tones, but of the sound as a whole, i.e. where an interval becomes a mental representation based on sensations.

At root, the theory links intervals to ideas of universality, where perfect consonances become, in effect, metaphors for fundamental truths about music and the human race. The intuitive attraction of a theory of music's origination via consonant signalling (the enhanced vocal cries of simultaneous sustained pitches that led to the perfect consonances) has ensured that Stumpf's theory is regarded to this day as markedly more plausible than most.[12] (By analogy, Richard Wagner had presented the poetic side of such a theory in 1854 by using the perfect consonances to depict the origins of the world in the opening bars of *Das Rheingold*, even if he also admitted the fifth partial, the major third, in his sonic vision of our mythic prehistory.)

Stumpf presumes fusion to be immanent in music. It is based on both the physical reality of acoustics and the physiological reality of 'brain processes', i.e. carefully distinguished from Helmholtz's reliance of the structure of the inner ear, which famously gives a Fourier analysis of

---

[12] See, for example, Bruno Nettl, *The Study of Ethnomusicology: Thirty-One Issues and Concepts*, 2nd ed. (Champaign, IL: Univ. of Illinois Press, 2005), 262.

compound sound waves.[13] But, as Rehding points out, it remains unclear whether fusion is physiologically innate or an aspect of external reality, a telling ambiguity given the weight placed on this phenomenon for his theory of music's origins.[14] Indeed, it is a concept that links hard acoustic science to cognitive psychology, forming a critical bridge between mind and matter, or as Stumpf characterizes his study: 'the cognitive penetration of matter'.[15]

Stumpf's classical leanings are revealing here. His essay on pseudo-Aristotelian problems about music (1897a) clarifies that the concept of fusion is expressly borrowed from Aristotle's discussion of the octave in *De sensu*, where the two notes 'are not exactly homophonous but only analogous to each other.'[16] Here again, Stumpf distinguishes mental from physical elements, arguing that 'this mixture or fusion of simultaneous sounding is common to all consonance according to [almost all writers on music from antiquity], and characterizes its constitutive property in a psychological sense, while the frequency ratio does so in a physical sense'.[17]

But where did this distinction originate for Stumpf? During his early doctoral work on Plato, he reports that he was 'tormented' by difficulties arising from Aristotle's critique of the theory of forms, proposing that the very name 'form' should be banned from metaphysics. Might the consonant dyad serve as precisely such a problematic form? Stumpf's familiarity with Plato gave rise to the application of the term 'heterophony' to the looping of simultaneous melodic paraphrases in indigenous musics, and so there may be good reason to return, via

---

[13] Hermann von Helmholtz, 'On the physiological causes of harmony in music' [1857], in *Science and Culture: Popular and Philosophical Essays*, ed. David Cahan (Chicago and London: Univ. of Chicago Press, 1995), 46–75.

[14] Rehding, 'The quest for the origins of music in Germany circa 1900', 354.

[15] See this volume, 65. For a discussion of this topic, see Martin Ebeling, 'Tonverschmelzung, neurologisch—mathematisch—musikalisch', in Martin Ebeling and Margret Kaiser-el-Safti (eds.), *Die Sinne und die Erkenntnis* (Frankfurt amMain: Peter Lang, 2011), 125–161.

[16] Carl Stumpf, *Die pseudo-Aristotelischen Probleme über Musik* (Berlin: Königliche Akademie der Wissenschaften, 1897), 9.

[17] Ibid., 7.

Aristotle, to the subject of his doctoral 'torment' for the deep context of fusion.

The celebrated section in Plato's *Republic* on educating philosopher kings distinguishes sensations that inspire thought from those that do not. This, it would seem, offers a prototype for the concept of fusion as that perception of two separately sensible sounds, fused as one indistinguishable sound, where the sound retains both its compound and its singular identity. Since not everyone agrees that Plato even has what can properly be described as a theory of forms, let alone an accurate conception of what this theory would be,[18] it is worth quoting Plato's explanation of this specific instance of form at length:

> I'm sure you'll see what I mean if I say that at the level of the senses, some things don't encourage the intellect to explore further, because the situation can be adequately assessed by the relevant sense, while other things can't help provoking an enquiring attitude, because sense-perception fails to produce a sound result. . . . [I]n order to count as thought-provoking . . . they have to produce contradictory sense-impressions at the same time; otherwise, they aren't thought-provoking. The impression sense-perception has to give of an object is that it is no more X than the opposite of X, however close or far away it is when you encounter it. . . . I mean, here's how each sense works: the main point is that the sense into whose domain hardness falls is inevitably also the sense into whose domain softness falls; and the message it passes on to the mind is that, in its perception, the same thing is both hard and soft. . . . It makes sense to suppose, then . . . that these are the circumstances in which the chief thing the mind does is summon up calculation and thought to help it examine whether in any given case it's being informed about one object or two objects . . . If each of them is single, then, and it takes two of them to make two, then it'll think about them as two separate objects. I mean, if they were inseparable, it wouldn't be thinking about two objects: it would be thinking about one object. . . . [S]ight sees both big and small as a kind of mixture, not as separate from each other . . . and in order to clarify the situation, the intellect is forced in its turn to look at big and small as distinct entities, not mixed together, which is the opposite of what sight does.[19]

---

[18] Verity Harte, 'Plato's Metaphysics', *The Oxford Handbook of Plato* (Oxford and New York: Oxford Univ. Press, 2008), 191–216, here 193.

[19] Plato, *Republic*, trans. and ed. Robin Waterfield (Oxford and New York: Oxford Univ. Press, 1998), 523b, 524a–c.

Following Aristotle's analogy between visual colour mixtures and consonant tones,[20] if we substitute sight for audition here, this would seem a lucid, if abstract, explanation for the phenomenon of a dyad heard as a single entity (owing to its 'consonant' frequency ratio) but intelligible as two separate pitches. It is beside the point whether or not Stumpf had this particular passage in mind while exploring Aristotle's theory of octave pitches. In any case, the metaphysical difficulty of a form that is not consistently identical with itself, potentially even existing in a state of self-contradiction, plays no part in Stumpf's fusion; the outline of the concept nevertheless offers a blueprint for a phenomenon at once acoustic and mental, i.e. one that endlessly solicits cognitive persistence. The pleasure that Stumpf finds in perfect consonances acts as a catalyst for the historical development of consonances among primordial humanity. This, again, is supported by an argument arising from Wallaschek's neurological research during the 1890s (into language and music in patients with aphasia), namely that emotion and intellectual activity are differentiable, separate brain processes.[21]

2.4. The phonograph

The corollary to holding metaphysics in abeyance here is a turn towards materialism and positivistic investigation. In a lecture in 1907 Stumpf recounted how materialism supplanted Hegelian idealism to become the dominant philosophy of the second half of the nineteenth century. (Many writers deemed this a 'catastrophe', he added, that signalled the end of philosophy as such.)[22] Against this traffic, music continued to retain its metaphysical identity in many circles. But from 1877, Thomas Edison's phonograph ensured that the new scientific perspective directly and irreversibly challenged the special character of sound. By capturing the fleeting

---

[20] Stumpf, *Die pseudo-Aristotelischen Probleme über Musik*, 8–9.

[21] Richard Wallaschek, 'Über die Bedeutung der Aphasie für den Musikalischen Ausdruck', *Vierteljahrsschrift für Musikwissenschaft* 7 (1891): 53–73; and 'Die Bedeutung der Aphasie für die Musikvorstellung', *Zeitschrift für Psychologie und Physiologie der Sinnesorganie* 6 (1894): 8–32.

[22] Carl Stumpf, 'Die Wiedergeburt der Philosophie', in *Philosophische Reden und Vorträge* (Leipzig: J. A. Barth, 1910), 161–196, here 164–165.

moment, the recording apparatus reified musical practices as never before, making performances scrutable by quite literally objectifying the moment in wax (though, until the use of copper negative—as noted above—this was never as permanent as its concept might suggest). Ironically, the new technology only underscored the impermanence of life and art, becoming at once a means of storing time and a signifier of transience. In 1878, for instance, Edison recommended capturing the dying words of relatives along with treasured family mottos.[23] It is perhaps no coincidence that part of Stumpf's rationale for establishing an archive of phonographic recordings in 1900 was that the opportunity to record music pertaining to 'originary conditions . . . will shortly have been lost forever through the modernization of primitive peoples'.[24] Treating present-day indigenous tribes as sources for accessing the evolutionary past was common enough during the later nineteenth century, but the phonograph served to highlight their status as the final living trace of tantalizingly impermanent developmental stages. To be sure, technology for transcribing sounds had been in use since 1857 with Édouard-Léon Scott de Martinville's phonautography, though this lacked any form of playback mechanism at the time, becoming merely another means of acoustic writing.[25]

In a sense, the phonograph transformed the young discipline of musicology from a data-poor to a data-rich field, where data (hard evidence) are distinct from facts (the interpretive criteria extrapolated from data for purposes of historical assessment). In the same vein, the new 'cents' system formally put into practice by Alexander Ellis (1814–1890) in 1885 presented a means of determining pitch by dividing the equal-tempered semitone into 100 equal logarithmic units, i.e. more precisely than human ears could detect.[26] This materialist turn and its embrace

---

[23] Thomas Edison, 'Phonograph—the wonderful possibilities of Edison's invention', *North American Review* 126 (May–June 1878): 527–536, here 533.

[24] See this volume, 33.

[25] Martinville's scientific papers are housed at the archives of the Société d'encouragement pour l'industrie nationale, Paris, and are also available online: http://firstsounds.org/features/scott.php [accessed 15 March 2012].

[26] Alexander J. Ellis, 'On the musical scales of various nations', *Journal of the Society of Arts* 33 (1885): 485–527.

of empiricism is predicated on the dependence on objects of research, whether wax cylinders, tonometric instruments and the transcriptions of explorers, or the vocal organs and brain processes of indigenous musicians. Viewing the body as the product of evolutionary biology did not entail a loss of inner life, however. The knowledge won by research in physiology and anatomy did not void the human form of spiritual or mental attributes. It is worth recalling that Stumpf trained at a seminary and remained a Christian throughout his life. It took an egregious insult from a priest for him finally to sever all ties with the Catholic Church.[27] Thus, the physical body was not merely a complex machine in an atheistic universe, and we might liken Stumpf's investigations into the processes of cognition to what Andreas Daum has called 'strategies for enchantment' in the discourse of nineteenth-century science, for in the rise of psychology they present a counter-narrative to the view of humanity's desacralization as a linear process against the growth of atheistic materialist thought.[28]

The continuing relevance of Stumpf's work is evident both in the ongoing digitization of his archive, which swelled to some 30,000 cylinders dating from between 1893 and 1954,[29] thereby bestowing a new degree of permanence on the collection; and in the recent re-emergence of comparative approaches to music via new technologies such as recording analysis software, e.g. Sonic Visualiser, which allows digital recordings of the same piece to be compared with a degree of precision unavailable to the naked ear.[30] Such comparative investigations have increasingly become part of modern performance studies, whose subject

---

27 See this volume, 218.

28 Andreas Daum, 'Science, politics, and religion: Humboldtian thinking and the transformation of civil society in Germany, 1830–1870', *Osiris* 17 (2002): 107–140, here 116.

29 Susanne Ziegler, *Die Wachszylinder des Berliner Phonogramm-Archivs* (Berlin: Staatliche Museen zu Berlin, 2006), 51.

30 Chris Cannam, Christian Landone, and Mark Sandler, 'Sonic Visualiser: An open source application for viewing, analysing, and annotating music audio files', in *Proceedings of the ACM Multimedia 2010 International Conference*. http://www.sonicvisualiser.org/ [accessed 28 September 2011].

is far from restricted to Western art music.[31] The fleeting references to Beethoven's Ninth and Brahms' First symphonies in Stumpf's 1911 text indicate that he viewed the German musical canon as one musical culture among many in the world, albeit the most developed. It would arguably take another eighty years for mainstream research within historical musicology to accept the implications of this comparison with emphatic declarations such as: 'We are all (ethno)musicologists now', underscoring the fact that the methodologies established by Stumpf's *Origins of Music* continue to enjoy a rich afterlife.[32]

Finally, a few words on this translation. Stumpf's German is flowing and clear, with moments of joviality; I have sought to replicate that balance in my translation. Part I of *The Origins of Music* was originally a lecture, to which Stumpf appended thirty-two endnotes. For the convenience of the reader I have filled out all references to academic literature, however brief, to include year of publication, publisher, and all volume numbering and pagination; I have also supplied forenames for researchers whom Stumpf references only by surname. For clarity, I have provided example numbers in chapters 3 and 4, and have made very minor adjustments to Stumpf's text in order to accommodate this numbering. Editorial comments, where necessary, are included as footnotes. Stumpf also occasionally added his own footnotes, however. In order to differentiate his footnotes from editorial footnotes, all notes by Stumpf are denoted by [SN], and all in-text references he gave have been normalized as footnotes with the designation [SR].

Acknowledgement

I am grateful to Karola Obermüller for her generous assistance with parts of this translation.

---

31 A recent example is Nicholas Cook, Eric Clarke, Daniel Leech-Wilkinson, and John Rink (eds.), *The Cambridge Companion to Recorded Music* (Cambridge: Cambridge Univ. Press, 2009).

32 Nicholas Cook, 'We are All (Ethno)musicologists now', in *The New (Ethno)musicologies*, ed. Henry Stobart (Lanham, MD: Scarecrow Press, 2008), 48–70.

Section II

The origins of music (1911)

By Carl Stumpf

Preface

This book is based on a lecture delivered at the Urania in Berlin.[1] The previously published text is elaborated here: notes have been added pertaining to scholarly explanation and substantiation of individual points, there are also numerous reliable examples of primitive melodies with technical analyses, and finally, some illustrations of primitive instruments.

The ethnological study of music has frequently occupied my time over several decades and the arrival of the phonograph has served to increase this further. I wanted to summarize the fruits of this work for experts and for a wider audience. This would not have been possible without the help of my young assistants at the Berlin Phonogram Archive, and above all without the help of [Erich von Hornbostel] to

---

[1] Stumpf gave his lecture on 24 November 1909 at the Urania, a public educational institute founded in Berlin by Wilhelm Foerster, Wilhelm Meyer, and Werner Siemens in 1888. The original lecture text is published as 'Die Anfänge der Musik' in Stumpf, *Philosophische Reden und Vorträge* (Leipzig: J. A. Barth, 1910), 225–261.

whom this treatise is dedicated.[2] There is no line we did not discuss, no melody he did not check note for note. I can only leave this little book with the wish that it will shortly be superseded by a comprehensive work in his hand.

In addition to him, I must gratefully thank Erich Fischer for his assistance with the troublesome transcription of several phonographic recordings that remain unpublished.

Berlin, April 1911, C. Stumpf

---

[2] Erich Moritz von Hornbostel (1877–1935) was Stumpf's assistant at the Berlin Psychological Institute, and became the first director of the Berlin Phonogram Archive in 1905. For a study of Hornbostel's work, see Sebastian Klotz (ed.), *"Vom tönenden Wirbel menschlichen Tuns". Erich M. von Hornbostel als Gestaltpsychologe, Archivar und Musikwissenschaftler: Studien und Dokumente* (Berlin: Schibri, 1998).

Chapter 3

Part I: The origin and archetypes of music making

Over the course of many millennia the human race has brought about developments in language, science, art, and in ethical, social, and technical practice, which raise the question time and again of how all these glorious things have arisen, and what divine spark—glowing inconspicuously at first—gradually kindled this wealth of light. Without wanting to delve deeper into the depths of human nature here, or even into metaphysical secrets, I want to try to get closer to the question of the origins and first manifestations of music, using the experiences and knowledge afforded us by today's ethnology, comparative musicology, and experimental psychology.

This will always be a matter of hypotheses. But we are better equipped to put forward credible hypotheses today than our predecessors. While Rudolf Virchow[3] complained as early as 1886 that the lack of any interest in the prehistory of music was the single unmitigated gap in the efforts of Berlin's Anthropological Society—a degree of apathy excused by the scarcity of reliable material—Heinrich Waldeyer[4] in 1903 could characterize as a field of undreamt-of dimensions and significance the research in this area enabled by a new aid, the phonograph, and by the measuring of exotic instruments. Indeed it is imperative now to raise an inventory of everything still available from originary conditions. Unless we arrange a systematic collection and safe-keeping of documents through which we can visualize the dim and distant past, the modernization of

---

[3] Rudolf Virchow (1821–1902) was a German anthropologist and biological pathologist, who founded the field of cellular pathology.

[4] Heinrich Wilhelm Gottfried Waldeyer-Hartz (1836–1921) was a nationally celebrated anatomist and pathologist; he held university appointments at Breslau, Strasbourg, and Berlin.

primitive peoples and the extinction of many tribes means that the opportunity will soon have been lost forever. Even the material at hand, however, allows the outlines of primitive musical practice to be seen far more clearly than before.[i]

3.1. Recent theories

Let us first recall briefly, and with some critical remarks, the hypotheses that have recently been put forward concerning the origins of music.[ii]

3.1.1.

According to Darwinian doctrine, in which all advance must be understood essentially from the principle of natural selection or survival of the fittest, music initially forms a curious anomaly. Saint Cecilia looks aloft to heaven—how does she help us in the struggle for existence? Her disciples certainly earn plenty of money from time to time; some earn a living playing the piano with their well-trained fingers. For the majority of people, however, the indefinable, abstract structures of air [*Luftgebilde*] that we call music are not connected to the real utilities and needs of everyday life.

Nevertheless, Darwin had a suggestion. His solution can be expressed with the words: 'In the beginning was love'; admittedly not the heavenly kind, but earthly, sexual love. Males endeavoured to please females, and females selected the one who offered the greatest advantages. Just as the males who are considered the most beautiful in terms of build and colour have always been selected, so also the best singers or wailers. Hence, in animals we find the male sex more colourful and fond of singing. Among humans, initially only males were productive artists, but females added critical discernment. Nowadays both genders sing and play, the female almost more than the male. But, indisputably, men still remain more musically productive, and 'sweet love thinks in sound'—that applies today just as it did in ancient times.

Admittedly, great difficulties arise if one goes into details. I do not want to dwell on the facts that birds also often sing outside periods of courtship; that their calls may also be signals for other purposes, or mere expressions of a general awareness of life; that animals closer to humans do not sing, but only utter harsh cries; and finally, that the songs of primitive peoples are in fact not predominantly love songs, but are in the majority of cases military, medical, and religious songs. I only wish to examine one point—a crucial one nonetheless—a bit more closely.

Music is not the mere production of tones, but rather the production of certain arrangements of tones, however simple they may be. It is an absolutely essential feature of music in the human sense that these arrangements can be recognized and reproduced independently of absolute pitch. A melody remains the same whether it is sung by a bass or soprano, whether in C or in E. As far as we know, we find this capacity to recognize and to transpose melodies universally among primitive peoples. An Indian or a South Sea islander does not mind beginning his song a little higher or lower; so long as it is comfortable for his vocal range, he pitches the intervals just the same. For the purposes of phonographic recordings a small pitch pipe is blown as prescribed into the recording horn by explorers, in order later to be able to reproduce the original speed of the cylinder, and hence the pitch and tempo of the song. In the process, it was observed that the native singers frequently adjusted the intonation of their song to the pitch of the little pipe.

So what about animals? To my knowledge it has not previously been observed that a bullfinch or starling to whom one has taught a particular melodic motive, say 'Morgen muß ich fort von hier' [tomorrow I must leave this place] or 'Dein ist mein Herz' [my heart is yours], has ever repeated these illustrations in a different key, be it merely a whole tone higher or lower, during its many hours of leisure, although its vocal apparatus would allow it to do so.[5] Otto Abraham[6] carried out

---

5 'Morgen muß ich fort von hier' is a seventeenth-century folk song recorded in the Arnim / Brentano collection *Des Knaben Wunderhorns* (1808); it was set to music by Johannes Brahms (WoO posth. 38 no. 17), Wilhelm Goldner (Op. 7 no. 2), Friedrich Silcher, and Max W. K. Vogrich. Wilhelm Müller's strophic poem 'Ungeduld', containing the memorable refrain 'Dein ist mein Herz', was set to music by Karl Friedrich Curschmann (Op. 3), Josephine Lang (Op. 6), Leopold Lenz (Op. 22), Franz Schubert (D. 795), and Louis Spohr (Op. 94). Stumpf gives no indication which musical settings he is referring to, but the most prevalent would seem to have been Silcher and Schubert, respectively.

6 Otto Abraham (1872–1926), was a physician and colleague of Stumpf's at the Berlin Phonogram Archive. Together with Erich von Hornbostel, he published collaborative

experiments with a parrot aiming at this for years, but without any success. I do not want to claim that there might not be small changes in the pitch of a bird's call or a bellowing cow for those individuals in question. On the contrary, it is clear from the outset that mathematically equal intonation is only the exception; the rule, however, will be the existence of deviations which move around a middle point within certain boundaries. But these random fluctuations—which result from differing strengths of expiration that may depend on the animal's momentary physical feeling and condition—should not by themselves be confused with actual transposition.

As far as one can conclude from the above, a bird's feeling of pleasure—if it is linked to the sounds themselves (for muscular sensations probably also contribute to this)—may well be substantially different from that of human beings' listening to human and avian music. The animal feeling of pleasure appears to be quite dependent on this specific succession of absolute pitches, whose slight displacement might escape a singer's attention; the human feeling of pleasure is determined first and foremost by the pitch relationships whereby huge displacements of the absolute pitches occur with the full consciousness of the singers and listeners, without rendering the melody unrecognizable or unenjoyable.[iii] We say: first and foremost. It cannot be denied that absolute pitch can effect significant differences. Absolute pitch plays a significant role for the Chinese.[iv] We ourselves invoke 'key characteristics',[7] on the other hand, and the aversion of sensitive types to the transposition of a song written for a particular key. However, the

---

works based on the study of recordings, such as *Studien über das Tonsystem und die Musik der Japaner* (Leipzig: Breitkopf & Härtel, 1903); *Phonographierte Indische Melodien* (Leipzig: Breitkopf & Härtel, 1904); and 'Vorschläge für die Transkription exotischer Melodien', *Sammelbände der Internationalen Musikgesellschaft* 11 (1909): 1–25. Eng. trans. George and Eve List, 'Suggested methods for the transcription of exotic music', *Ethnomusicology* 38 (1994): 425–56.

[7] Stumpf refers obliquely to Christian Friedrich Daniel Schubart's (1739–1791) *Ideen zu einer Ästhetik der Tonkunst* (1784–1785), whose well-known final section on the characteristic identity of keys argued that sharp keys reflect passion and drives, flat keys evoked gentle feeling and repose. A useful overview of this belief is given in Rita K. Steblin, *A History of Key Characteristics in the 18th and Early 19th Centuries* (Ann Arbor: UMI Research Press, 1983). See also, T. A. Dubois *Christian Friedrich Daniel Schubart's*

piece still remains just as comprehensible and will readily be recognized by us as the same work. To dispute the *possibility* of transposition will occur to nobody. Only the expression and the effect appear to be influenced by absolute pitch.

That is the salient point, and Darwin's comprehensive scientific vision has not considered it, just as—strangely enough—it is commonly treated by zoologists in general as if its effects are negligible.[v]

Music's situation is similar to that of language. Animals also have language. But language in our sense begins only where vocal sounds are used as symbols of general concepts, and there is just as little evidence for this as the usage of transposed intervals by animals. What we have inherited from animal ancestors in both regards is merely the larynx and the ear.

Our current understanding would suggest that, should any as yet unexamined human tribes find themselves entirely inept at melodic transcription in this respect, we would simply deny them a capacity for music in the narrower sense. Contrariwise, should talented animals just once verify or instil this ability, we would instantly consider them as our rightful brothers in Apollo. For the moment, though, neither of these is the case, and indeed our physical next of kin, the mammals, offer particularly meagre prospects.

If music in general is to be derived from the animal kingdom, old Democritus' idea would almost have more to commend itself than Darwin's: namely, that one reaches the origin of music by *imitating* birds.[vi] Then, of course, genealogy would have nothing to do with it. In fact, one finds such avian imitation in primitive peoples; the Berlin Phonogram Archive owns reference samples of this. But the only or even the main source of music cannot lie here. The samples available to us in no way relate to bird-likenesses, particularly of a melodic, musical kind. It is more the rhythmic element, and the trilling and chirruping, that entices primitive men to imitate birds. Yet if more melodic tunes were indeed imitated in ancient times, this would immediately raise the

---

Ideen zu einer Ästhetik der Tonkunst: an Annotated Translation (doctoral dissertation, Univ. of Southern California, 1983).

question: how did we arrive at this choice? Why did we prefer melodic material with distinct intervals? Thus, the question is only deferred.

3.1.2.

Without knowledge of his predecessors, Herbert Spencer[8] has advanced another modern hypothesis that we already find in Rousseau and Herder, among others. We can express it in the formula: 'in the beginning was the word.'[9] It teaches that music arose from the accents and intonation of human speech. These tonal characteristics become considerably more prominent in excited speech, under the influence of strong emotion. If we call someone, and call him again for a second and third time when he fails to appear, or if we ask or demand with rising feeling, if we celebrate or mourn through words: speech always becomes musical according to Spencer, one already begins to sing. This pitch movement of excited speech would later be separated entirely from words and transferred to instruments, and thus absolute music came into existence.

There is much truth in this, to which we will return later: 'intoned speech' [*Sprachgesang*] forms a widespread form of recitation among primitive peoples. But on the actual central issue, Spencer is wide of the mark. For music is differentiated entirely and essentially from sing-song speech [*singendes Sprechen*] by its need of fixed steps, whereas speech—admittedly of varying degrees of pitch differentiation—knows no fixed intervals and in many cases occurs in the form of continually gliding pitch movement. Human speech acquires its unbounded capacity for expression from precisely these tiniest nuances and continuous transitions, which absolutely cannot be reproduced in music. By enlarging and analysing precisely the curves that a spoken sentence inscribes

---

[8] Herbert Spencer (1820–1903) was an English sociologist and philosopher, a staunch advocate of evolutionary theory, a critic of utilitarian politics and colleague of Charles Darwin's. His writings include *The Principles of Psychology* (London: Longman et al., 1855); *Education: Intellectual, Moral, Physical* (London: Williams and Norgate, 1861); and *Principles of Sociology*, 3 vols. (London: Williams and Norgate, 1876–1896).

[9] Spencer, 'The origin and function of music', *Essays: Scientific, Political, and Speculative* (London: Longman et al., 1858), 359–84.

on the gramophone, Edward W. Scripture[10] proved (something not inaccessible to a fine ear, incidentally) that often a considerably fluctuating pitch occurs even within a single syllable, which—musically speaking—would be a flagrant mistake.[vii] (See figures 3.1–3.3)

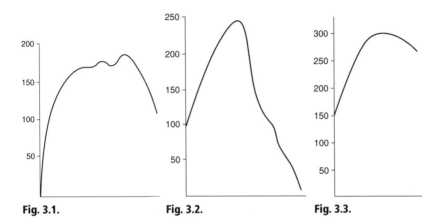

Fig. 3.1.   **Fig. 3.2.**   **Fig. 3.3.**

In each of these pitch curves, only the interjection 'O!' was spoken. The first was sorrowful, the second was adulatory, the third interrogatory. In doing so, the voice—starting at different absolute pitches—rose two octaves the first time, a twelfth the second time, an octave the third time (always only approximately, of course), only to fall down again. This continuous pitch movement is narrower in less emotive speech, but still spans a fourth with a single vowel or diphthong, as shown by Wilhelm Effenberger's examples—using Scripture's method—of two individuals who had to say the verse 'I remember, I remember the house, where I was born'[11,viii] (See figures 3.4 and 3.5).

---

[10] Edward Wheeler Scripture (1864–1945) was an American psychologist and speech scientist, whose doctoral supervisor at Leipzig University was Wilhelm Wundt, a pioneer of experimental psychology. In 1892, Scripture co-founded the American Psychological Association, and served as the director of the Yale Psychological Laboratory between 1892 and 1903. Other positions held include at Columbia University, the University of Vienna, and the West End Hospital in London. His major study of the mind was *The New Psychology* (London: W. Scott, 1897).

[11] The opening lines of Thomas Hood's (1799–1845) poem 'I Remember, I Remember.'

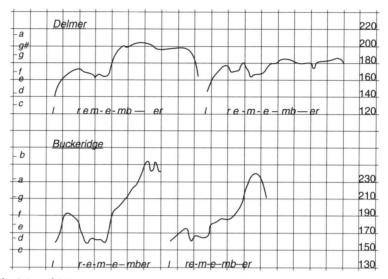

Fig. 3.4. and 3.5.

As is well known, the symbol for the ancient Greek circumflex (peris-pomenon) signified just such a rising and falling of the voice on a vowel or diphthong. Its original form ʌ (analogous to Scripture's curves) illus-trated this vocal movement. In fact, Dionysius of Halicarnassus speci-fies the span of a fourth for this.[ix] With actors, admittedly, one also frequently finds an entirely constant pitch on one syllable, even for an entire sentence if a particular effect is intended.

That the weighty English 'I', for instance, whose movement we just tracked, can be sustained by an artistic orator appears to be proven by the course of the gramophone curves resulting from the 'I' in the actor Jefferson's sentence 'I, said the owl'[12,x] (See figure 3.6).

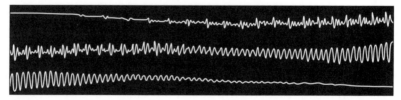

Fig. 3.6.

12 Joseph Jefferson (1829–1905) was a well-known American comedy actor. The sentence Stumpf remembers Jefferson reciting occurs midway through the nursery rhyme 'Who killed Cock Robin'.

Here we see the individual, original wavy lines whose measurement served to produce the earlier pitch curves. Here also, the pitch waves incur sizeable alterations in a short space of time. But from the second third onwards, these alterations only concern the wave form, i.e. the timbre, not the wave*length*. If we measure the distances between successive peaks, we find a significant (indeed, a constant) decrease, i.e. an increase in pitch, only in the first third of the whole curve. From then on we have sing-song speech, without continuously gliding pitch movement. In exceptional cases this is acceptable and useful for producing particular effects, but it is not generally gratifying. It is particularly unpleasant when not only are single accented syllables and long syllables sustained at a constant pitch, but also when fixed musical intervals are frequently used in the succession of pitches without actually being sung. Habitual for many people, and customary in certain regions, sing-song speech is unattractive precisely because it approaches music's fixed intervals and thereby gives up the special asset of language without attaining that of music.

Admittedly, if we examine the pitch movement of a good singer closely, we still do not find a perfectly sustained pitch, but often a precarious fluctuation on a note, and numerous deviations when intoning an interval, sometimes intended, sometimes unintended.[xi] Moreover, a more extensive sliding of the voice (portamento) here and there is famously popular. Such a sliding movement is common among primitive peoples, and is often employed intentionally in particular places and for particular effects.[xii] But there is no doubt: the rules and the spirit of music demand fixed pitches and intervals in principle; the intention of singers and instrumentalists—except in exceptional cases—is directed towards their creation. With speech, by contrast, such an intention does *not* generally exist and *may* not exist if speech does not wish to sacrifice its prime quality.

The renowned status of fixed, pure tonal relationships 1:2, 2:3 etc. must therefore have an origin that is not purely linguistic in nature. Whether or not speech helped in some way at the birth of music or during its nurturing, it certainly was not the mother of music. That which essentially separates music from speech cannot be extracted from speech.[xiii]

3.1.3.

Hans von Bülow's words can serve as a basis for a third opinion: 'in the beginning was rhythm'; namely, rhythmically ordered movement.[13] The connection between dance and song is often emphasized among primitive peoples. The music researcher Richard Wallaschek[14] found much of the origins of music specifically in the singing that accompanied military and hunting dances, and in the necessity of rhythmic forms for communal singing. Then the Leipzig economist Karl Bücher[15] arrived at the same conclusion from a quite different point of view in his interesting and substantial book *Labour and Rhythm*.[16] Ordered movement, which for him forms the origin of all arts, is none other than physical labour, particularly communal labour. Many of the actions that are necessary for daily living—for production of foodstuffs, for farming, rowing, hammering, etc.—are more effective if they are carried out rhythmically. This leads to the accompaniment of labour with all kinds of verses (which Bücher collected in large numbers) and not least with drums and with singers. Poetry and music arise jointly from the necessity of rhythm, and this is itself a natural consequence of the alleviation that it brings to labour, and of the movement in which the work is carried out, the stamping, striking, lifting, etc.

But even a theory of rhythm, however plausible, does not solve our main problem. It notes most occasions and motives that could lead to singing, but the explanation fails again precisely where music's specific difference begins, namely with the question of how humankind came

---

[13] Hans von Bülow's statement occurs at the opening of his essay 'Musikbibel', in *Ausgewählte Schriften 1850–1892*, 2nd ed. (Leipzig: Breitkopf & Härtel, 1911), pt 2: 273.

[14] Richard Wallaschek's (1860–1917) work helped to develop the fields of comparative musicology and music psychology, particularly through his theories about the perception and production of music. He served as a music critic in Vienna between 1896 and 1909, and followed his modern history of music aesthetics, *Ästhetik der Tonkunst* (Stuttgart: W. Kohlhammer, 1886), with an exploration of the origins of music in *Primitive Music* (London and New York: Longman, Green and Co., 1893).

[15] Karl Bücher (1847–1930) was a celebrated German economist and founded the Institute for Newspaper Science in 1916. In addition to *Arbeit und Rhythmus*, Bücher's most influential text was *Die Entstehung der Volkswirtschaft* (Tübingen: Laupp'schen Buchhandlung, 1893).

[16] Bücher, *Arbeit und Rhythmus* (Leipzig: Hirzel, 1897).

to structure in definite intervals a line of pitches that is, on the whole, entirely continuous. Humans could express rhythm just as well if not better through clipped, inarticulate sounds. Emphasizing an accented syllable led naturally to a raising of the pitch for this syllable and hence to a differentiation of intonation; but the consonant intervals on whose origin music particularly depends in no way stand out as particularly suitable for rhythmic purposes, no more so than any other frequency ratios. In instrumental music, training in the art of rhythm would only have led to drumming. But even the most subtly differentiated drum sonata is still not music, at least not *the* music whose origin we seek. After all, rhythm exists not only for hearing, but also for the feelings generated by muscular movement itself; and if the whole of the human race had remained forever deaf, it would certainly still have been able to cultivate dancing, but not music. The essential ingredients of musical scale formations must have arisen independently, for only then could melodic necessity work together with rhythmic necessity (which may have developed first anyway).

It seems to me that another reservation arises from the fact that while work songs are to be found among the unendingly numerous songs of primitive peoples (e.g. boat songs of the Indians or South Sea islanders, marching songs in Africa), they only constitute an extremely small fraction. One only has to compare the melodies in our musical appendix [pp. 107–174]: they were not chosen with regard to purpose or occasion, but for musical structure. Yet there is not a single work song among them, unless one counts (with Bücher) songs of priests and doctors, which seems altogether too modern to me. Proper rhythmic and in particular communal labour only occurs among peoples who are no longer entirely primitive; it is here that work songs in fact increase in quantity, and the majority that Bücher collected come from such peoples.

So, none of the formerly established theories offers an adequate answer to the question at hand.

3.2. The origin and archetypes of singing

We now understand music as the art whose material consists essentially of fixed and transposable tonal steps. If we wish to make the origin of the art comprehensible, we need to distinguish two questions:

(1) How did we develop the ability to recognize relationships of sensory perceptions [*Sinnesempfindungen*] independently from the particular properties of these perceptions [*Empfindungen*]?

(2) And how did we arrive at the particular intervals that we actually find in the music of different peoples and times?

The first question concerns the faculty of abstraction, which is practised vis-à-vis other sensory impressions, for instance when we recognize an ornament or image in reduced form. This general question appears to be related to the definition of our entire human inner life as it differs from that of animals. To what extent are animals in a position to recognize and educe similar relationships in dissimilar material? To what extent could they, for example, abstract the momentary size of phenomena (and so forth) while recognizing people, objects, and localities by the difference of colour and illumination? Certainly we cannot say at the outset that animals are incapable of this. But on the other hand, the uniform reaction if, for example, a dog recognizes its master—not without hesitation—at different distances or in different lighting, proves that the dog has managed to separate the form mentally from the different circumstances. Even when neither the master's scent nor his voice are involved, when exclusively visual clues trigger movement, one can only conclude—initially—from this fact that the organ of perception and the nervous system have become accustomed to certain stimuli that still have their effect under markedly changed circumstances. Admittedly this also goes for us humans in many cases, when we react in the same way to markedly weaker impressions. In our developed inner life, however, that recognition also occurs in a truer sense, meaning not merely the same *reaction* but also *recognition* of the sameness or identity.

That animals always behave in this way may reflect the fact that this faculty of abstraction is already developed to a great extent in primitive peoples, and we must assume its presence to some degree in primordial humans if we do not wish to completely relinquish an understanding of its development.[17] For here lies one of the roots of all human progress. Another, closely related, lies in the generalization of the formation of concepts. Together these lay the basis for our intellectual life, and also our feelings and will. This is the divine spark of which we spoke at the beginning. Quite how it entered the soul and how its glow adapted itself to the framework of evolutionary theory is not something we will expect to research or shed light on here. We assume the existence of a faculty of abstraction [*Abstraktionsfähigkeit*] in primordial man and now put the concrete question of how it is that humans may first have come to separate tonal steps particularly appropriate to transposition from others.

Two secondary questions are also implied here: what was the cause? And: what makes the tonal steps suitable for transposition? We can answer the first hypothetically, the second with certainty.

Let us take as a basis for the hypothesis the oft-pronounced thought, which also presides over books, that all arts are born from the praxis of life. The formula in Goethe's *Faust* ought to be ours: 'In the beginning was the deed'.[18] But which deed, and which practical need, was the origin of music? It is possible that several different causes were involved. I want to suggest, however, that the supposition that a need for *acoustic marking* [*Zeichengebung*] was in play, is not improbable. In doing this we take for granted that the human voice is a musical device.

If one tries to give someone a vocal signal from a great distance, the voice lingers on a high, fixed pitch at great volume—as produced naturally simply by the greatest tension of the vocal folds—while this decreases at the end with diminishing pulmonary strength, as we see in

---

[17] Stumpf's distinction between primordial humans [*Urmenschen*] and primitive peoples [*Naturvölker*] is worth bearing in mind: the former is temporally prior to modern humanity, the latter are culturally prior to, but temporally simultaneous with, Western civilization in 1911. Primordial humanity is of course also prior to modern humanity in evolutionary terms, while primitive peoples are only so in the sense of cultural evolution.

[18] In Part I of Goethe's *Faust*, the protagonist famously rejects the word, meaning, and mental power before stating: 'Mir hilft der Geist! Auf einmal seh' ich Rat / Und schreibe getrost: Im Anfang war die Tat.'

yelling, when herdsmen call out to each other in the mountains. This lingering on a fixed pitch is, I believe, the first step towards singing; it demarcates the boundary separating it from mere speaking.

The second step, the actual creative act for music, is then the need of a fixed and transposable interval to which acoustic signals could lead. Indeed, if the voice of an individual is insufficient, several will call together. Men and boys or men and women will produce sounds of unequal pitch because each only achieves the highest volume within their vocal range. Thus numerous harmonies arise accidentally.

Of all the combinations, only one has the virtue of pitch simultaneity [*Zusammenklang*][19] that is similar to the point of confusion with the impression of a single note: the *octave*. Hence we still call singing together in octaves by men and women monophonic singing, although it would have to be called polyphony if the disparity of pitch is observed. In psycho-acoustics we know this characteristic by the name fusion [*Verschmelzung*],[20] and even Greek music theorists found the essence of 'consonance' in it. This unity of simultaneous pitches in the octave did not arise initially through music itself. It is not the result of a musical development, rather a phenomenon that is necessarily conditioned by the nature of tones or the brain processes on which they are based.[xiv] It is therefore likely that this also exists in animals, but that animals have not been aware of it and have done nothing with it. Primordial humans, however, may have noticed this uniformity and may have particularly liked using simultaneous pitches of this kind while having the impression of singing the self-same note, i.e. a strengthened note. (Whether an actual strengthening or just a greater fullness of sound was achieved

---

[19] The concept of *Zusammenklang*, in its widest sense, denotes the simultaneous sounding of two different pitches, neither of which need be regulated by tempered tuning or any other harmonic framework.

[20] Stumpf's concept of fusion or *Verschmelzung* refers to the quality of a relationship between two pitches that the listener perceives in the fundamental consonances: the octave, pure fifth, or pure fourth. The term does not denote a gradual procedure (a fusing, if you like), but an instantaneously existing state, whose sensations—the combined sensations of hearing the individual pitches—integrate at a cognitive level, giving a pleasing experience. This defines consonance, for Stumpf, and refers to the perception of one sound comprising two pitches that are 'fused' together.

remains an open question.) Even today we can see that unmusical people regard the octave as a single note. Experiments have shown that this occurs about seventy-five times out of a hundred.[xv] Thus precisely those who are at least influenced by musical education are subject to this illusion.

But there are other simultaneous pitches that possess the same characteristic to a lesser but still noticeable extent: particularly the *fifth* and the *fourth*. One can expect the intervals to be confused with a single note by unpractised and unmusical people in 40–60% of cases with the fifth, and 28–36% of cases with the fourth. These simultaneous pitches could gradually make themselves noticeable through their unified effect. Even with our church organ the fifth is added to each and every note in certain registers without anyone noticing it. The sound becomes fuller without forfeiting its unity.

That signalling [*Signalgebung*] was the cause, or one of the causes, for the selection of particular intervals is hypothetical, as I mentioned earlier. That the striking fusion of two simultaneous notes approaches certain frequency relationships independently of absolute pitch—thus making them suitable for transposition—is certain, however.

Since language must have arisen from the need for signalling (initially in the form of aural and gestural signs which are closely interrelated and made comprehensible through each other), our hypothesis thus sets out a common root for music and language.

If, in addition, we effectively consider religious needs at the very dawn of humankind, we can accept that beyond signalling to people, the invocation of gods, e.g. the demonic magical powers of air and water, is among the commonest causes of the most vigorous vocalization. In this way we can also position that aspect of human nature in relation to the origins of music.

Another effect now comes into play, one to which we must ascribe a significant role in humanity's earliest history at any rate, and which is already apparent in more evolved animals, namely monkeys: *curiosity*. Alongside accident and necessity, this is the source of all discovery and invention; it is also the wet nurse to that which gave birth to accident or necessity. When two voices meet at the octave, the fifth, or the fourth, a listener with superior hearing could not fail gradually to notice that there are actually two different notes involved. If one sang the notes one after the other, this would be quite clear. One might rejoice at producing such dyads that were in unison; one then sang the same notes one after the other intentionally in order to commit their impression to memory in this form. At the same time the empty gap still presented by even the smallest of these intervals, the fourth, is then intentionally closed up with intermediary notes. And so we can imagine how the first melodic phrases as well as the first seeds of a scale were formed. Here the octave will have been employed less for melodic usage. Although octave leaps occur in truly primitive songs, they only turn up naturally in a few places. Small steps are more suitable for melodic use. Hence fourths or fifths are the largest intervals in many primitive songs that are sung directly as two consecutive pitches. But equally, the entire ambitus of a song, the range from its lowest note to its highest, rarely exceeds this boundary.

One could well ask whether the first consonant intervals would not also have been marked in the consciousness of primordial humanity by the mere succession of notes. With octaves, for instance, we speak of a certain relationship or similarity or even an identity of the two notes, which could also have attracted the attention of primordial humans. I do not want to exclude such a possibility but regard the fusion that occurs at the simultaneous sounding of notes as the more insistent phenomenon. And for that reason, especially since it could simultaneously have that practical significance, I regard it as the most likely starting point for the development of music.[xvi]

Merely by using certain *small* intervals one could succeed much sooner in singing successive notes without needing any consonant simultaneous pitches at all. People sang notes that were clearly differentiated from each other—perhaps only in response to the play drive[21] or again

---

21 In Friedrich Schiller's treatise *On the Aesthetic Education of Man in a Series of Letters* (1794), the notion of a play drive [*Spieltrieb*] emerges as a concept—borrowed from Immanuel Kant's *Critique of Judgement* (1790)—to transcend the dualism of the sensuous drive [*Sinnestrieb*] and formal drive [*Formtrieb*]; for Schiller, it is defined precisely by the interaction of these two fundamental, opposed drives of the psyche. He characterizes

for the purpose of signalling—meaning that songs were thereby already possible that could be repeated starting on a different note (one also gained a kind of training by producing such steps which could then intentionally be made a little larger or smaller). For such small steps can in fact allow themselves to be produced with exactitude in equal sizes from any starting pitch, and we thereby achieve a type of transposable interval.[xvii] Their tuning, admittedly, will not easily achieve the precision and regularity of intervals based on the principle of consonance.

Many of the most primitive songs, e.g. those of the Vedda of Ceylon,[22] are of this type and certainly originated in this way. One may label them as mere preliminary stages or even as the origins of music; in any case, what is true is that this trend, emanating from small tonal steps, must have united with the foregoing [transposable intervals based on octave fusion], flowing from experiences of consonance, before further development was possible. If such songs with arbitrarily small steps were temporally prior, which is possible, indeed highly probable, we would say: the secondary stream has a longer course but it does not thereby become the primary stream. It is this, the use of consonant fundamental intervals, that increasingly reveals itself as the essence of music, whose source is the source of music.

Moreover, one can easily imagine the manner in which the two streams of this river must soon meet. Short melodic motives made from small steps are pre-eminently suitable for the purposes of signalling, particularly since a wealth of different signs arise from a few notes through the differences of accentuation, which can be used as a family summons, for example. Now when men, women, or boys produced such a signal composed of two or three notes, the cases in which parallel octaves or fifths were sung together must have stood out from the others and gradually become favoured through the

it as the fount of all art, as well as the foundation of 'the much more difficult art of living.' See especially letters 12–14 in Schiller, *On the Aesthetic Education of Man*, trans. and ed. Elizabeth M. Wilkinson and L. A. Willoughby (Oxford: Clarendon, [1967] 1989), 78ff.

[22] Ceylon was renamed Sri Lanka in 1972.

impression of the unison. If this happened a lot, an individual could easily be tempted to try and imitate in their own voice (or by whistling) the call of a current partner whom he had just heard, transposing his own call by an octave, or a fifth or fourth higher or lower. The use of falsetto, often found among primitive peoples, could be related to such attempts at imitation, among other things. Thus singing in parallel was at the same time good training for the ability to transpose.

Once motifs of two or three notes were expanded into larger forms, to which we could already attach the name melody, then the same process could, indeed must, repeat itself. In fact we find that not only the singing of entire melodies in parallel, but also the singing and playing in parallel fifths or fourths, is widespread among primitive peoples. Even in our civilized Europe one still often observes untrained singers [Natursängern] who sing in fifths while believing they are singing in unison. In a moment of distraction or under unusual circumstances the same can even happen to a [trained] musician. If we now separate what was sung simultaneously, it becomes apparent that the melody has been displaced by one of the consonant intervals. There are even early examples of such repetitions. In later Greek and early Christian music, this was called antiphony. Even today, there is—alongside the octave shifts that can hardly count as transposition any more—the regular shift by fifths of fugal themes and other contrapuntal forms. It may sound ridiculous but it is literally correct that the origins of counterpoint reach back to prehistoric times.

In view of this von Hornbostel pointed out that polyphony could have arisen conversely from antiphony, which might first have been completely unregulated. We frequently find among primitive peoples that when two singers or a singer and choir alternate, the second partner begins while the first is still singing his last notes. Perhaps they found a certain attractiveness in this bad habit—probably only arising from the singer's impatience—just as it is used in the art of music to beautiful effect; and perhaps they practised it deliberately and thereby discovered afresh the impression of consonant intervals from a higher and already artistic standpoint.

3.3. Primitive instruments and their influence

Without a doubt, exactly the same process in singing was put into effect very early on with the use of *instruments*. We must expect, however, that many of the ostensibly primitive musical instruments we find today may be regressions from more evolved instruments that migrated from civilized peoples to primitive peoples. For instance, the African harp might stand in this relation to the old Egyptian harp, just as the Kubu pipes on Sumatra stand in relation to those of the civilized people of Java.[xviii] All the same, we can still use those instruments discovered among primitive peoples to give us a rough picture of the original situation.

Pipes are, if not the oldest, at least very old musical devices [*Musikwerkzeuge*]. We find perforated bones of slain animals, particularly of birds, alongside stone tools in European (as well as American) graves and caves. The horns of an antelope or aurochs and hollowed-out mammoth teeth were also used; bamboo cane was particularly common, later also artistically crafted terracotta pipes. They were either blown at the open end or furnished with a hole at the side. At the open end, even in ancient times, a mouthpiece with a narrow fissure would be mounted using a quantity of asphalt, corresponding to the principle of our flageolet.

Such pipes (intended to give just one note) might in turn now find a signalling application, just as today's primitive peoples use pipe signals in countless configurations.[23] That amplification was needed is demonstrated by the frequent occurrence of double pipes. If pipes of different pitch were blown together by several individuals, those three fundamental intervals [octave, fifth, fourth], whose uniformity attracted the attention of our hearing, could again gradually be singled out, even if one did not already know them through singing. In contrast to the untrained human voice, pipes have the advantage that they hold their pitch better while the voice easily wanders within wide boundaries.

---

[23] Stumpf is alluding here to Erich von Hornbostel, 'Über einige Panpfeifen aus Nordwest-Brasilien', in Theodor Koch-Grünberg (ed.), *Zwei Jahre unter den Indianern*, 2 vols. (Berlin: Wasmuth, 1910), 2: 378–391.

Consonant relationships could manifest themselves more easily here, and were perhaps also actually first discovered in this way.

Different pitches were then produced on a single instrument when a resourceful prehistoric instrument maker added several holes. But these holes were not simply added out of acoustic need, as though one wanted to hear the pitches. Rather, they were first bored at random or for superficial reasons (such as how holes could best be set in bamboo nodes, and especially according to the holes' spatial symmetry) and the pitches then blown in such a way that they were found pleasant as they then emerged. A comfortable position for the three or six most frequently used fingers has also been seen, of course. Our sense of hearing, by now perfected, gradually intervened correctively, and brought acoustically perfect intervals to bear on pipes as well, at least with the help of playing technique.

What is more, the system of panpipes—stringing together a number of differently tuned pipes—was probably used very early on to create different pitches. One finds them among primitive peoples in all parts of the world. The pipes are tuned according to different principles. Initially it is likely that no tuning at all took place, and superficial motives or accidents were decisive for the assembly. One finds acoustically perfect intervals on most present-day panpipes, however. Here the pipes are either ordered consecutively by pitch, or they form groups that seem to us like broken chords. Finally, in certain cases a particular melody appears to be fixed once and for all in the ordering of the pipes, or one becomes fixed ad hoc.[xix]

In addition, double pipes are particularly noteworthy, consisting of a front and a back row. The two pipes that belong together are always the same size but one is open, the other closed; as a consequence they have an octave relationship. One can see from this how acoustic know-how increases.[xx]

With wind instruments (including trumpets of various kinds, which were gradually emerging), still another phenomenon was observed that must have directed attention to consonant intervals independently of the experience of simultaneous pitches: namely, *harmonics* caused by 'overblowing'. Swiss shepherds still produce them today on the alpenhorn. The intervals of the harmonic series are first the octave, then the fifth, fourth and [major] third. The first three intervals are identical with those that exhibit the greatest fusion in group singing and group piping; and it had to be this way for them to become fixed in our consciousness afresh. Indeed, it is certainly quite conceivable that in many cases the makers were guided by harmonics while assembling panpipes. Sequential overblown pitches could not have been the only source of consonant intervals, however, because those intervals also occur in tribes who do not have wind instruments; because, further-more, the use of *simultaneous* pitches at the octave or fifth must have been motivated by the particular characteristics of these pitch simulta-neities; because, finally, overblown pitches often come out impure and somewhat flat, while the ear presses for purity. Hearing complies not with the permanence of instruments, but with that of the instruments of audition.[xxi]

The invention of pipes with several holes and the first panpipes must have given music making a significant boost. The creation of ever new alternating pitch sequences, even if with just a few notes, must have provided great stimulus to those who took pleasure in tones (and in this respect individuals were probably as diverse as they are today). The first instrumental melodies arose. Dances, sacrifices, and any other ritual or non-ritual events could now be used for practising this art. At the same time, the fixed pitches of instruments offered a welcome support for singing. It was now possible to fix musical phrases [*Tonwendungen*] that imitated those used in singing. With the help of pipes one could hand down melodies from generation to generation more accurately than merely by singing. 'He carves himself a pipe from reed and plays the children pretty dances and songs.'[24] The fixing of pitch in instru-ments provides support to singing in a similar manner to the way script did to speech later on.

---

[24] Stumpf quotes again from Wilhelm Müller's poetry (here: 'Eifersucht und Stolz'), which Schubert set as the fifteenth song in his cycle *Die Schöne Müllerin*, D. 795. This second reference to a poem from that cycle strongly indicates he had Schubert's musical setting in mind both here and in the instance from footnote 5 (p. 35).

In addition to pipes, primitive forms of string instruments are widespread, though they certainly developed more slowly. A likely hypothesis is that they arose from the hunter's tensile bow. You could quickly see that the pitch of the bowstring changes with the tension, and you might find yourself driven to all sorts of experiments. Thus arose the so-called musical bow, the very first string instrument that still exists in many parts of the world. The string is struck with a small stick, it can also be plucked, but is only rarely bowed. The insubstantial tone produced is frequently amplified by the player holding the string in their open mouth, which thereby functions as a resonator. But amplification through objectively hollowed spaces has long been known to primitive peoples. Hollowed-out pumpkins in particular serve this purpose for musical bows. The pitches are then multiplied, just as with the pipes, by fitting strings of different tension or length. The harp and the lyre were built with tortoise shells as primitive resonance boxes. Thus here, too, the basis of instrumental melodic formation was achieved.

Finally, percussion instruments,[xxii] which originally only depended on volume, were also rendered subservient to musical hearing. The first step towards this points to a combination of two wooden blocks, boards of unequal pitch, which are struck alternately. The signalling drum is more artistic, a hollowed-out block of wood where incisions on the upper side form two reeds. It is used in Africa and elsewhere for the language of drums [*Trommelsprache*], i.e. communication across wide distances through particular sound signals, partly modelled on formal, partly on ordinary language. The two reeds have different diameters and hence produce different pitches. The same instrument, artfully developed, was common in old Mexico at religious concerts. But even the use of tuned membranes is all-pervasive. We find a great variety of timpani tuned to different pitches. There are certainly no consonant intervals to be found on these instruments; they have only been transferred onto them.

The much-used xylophone and metallophone exhibit a higher stage of development, though they appear, like the musical bow, first to have been imported from Africa to America. There, quite a number of sonorous wooden or metal bars are brought together and will often be coupled to corresponding resonators. These instruments are extraordinarily valuable for music researchers because we can measure with physical precision the scales represented in well-preserved exemplars. In Africa the handy little thumb piano,[25] whose wooden or metal bars are made to vibrate by pressing down with the thumbs, is as popular as the piano is with us.

One can raise the question of whether instruments are utterly indispensable for music, or whether tribes exist that have only developed vocal music. In point of fact there are such, e.g. the Vedda in Ceylon have no instruments. But their songs are also at an extremely low level, while the North American Indian tribes that only use a few, meagre instruments have very developed vocal music. We have to regard the purely vocal development of music as possible, up to a certain level.

3.4. Polyphony, rhythm, and intoned speech

We now want to briefly characterize primitive music (empirically speaking, the music of primitive peoples) in three ways: in terms of the first demonstrable forms of polyphony; in terms of rhythm; and in terms of the conjunction between singing and speaking.

3.4.1.

First of all, what about the origins of harmony, which for us belongs so essentially to music that we understand monophonic, unaccompanied melody in a harmonic sense, and that all melodic tension and release likewise implies for us harmonic tension and release? Are triads, and chords in general, a fairly late product, a gothic barbarism, as Rousseau put it?[26] Or are they as old as music? Is original melody also perhaps

---

[25] The sansa or mbira. Two recent studies of this instrument are Chartwell Dutiro and Keith Howard, *Zimbabwean Mbira Music on an International Stage* (Aldershot: Ashgate, 2007); and Paul Berliner, *The Soul of the Mbira* (Berkeley: Univ. of California Press, 1978).

[26] Jean-Jacques Rousseau, 'Examen de Deux Principes Avancés par M. Rameau', in *Oeuvres Complètes*, ed. Bernard Gagnebin and Marcel Raymond (Paris: Gallimard, 1959–1995), 5: 345–370.

to be traced in just the same way as our modern melody: from harmony?

We can take it as read that pleasure in the manifold combination, complication, and release of chords has been an achievement of modern Europe since about the thirteenth century. The ancient Greeks, who came to know the deepest, most spiritual effects from their evidently richly developed musical system, still knew neither major nor minor chords, never mind a harmonic system. Popular harmonizations of surviving fragments of Greek melodies are falsifications. The same goes for primitive peoples of the present, as far as we can tell from existing knowledge. But lying between the modern European system of chords and strict monophony are a variety of forms of polyphony, whose origins must go back a very long way. If our supposition about the origin of music is correct then this lies precisely in polyphonic (even if unconsciously polyphonic) singing or playing. And it is no small confirmation of this that, as mentioned above, alongside the octave, fourths and fifths occur among present-day primitive peoples. After initially creeping in unnoticed, gradually with the performers' intent they caused the sound to gain in fullness—for something attractive was found in them—without forfeiting its unity. They occur regularly in particular places within the songs and can be seen as spontaneous collisions [*Entgleisungen*]. In Asia (China, Japan, Siam,[27] Sumatra, etc.) it is quite normal for instruments to play below or with the voice in fifths and fourths. This playing at the fifth is all the more remarkable in that undeniable reports testify it was practised in exactly the same way—and was regarded as beautiful—in the ninth and tenth centuries AD (even in the thirteenth century among Carthusian monks). The whole of our polyphonic music originated from this; now, admittedly, such parallels are no longer permitted. Passages in thirds arise now and then, particularly in Africa; whether or not this is independent of European influence is questionable.

Hence it is certainly fair to say that the roots of harmony are to be found in primitive peoples. They simply did not grow any further;

---

[27] Siam was renamed Thailand on 12 May 1949.

harmony itself failed to materialize. Indeed, a primitive person does not find a major chord objectionable, though he does not long for one, certainly not for triads; and where he uses a dyad, our sense of hearing will typically perceive this as out of place. One finds open dissonances without resolution between vocals and accompaniment, or between instruments, in conspicuous places. This is still particularly the case in Chinese and Japanese music, and appears to have been just the same in ancient Greek music, according to Plutarch.

Originally, there were probably quite different reasons for taking pleasure in polyphony than there are for us now; we are thoroughly under the influence of the enormous developments of the last millennium. Originally, people simply rejoiced merely at the simultaneous production of different pitches in general, and to some extent at the full and unified impression that arose from certain combinations [*Verbindungen*]. Occasionally we even seem to foresee how parallel seconds arise among primitive peoples in a certain roughness of pitch simultaneity through the production of adjacent pitches floating alongside one another.[xxiii]

In addition to parallel singing in consonant intervals there is yet another basic approach to polyphony among primitive peoples: the sustaining or repetition of a pitch throughout an entire melody. We even find this kind of discanting at the beginning of our musical epoch; it is called diaphonia basilica.[28] The old hurdy-gurdy with its drone strings and the bagpipes (particularly widespread in the Orient) are late arrivals to this primitive type of polyphony.[29] The organ pedal and the basso ostinato are analogous in present-day music. Indeed, in the greatest instrumental work of the classical period, Beethoven's Ninth Symphony, the trio of the second movement offers a performance of a bagpipe tune: primitiveness as an appealing element of the highest, holiest art.

---

[28] A term used by Johannes de Muris (*c.* 1320) for *organum duplum* in which the tenor line sustains long pitches. The Greek etymology is *basis*, base, foundation. A more common, thirteenth-century term for this two-part polyphony is discant.

[29] In 1911, Stumpf's European notion of the 'Orient' would have included the whole of Asia, the Near and Middle East, as well as modern East Asia.

3.4.2.

So much for the first traces of polyphonic music. Although the tremendous impact of this factor only became fully developed very late on, the situation is the other way around with rhythm. This aspect of music, whose fundamental significance we do not underestimate,[xxiv] thrived very early on as a remarkable, rich design. It relates partly to practical need, for with signals, especially the language of drums, rhythmic alterations offered the simplest means of producing the most varied sound signals with few pitches. By the same token, however, it also relates to the lagging behind of polyphony. Rhythm can develop much more freely in music that is essentially monophonic than it can in that which is essentially polyphonic or harmonic. For when many make music together, and when voices sing completely different melodies, they must adhere all the more strictly to certain stereotypical and easily retained rhythms if total chaos is not to ensue. Thence polyphony led soon afterwards to mensural music, and thus we confine ourselves to a few unchanging metres, like 4/4, 3/4, and maintain them throughout an entire piece. Even among the Chinese, Japanese, and Siamese, where some kind of polyphony is common, we only find these simplest of metres, particularly duple metres. On the other hand, in music that was originally essentially homophonic the door was open for the most divergent rhythmicization. In this, the Greeks were superior to us. But even primitive peoples are superior to us. We find that among Amerindians, for example, 5/4 and 7/4 metres are common; but in our music these have always been somewhat audacious, even if they occur more frequently in European folk music. Indeed, these metres alternate in rapid succession with each other as well as with even metres within a piece. If a whole choir sings, these complex rhythms are performed unanimously because everyone simply sings in unison, and they are practised in the particular rhythmicization of the song in question. It is the same with many other primitive peoples. Many South Asian peoples appear almost to have a preference for septempartite grouping. But there are also rhythms of such complexity that we can no longer grasp them aurally; instead, we only discern them by meticulously checking the relevant durational units at hand.[xxv] Furthermore, a peculiar and extremely widespread habit is to play on parts of the bar we would denote as 'weak'. One finds this just as much among American Indians as among the civilized people of Siam and Java. Moreover, several entirely different rhythms run along independently in parallel (rhythmic polyphony, polyrhythmics), e.g. between the singing and the accompanying timpani, the simultaneous perception of which is impossible or very difficult for us.[xxvi]

We can only conclude from these facts that the majority of music observed among primitive peoples in no way represents the most primitive [musical] conditions. Rather, it has a long history behind it, at least with regard to rhythm and the whole design, as raw and barbaric as it sounds to us. I only want to draw on the simpler rhythms used in rhythmicized work singing, which Bücher rightly emphasizes as a driving force for the development of a rhythmic feeling. Those complicated rhythms and their artistic assemblage must be traced right back to things other than mere practical needs. Here again we have to take into account curiosity, the need for play, joy in experimentation, and an advancing capability for conception and synthesis of developed forms; we should think about the need for suitable expressions of religious ideas and ritual ceremonies, and for everything that moves the soul. In short, we must increasingly consider the motives arising from the higher nature of human beings.

3.4.3.

Just as rhythm did not constitute the origin of music but proved a particularly rich and rapidly advancing characteristic of primordial music, so language—in which, equally, we could not find music's origin—has become very important for its development. Musical intervals were often used in speaking, once they had been absorbed into our consciousness. In fact, a kind of intoned speech [*Sprachgesang*] arose, i.e. recitation and declamation, in which the voice lingers on particular notes for longer than usual, delivers entire sentences in an unchanging pitch, and in exceptional passages uses musical intervals as an aid. We have a large number of specimens of this among primitive peoples, but also some among the civilized nations of East Asia. The boundary with normal speech is not always easy to draw, but I wish to denote culti-vated intoned speech as absolutely true singing. An example is provided for us by the singing of cathedral canons and monks who recite vespers or matins in church. The rhythm and tempo of speech is carried over from normal speech largely unchanged, hence we have the impression of only slightly modified speech. Nevertheless, a crucial new element has entered through the fixed pitches and intervals.

Musical intervals are not imported arbitrarily into speech; rather, those intervals with the greatest similarity to speech inflections are selected. This is well known in liturgical singing. But such transferals already take place among primitive peoples. Thus, the native people of Togo transferred their speech intervals (which have a particular impor-tance for them because the same word has a number of meanings through different inflections) to the language of drums, which is trans-mitted by means of tuned percussion instruments. Their acoustic signs are therefore easily comprehensible to natives. Phonographic record-ings put this connection beyond doubt.

Experience of spoken songs [*Sprachgesänge*] cannot be cited in support of the hypothesis that music originated in language, a hypoth-esis we do not endorse. To my mind, there is no reason in existence to think that speech singing [*sprechende Singen*] preceded actual—I want to say, musical—singing. The latter differs from intoned speech [*Sprachgesang*] by the use of fixed rhythmic forms, by shifting emphasis to the melodic aspect (the song texts frequently present only meaning-less syllables, and we find songs among many tribes in which they import texts from other tribes), but especially through the appearance of fixed and transposable intervals. It would be conceivable—psycho-logically speaking—that the intervals whose emergence signals for us the beginning of music, had first been used in the form of spoken sing-ing, namely in the first and last phrases of a passage of recitation that normally lingered on one pitch.[xxvii] But it is not at all evident why just the octave or fifth were used and not simply a random mixture of all possible tonal intervals. So specific causes for this must be sought, and it is here that one first encounters the origins of music. I regard it as more likely that the first use of musical intervals occurred entirely independently of language, and that over time the narrative and dramatic form of speech drew on the new means to enhance their effect only after singing and playing in melodic intervals had been established.

If one wants to say that intoned speech is a menial, inferior form, and hence should be seen as the precursor [to melodic intervals], we would not altogether agree. One would also have to disapprove somewhat of the recitatives in our classical operas and oratorios, and disapprove greatly of the wholesale displacement of the Lied form by recitative: anyone who has once heard the ritual preface in the Catholic mass that precedes the mystical silence of transubstantiation recited in a worthy manner will not deny its tremendously expressive power, and will be able to form a picture, admittedly not of Greek music itself, but of its effects and agents.

3.5. Paths of development

Now let us review the discussion. We refrained from establishing an exact chronological sequence for the emergence of the first vocal utterances that can be described as musical. It was more a question of laying the roots bare, gauging their driving force, tracking their connection to the main trunk. But in this summary we now want to take into account the alleged temporal ordering and, for the sake of brevity, even speak categorically. The hypothetical proviso is self-evident in these matters.

Work and dance rhythms were already marked, prior to all music, by percussion instruments and inarticulate vocal sounds. But as an element of music, rhythm was introduced only after musical intervals, not just tones [*Töne*], had taken the place of noisy sounds [*Geräusche Töne*]. For the purposes of signalling as well as simply a need to play, small intervals were used initially, which these early musicians learned to reproduce in an approximately similar way at other absolute pitches. Such intervals were produced by voices as well as by primitive instruments (wood blocks and the like). But music in the narrow sense first arose when consonant intervals were discovered, particularly the octave, which at the same time specified a fixed space for smaller steps. This discovery was made because of the nature of fusion during simultaneous signalling between several individuals. In the process, the voice, and instruments too, could be carriers of tonal space: the same fundamental intervals must be produced by both sound sources. In any case, by fixing intervals objectively, instruments were exceedingly important for the further development of singing. Beyond the phenomenon of fusion, the sonic relationship [*Klangverwandschaft*] between successive pitches, at least among pitches rich in harmonics, could lead to the fundamental intervals. With wind instruments, the overblown pitches play a part in imposing these intervals in our consciousness; but these were not the principal cause.

At the same time as the introduction of fixed intervals, small and large, the rhythmic characteristics of the tonal space became increasingly differentiated in the service of signalling, but also because of artistic interest (in this case, in connection with dance and poetry during ritual acts and the like); and the first melodic forms arose. Lingering on fixed pitches and the use of fixed intervals was also transferred to raised speech; thus intoned speech [*Sprachgesang*] was created as a special form of music.[xxviii]

It is now the task of comprehensive analyses and comparisons to discover the main forms of primitive melodic formation and their gradual refinement. The rule-bound practices [*Gesetzlichkeiten*] of the rhythmic course of melodies will have developed partly in relation to the metre of natural and artistic speech, but also partly independently of them. The different frequency and duration of individual notes, the size of the steps, the tuning of the intervals, the equality of their intonation, the length of individual melodic motives and of the whole melody, the nuances of performance—in short, all melodic features must be investigated statistically and psychologically in material that will hopefully be obtained in the future. At present we are far off such an essence of melodic form [*Melopöie*] among primitive peoples; only the very earliest stages are available and we cannot yet provide an overview.

In just a few words I would like to outline which paths the further formation of the tonal system itself pursued, following its initial beginnings, or—drawing on the empirical material available—which essentially pure disparities of tone we find at present among non-European peoples, disparities from which we can more or less create a picture of the course of development.

First, we notice a progressive centralization of tonal material. A principal note gradually becomes apparent in melodies. We now call it the tonic. For us, there are no melodies and no chords that do not stand in relation to this principal note. As soon as we relate a note to another tonic, we change its musical character. But this rigid centralization, this particular position of the principal note as the lowest on the scale, and that of its harmonic and melodic functions, are later achievements.

Furthermore, scales increasingly fixed within the compass of an octave gradually form; five-note and seven-note scales circulate most widely. These scale forms occur as a result of different points of view, and there are probably two paths to be followed. First, the logical design of a principle of consonance, in which one utilizes pure fourths and fifths; much later pure thirds as well, for the production of new intervals and for precise fixing of the steps. Secondly comes the principle of distance. Here one simply asks which note lies in between the two given notes, in the middle of them. So we can interpolate a note in between the fourth or fifth, and produce either an oversized whole tone or a neutral third. We first realized that things in fact proceeded in this way by studying Siamese and Javanese music. Equally spaced scales arose in this way (without the difference between whole tones and semitones). There are five-step as well as seven-step scales of this kind, which have not a single note in common with ours, and seem completely out of tune to a keen European ear.[xxix] But these are certainly not early stages, rather they are highly developed cultural creations, just of a different kind to ours. One can glimpse in these scales—formed according to the principle of mere tonal distance—a continuation of those origins, as we found them among the Vedda; a continuation of the formation of smaller tonal steps, not with regard to consonance, but simply on the basis of an equal difference in pitch, roughly estimated. So this root too has forced its way through; its outcome is the ability to recognize equally spaced steps—cultivated to the point of virtuosity—just as with us it is that of recognizing and differentiating grades of consonance. But this was not for its own sake, and it did not happen purely by dint of its own force. For we know, at least, that the Siamese and Javanese always set out from the octave. This forms the space within which the steps are then partitioned into a given number in accordance with the principle of distance. Even fourths and fifths are probably also partitioned indirectly.[xxx] Therefore, there are no scale forms that were based *purely* on the principle of distance.

Thirdly, very different styles of melodic construction developed. While this resembles ours in many cases among primitive peoples (even Siamese melody is thoroughly comprehensible to us), the analysis of phonographic recordings of south Chinese music showed principles of formation and alteration of melodies that would be impossible to our taste (removal of individual bars, substituting individual notes with their fifth, and so forth).[xxxi] Perhaps these are the product of a decadent art, but one way or another they seem entirely unfamiliar and peculiar to us.

Finally, there are differences in the use of simultaneous pitches and musical sequences. What we have already said about this also goes for relatively primordial phenomena. On the other hand, a kind of polyphony has developed into a system among the civilized peoples of Asia, one which is very different to ours. In China, Japan, South East Asia, and the Sunda Islands there are whole orchestras that more or less play a melody as though several variations on a theme were taking place simultaneously rather than one after another. One instrument plays the theme unchanged, the others contribute more or less free paraphrases. But in the aggregate, the basic melody resounds through. In the process, bad pitch simultaneities occur to our ears, of course, if one analyses closely. That these peoples have in no way developed a feeling for harmony is not hard to explain in light of such pitch simultaneities. I have called this type of polyphony *heterophony* in comparison with harmonic music, recalling an expression Plato once used to describe a certain multi-voiced musical practice in ancient Greece, and in fact it is quite possible that Siamese and Japanese music gives us a picture of this form of ancient Greek musical practice.[xxxii] Although our present European music displays individual cases of similar phenomena, it is now, by contrast, entirely built on the chordal system which is derived by consistently and exclusively carrying through the principle of consonance. Since this is the primordial phenomenon out of which music arose, which forms its flesh and bones, and since it has brought this elementary fact most purely and perfectly into being and thereby established the stylistic principle for the whole imposing design [*Bau*], we may regard it as the highest form of music so far, without being narrow-minded from the perspective of either ethnopsychology or developmental history.

I want to confront certain misunderstandings that sometimes limit comparative investigations of this kind: that all value of difference should be denied or even that the primitive should be held up as a model for imitation. This Rousseauian non-thought [*Ungedanke*], which is often found in aesthetic as well as ethical discussions, consists in nothing less than contradiction with evolutionary thinking. We really do not want to regress. The golden age lies not behind us but ahead of us, at least we hope and wish as much. If we glimpse the essential attributes of human brainwork [*Geistesarbeit*] already in apparently animal-raw products of primordial humankind, if the fond contemplation of what is most simple, the 'devotion to small things' discloses a structure to us, a summary of parts, a different evaluation of individual parts, a transfer of similar relationships to dissimilar materials, in short, all features of the cognitive penetration of matter, then we do not thereby forfeit but first gain the right measure for the assessment of later cultures. All authentic greatness only grows through comparison and understanding. Comparative observation of the arts leads to fairness and objectivity of judgement by placing an unimagined multiplicity of possible artistic styles within our field of vision; it can thereby even sustain creative artists (one only has to think of the excitement that Goethe and our recent painters derived from the Orient): but it demonstrates, at the same time, the world of differences in the realization of the paths taken and the disparate fruitfulness of different artistic principles. Among many kinds of artistic practice, equally possible and equally justified in themselves, only a few blossom richly. Thus we only really learn to treasure the glorious last epoch of music and likewise to trust—in every sense of the word—the unfathomable potency that still allows marvels to arise along new paths, even after the most sublime creations of the past.

Endnotes

i   The founder of comparative musicology in accordance with the exact methods of the natural sciences is Alexander J. Ellis, who, in his essay 'On the musical scales of various nations', *Journal of the Society of Arts* 33 (1885): 485–527, first published numerous measurements of exotic musical instruments that were played by natives and deemed well-tuned; cents calculation (based on one hundredth of the tempered semitone) led to comparison of the results. He had also already undertaken aural tests with exotic musicians. I have reported extensively on his essay (offprints of which are no longer available) in the *Vierteljahrsschrift für Musikwissenschaft* 2 (1886): 511–523. Ellis' investigations are admittedly concerned less with primitive peoples than with exotic civilized nations; but the precision of his designations has become a model and must be adhered to with regard to primitive peoples, if only in order to establish the boundaries within which fixed intonation exists in general.

We gained a more stable basis for investigating melodies a few years ago by applying phonographic methods (B. I. Gilman ['Zuñi Melodies', *Journal of American Ethnology and Archeology* 1 (1891): 63–91] on the basis of recordings from W. Fewkes). Since that time, the utilization of this aid has assumed great dimensions.

My article 'The Berlin Phonogram Archive' (see endnote xiii) gives information about the purposes and development of the scientific Phonogram Archive in Berlin, which is preserved and administered temporarily at the University's Psychological Institute. My article also touches on some questions among others already discussed in the present book that can be investigated with the help of phonographic recordings. Meanwhile the participation of explorers and the number of cylinders admitted has increased substantially so that the latter already amounts to more than 3000. Travellers receive exact instructions about restrictions to be observed when making recordings, whereby scientific usability is guaranteed (see endnote xvii). Metal plates are produced from the delicately ephemeral phonographic cylinders by electroplating procedures, which enables the production of copies at will.

Through such copies, other collections in Cologne, Lübeck, Leiden, and Stockholm have been established in part or in whole from the collection here. But equally, our archive is also being augmented by copies, especially from America.

There is already a phonogram archive in Vienna at the Academy of Sciences, founded in 1900 [*sic*] at Sigmund Exner's instigation, and supported by the government (see the annual reports in the Academy papers), with a large collection of plate types that are produced by means of special 'archive phonographs' and can now be transferred to cylinders. Other collections have accrued in France, England, Russia, and America.

Of course, the ultimate goal is not the collection, but the utilization. Melodies must be ascertained note for note according to pitch and rhythm. This is quite an exhausting exercise; but apropos pitch it is solvable with physical exactness. There are also several aids which help to capture and define unfamiliar and complicated rhythms. In all cases, however, many years of training and the utmost diligence is required.

Hand in hand with the study of musical pieces must be that of possible instruments. Measuring instruments with sufficiently fixed pitches has even greater significance for discerning the tonal material that occurs in musical pieces; in the 'scales' if such exist. Panpipes and the xylophone and metallophone—all widespread— are particularly suitable for this.

In what follows I attempt to piece together the most essential new contributions to the knowledge of exotic music, provided that they are based on the author's listening, and carried out with ample dependability.

1. *Even before the phonographic era*, a painstaking study of American Indian music was published that can still be used as a source today, since the author, in listening to the songs, paid far more attention to the musical characteristics and described them in greater detail than was usual hitherto:

   T. Baker, *Über die Musik der Nordamerikanischen Wilden* (Leipzig: Breitkopf & Härtel, 1882).

Then I myself once tried to fix the songs of an Indian troup (one of Captain Jacobson's) with regard to the exact intonation of every note after repeated performances by the lead vocalist. I believe I correctly characterized the idiosyncratic deviation in intonation from our pitches in the attached description:

C. Stumpf, 'Lieder der Bellakula-Indianer', *Vierteljahrsschrift für Musikwissenschaft* 2 (1886): 405–426.

But explorers do not care to take the time for this kind of immersion in the detail of each melody, or for the time to train in doing so. Furthermore, transcribing live performance generally offers no possibility for checking and singling out the smallest sections at will, whereby one can study melodies like natural objects. Therein lies the infinite advantage of the phonographic method.

Among the pre-phonographic transcriptions of primitive melodies, I'll still mention:

F. Boas, 'The Central Eskimo', *Bureau of Ethnology* 6 (annual report to the secretary of the Smithsonian Institute, 1888).

A number of melodies are reproduced in the appendix. Likewise in the essay about north-west Indian tribes of Canada, *Report of the British Association for the Advancement of Science: Sixth Report on the Northwest Tribes of Canada* (London: Burlington House, 1890). The author is well known as a superb observer. Yet he appears to have paid much less attention to the deviations of intonation than the characteristics of rhythm and structure, for nothing is said in particular about intonation. He used the phonographic method later on. Similarly:

A. C. Fletcher 'A Study of Omaha Indian Music' (with John Comfort Fillmore), *Archeological and Ethnological Papers of the Peabody Museum* 1 (1893): 7–152.

2. In America Benjamin Gilman has published three instructive essays based on *phonographic* recordings:

B. Gilman, 'Zuñi Melodies,' *Journal of American Archeology and Ethnology* 1 (1891): 63–91

—the very first investigation that has used this method. Compare this with my essay:

'Phonographierte Indianermelodien', *Vierteljahrsschriften für Musikwissenschaft* 8 (1892): 127–144.

B. Gilman, 'Some Psychological Aspects of the Chinese Musical System', *Philosophical Review* 1 (1892): 54–78.

B. Gilman, 'Hopi Songs,' *Journal of American Ethnology and Archeology* 5 (1908) [entire issue].

Some rich phonographic material follows thereafter with:

F. Boas, *The Social Organisation and the Secret Societies of the Kwakiutl Indians*, USA National Museum, Report for 1895 (Washington: Govt. Print. Off., 1897)

F. Boas, 'Songs of the Kwakiutl Indians', *Internationales Archiv für Ethnographie* 9 (1896): 1–9

A. C. Fletcher, *The Hako, a Pawnee Ceremony*, Bureau of American Ethnology annual report 22 (Washington: Govt. Print. Off., 1904)

F. Densmore, *Chippewa Music*, Bureau of American Ethnology, Bulletin 45 (Washington: Govt. Print. Off., 1910)

In her large collection, *The Indians' Book* (1907), Natalie Curtis unfortunately rejects phonographs as 'inadequate and unnecessary' and thereby relinquishes all scrutiny—her own included—in her written accounts, even if they make a trustworthy and technically sound impression. At the very least, further information about the idiosyncrasies of intonation, of rhythm, and of performance would have been desirable. The melodies in the form they appear in her reproduction seem to me felicitous and meritorious.

3. The following works, on which our present account predominantly rests, have come out of the Berlin Phonogram Archive (they are later cited with: 'Ph.-A. no.'):

(1) C. Stumpf, 'Tonsystem und Musik der Siamesen', *Beiträge zur Akustik und Musikwissenschaft* 3 (1901): 69–138.

(2) O. Abraham and E. von Hornbostel, 'Studien über das Tonsystem und die Musik der Japaner', *Sammelbände der Internationalen Musikgesellschaft* 4 (1903): 302–360.

(3) O. Abraham and E. von Hornbostel, 'Phonographierte indische Melodien', *Sammelbände der Internationalen Musikgesellschaft* 5 (1904): 348–401.

(4) F. von Luschan, 'Einige türkische Volkslieder und die Bedeutung phonographischer Aufnahmen für die Völkerkunde', *Zeitschrift für Ethnologie* 36 (1904): 177–202.

(5) O. Abraham and E. von Hornbostel, 'Phonographierte türkische Melodien', *Zeitschrift für Ethnologie* 36 (1904): 203–221.

(6) _____ 'Über die Bedeutung des Phonographen für die vergleichende Musikwissenschaft (mit Diskussionsbericht aus der Berliner Anthropologischen Gesellschaft)', *Zeitschrift für Ethnologie* 36 (1904): 222–223.

(7) _____'Über die Harmonisierbarkeit exotischer Melodien', *Sammelbände der Internationalen Musikgesellschaft* 7 (1905): 138–141.

(8) E. von Hornbostel, 'Die Probleme der vergleichenden Musikwissenschaft', *Zeitschrift der Internationalen Musikgesellschaft* 7 (1905): 85–97.

(9) E. von Hornbostel, 'Phonographierte tunesische Melodien', *Sammelbände der Internationalen Musikgesellschaft* 8 (1906): 1–43.

(10) O. Abraham and E. von Hornbostel, 'Phonographierte Indianermelodien aus British-Columbia', *Anthropological Papers written in Honor of Franz Boas* (New York: G. E. Stechert & Co., 1906), 447–474.

(11) E. von Hornbostel, 'Über den gegenwärtigen Stand der Vergleichenden Musikwissenschaft', *Bericht über die II. Kongress der Internationalen Musikgesellschaft zu Basel vom 25-27. September 1906* (Leipzig: Breitkopf & Härtel, 1907), 56–60.

(12) E. von Hornbostel, 'Notiz über die Musik der Bewohner von Süd-Neu-Mecklenburg', in E. Stephan and F. Graebner, *Neu-Mecklenburg* (Berlin: D. Reimer, 1907), 131–137.

(13) C. Stumpf, 'Das Berliner Phonogrammarchiv', *Internationale Wochenschrift für Wissenschaft, Kunst und Technik* 2 (22 February 1908): 225–246.

(14) E. von Hornbostel, 'Phonographierte Melodien aus Madagaskar und Indonesien', *Forschungsreise der S. M. S. 'Planet' 1906/7* (Berlin, 1909), 5: 139–152.

(15) E. Fischer, 'Patagonische Musik', *Anthropos* 3 (1908): 941–951.

(16) E. von Hornbostel, 'Über die Musik der Kubu', in B. Hagen (ed.), *Die Orang-Kubu auf Sumatra* (Frankfurt am Main: J. Baer & Co., 1908), 243–258.

(17) O. Abraham and E. von Hornbostel in the 'Anleitungen für Ethnographische Beobachtungen und Sammlungen' produced by the Royal Museum for Ethnology (Berlin, 1908), section L: Music.

(18) O. Abraham and E. von Hornbostel, 'Vorschäge für die Transkription exotischer Melodien', *Sammelbände der Internationalen Musikgesellschaft* 11 (1909): 1–25.

(19) E. von Hornbostel, 'Wanyamwezi-Gesänge', *Anthropos* 4 (1909): 781–800, 1033–1052.

(20) M. Wertheimer, 'Musik der Wedda', *Sammelbände der Internationalen Musikgesellschaft* 11 (1909): 300–309.

(21) E. von Hornbostel, 'Über Mehrstimmigkeit in der außer-europäischen Musik', *Bericht über den III. Kongreß der Internationalen Musikgesellschaft* (Vienna: Artaria & Co.; Leipzig: Breitkopf & Härtel, 1909), 298–302.

(22) E. von Hornbostel, 'Über einige Panpfeifen aus Nordwest-Brasilien', in Theodor Koch-Grünberg (ed.), *Zwei Jahre unter den Indianern*, 2 vols. (Berlin: Wasmuth, 1910), 2: 378–391.

(23) E. von Hornbostel, 'Über vergleichende akustische und musikpsychologische Untersuchungen', *Zeitschrift für Angewandte Psychologie* 3 (1910): 465–487.

(24) E. von Hornbostel, 'Musik' entry in Richard Thurnwald, 'Im Bismarckarchipel und auf den Salomoinseln', *Zeitschrift für Ethnologie* 42 (1910): 140ff.

(25) E. von Hornbostel, 'Wasukuma-Melodie', *Bulletin de l'Académie des Sciences de Cracovie, Classe des Sciences Mathématiques et Naturelles* (1910): 711–713.

(26) E. von Hornbostel, 'USA National Musik', *Zeitschrift der Internationalen Musikgesellschaft* 12 (1910): 64–68.

(27) E. von Hornbostel, 'Notizen über Kirgisische Musikinstrumente und Melodien', in Richard Karutz, *Unter Kirgisen und Turkmenen* (Leipzig: Klinkhardt & Biermann, 1911), 196–218.

(28) C. Stumpf and E. von Hornbostel, 'Über die Bedeutung Ethnologischer Untersuchungen für die Psychologie und Ästhetik der Tonkunst', *Bericht über den IV. Kongreß für experimentelle Psychologie,* ed. Friedrich Schumann (Leipzig: Barth, 1911), 256–269; also printed in *Beiträge zur Akustik und Musikwissenschaft* 6 (1911): 102–115.

(29) E. Fischer, 'Beiträge zur Erforschung der Chinesischen Musik', *Sammelbände der Internationalen Musikgesellschaft* 12 (1911): 153–206.

(30) E. von Hornbostel, 'Über die Musik auf den Nord-Westlichen Salomon-Inseln', in Richard Thurnwald (ed.) *Forschungen auf den Salomo-Insel und dem Bismarck-Archipel* (Berlin: D. Reimer, 1912).

4. In addition to the above, there is phonographically supported work on primitive peoples by such European authors as:

G. Adler, 'Sokotri-Musik', in D. H. Müller, *Die Mehri- und Sokotrisprache. Südarabische Expedition der Kais. Akademie der Wissenschaft* (Vienna: A. Hölder, 1905), 6: 377–382.

P. Fr. Witte, 'Lieder und Gesänge der Ewe-Neger', *Anthropos* 1 (1906): 65–81, 194–209.

W. Thalbitzer and Hj. Thuren, 'Musik aus Ostgrönland', *Zeitschrift der Internationalen Musikgesellschaft* 12 (1910): 33–40.

C. S. Myers, 'Music' entry in C. G. and B. Z. Seligmann, *The Veddas* (Cambridge: Cambridge Univ. Press, 1911).

The phonographic method has also been used in Europe several times to record old folk songs, which expands the material of comparative musicology in important directions. Among the publications, I will mention in particular:

E. Lineff, *The Peasant Songs of Great Russia*, 2 vols. (St. Petersburg and London: D. Nutt, 1905–1912).

F. Kolessa, 'Ruthenische Volkslieder', in the communications of *the Ševčenko-Gesellschaft der Wissenschaften* (1906–1911).

Hj. Thuren, *Folkesangen* (Copenhagen: A. F. Høst & sons, 1908).

A. Launis, *Lappische Juoigos-Melodien* (Helsingfors: Finnische Gesellschaft, 1908)

F. Kolessa, 'Über die Sogennante Kosakenlieder (der Klein-russen)', *Bericht über den III. Kongreß der internationalen Musikgesellschaft* (Vienna: Artaria & Co.; Leipzig: Breitkopf & Härtel, 1909), 276–295.

5. In recent monographs and travel writing, the postulate of critical research has at least been observed more than before, even when no phonographic recordings were made. I cite, for example, the studies by:

F. Densmore, 'The music of the Filipinos', *American Anthropologist* 8 (1906): 611–632; J. Schönhärl, *Volkskundliches aus Togo* (Dresden and Leipzig: C. A. Koch, 1909); and H. Rehse, *Kiziba (am Westufer des Viktoria-Nyanza), Land und Leute* (Stuttgart: Strecker und Schroeder,1910).

6. For a clear round up of the general perspectives of musical ethnology to date, the following should also be mentioned:

C. S. Myers, 'The ethnological study of music', in *Anthropological Essays Presented in Honour to Edward Taylor* (Oxford: Oxford Univ. Press, 1907), 235–253.

B. I. Gilman, 'The science of exotic music', *Science* (new series) 30 (15 October 1909): 532–35.

How little we can rely on the numerous transcriptions that are impossible to check in travel writing, is illustrated by two very recent examples. A psychologist as famous as Wilhelm Wundt gives four specimens of primitive songs, of which the third and fourth, as they stand, could not possibly be real. (Regarding the first, see endnote xxvii). They go:

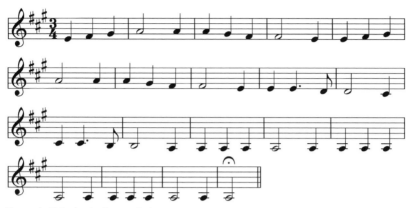

Example 3.1. Australian melody

From K. Lumholtz, *Unter Menschenfressern: Eine vierjährige Reise in Australien* (Hamburg: Actien-Gesellschaft, 1892), 59.

Example 3.2. Negro melody

From G. Schweinfurth, *Im Herzen von Afrika* (Leipzig: F. A. Brockhaus, 1874), 1: 450.

Regarding the latter, Wundt himself says it is already homogenous with our feeling for melody. In truth the two melodies differ in no respect from our popular tunes (excepting the close of the first). The first, which sounds nothing like cannibals, has 'Tempo di Valse. Allegro' written underneath in Lumholtz's original. As a piece, it sounds in fact like the main waltz from, for example, Oscar Straus' operetta *Walzertraum* (1907). Any expert will say that, as it is given here, it has about as much chance of originating with the primeval inhabitants of Australia as a silver soup spoon or a typewriter. Whether it migrated over from regions already under European influence, or whether Lumholtz's European sense of hearing played a trick on him while transcribing a real Australian melody must remain undecided. Both factors probably worked in tandem. Lumholtz says on page 198 of the same work that a good song wanders from tribe to tribe, and that he later heard a particular song (similar to that quoted here) being sung by the civilized Aborigines at Rockhampton, 500 miles south of the first location as the crow flies. It probably arose originally in the vicinity of Rockhampton and made this long journey before it arrived at the Herbert River Mountains where it is now sung without the words being understood. It is certainly conceivable that European songs also made similarly long journeys under such circumstances. (We see what happens in this respect when von Hornbostel recently discovered our 'Fox, you have stolen the goose' almost entirely unchanged on a phonogram recorded by the Kifghiz in western Turkey; only the major seventh had been changed to a minor seventh. Ph-A. no. 27). The European ear may have done much more in addition, it may have 'assimilated' the things heard; I regard only the close [of the melody], namely extended lingering on the low keynote, as a genuine product because we find this tendency very frequently among primitive peoples (while Wundt regards even 'the total lack of a melodic close' as characteristic). Lumholtz too remarks, 'to be able to pause for a long time on the final note is considered a skill in the art of singing'.

Since the example from Schweinfurth's book struck me as no less astonishing, I asked the great explorer of Africa by letter for information about the way in which he transcribed this song, and whether it might not have migrated to that region. He replied (27 December 1905): 'I reproduced the melody as it struck my ear. Perhaps this stylized the melody unconsciously in a European way. At the time it made a great impression on me. I often hummed it to myself on my travels; it was always my habit to sing in half voice [markieren] all the melodies I could get hold of while marching. I certainly believe, then, that I later reproduced it pretty accurately. A rhythmic song with a hundred voices must surely still have a melody that dominates, a diagonal cutting through [eine Diagonale], and I captured it in this way. ... The notation of the melody arose at that time (as I wrote my book) together with my brother Alexander, now deceased (whom Alexander Dorn declared an out-and-out musician). I performed the song several times for him; there was no other way to express it'.

I believe that everything necessary has been said. The report is certainly typical of a huge number of cases. What transformations must a melody undergo if one hums it to oneself on long marches, and what a complete transformation if, after this first unintentional arrangement, it is transcribed by a dyed-in-the-wool European musician who has perhaps never heard exotic melodies in the original! I do not want to reproach the highly distinguished researcher, who travelled and transcribed before the invention of the phonograph, and did not presume to undertake the precise recording on location. But what he sees as a guarantee for loyal transmission is in fact the opposite. To cap it all, my colleague Max Friedländer alerted me to the fact that there is an old soldier's marching song with a suspicious kinship to the Mitu song below, also sung on marches:

Example 3.3. 'Liederkranz von Erk', *Ausgabe für Berliner Gemeindeschulen* I (no. 115), 106. Cf. *Soldatenliederbuch*, ed. Hauptmann Maschke (1906), no. 189.

The original Mitu melody is certainly similar and perhaps even extremely similar to that published by Schweinfurth. In Africa, many such melodies with short two-part rhythms are to be found to which one could also sing 'Hurra'. I contend only that we cannot speak of the scientific exactitude of reproduction under the above circumstances. There can hardly be better evidence than

Wundt's two examples of how indispensable phonographic recordings are on location, and how little benefit there is— in terms of ethnopsychology—in getting advice from books alone.

In no way do I want to go so far as to condemn as unusable the purely aural transcriptions on location that we find in so much earlier travel writing. On the contrary, we are now more able to make good use of such musical examples. But this is only on condition that the user creates a picture of what really happens, informed by their own prior hearing of phonographic recordings and of nature (there are enough visitors from exotic places in European capitals, though it would defeat the purpose if they were already Europeanized). If, in addition, when travel writing is used the circumstances under which the traveller made the transcription, the method of transcription and further details are recorded, this offers some assurance for the accuracy of the reproduction. Travel reports usually offer no clues of this sort, and often their purely technical carelessness in notation already arouses doubts and misgivings. It is high time that the degree of conscientious criticism that new ethnography calls for in other areas is also bestowed on the field of music.

Of course, the greatest certitude will be achieved when explorers are themselves thoroughly trained in acoustics and psychology, when they study the whole musical culture of the natives on location, both making recordings and scientifically transcribing these after returning home. But that can only be the exception.

From the perspective of the old methods (we may say the old slovenly habits) the exact reproduction of exotic and primitive songs has been reproached as pointless, exaggerated meticulousness because the intonation of 'savages' fluctuates too much—it is said—to be worth the trouble of notating intervals that deviate from our own with diacritical signs, or even of measuring pitches in frequencies. I myself discussed this point as long ago as 1892 [with emendations to Gilman's 1891 transcriptions of Zuñi melodies], incidentally the first publication using phonograms, long before our critics Hugo Riemann and Richard Wallaschek. Of course, the existence of such fluctuations does not mean that we may trust the old form of notation any more than the new. It just means that—on analysing the material captured by a phonograph—we take the unavoidable fluctuations into account and should not simply declare all deviations from diatonic scales to be some kind of new and unheard-of scales. Our measurements, however, serve precisely to establish the range in between which those fluctuations occur in certain tribes or individual singers. For this purpose, explorers are instructed to record the same song sung on many occasions by several individuals, and also to record the same individuals at different times. Moreover, Otto Abraham has already begun, even before such objections were raised, to assess the breadth of fluctuation in the intonation of our own intervals during a song sung by our own singers, both trained and untrained, in order to have a yard stick to gauge within what boundaries, and with what constancy regarding the direction, such deviations occur. They were found to be quite large. But we cannot infer that [deviations of pitch] among primitive peoples must be the same size, or larger. They appear to repeat certain notes and intervals in their melodies with greater precision, while there are wide variations in other notes and intervals. All this can only be scrutinized on the path we have taken; someday, perhaps, it will turn out that we have actually, and with superfluous effort, fixed changeable and arbitrary pitches in some cases. Only one may not assume this at the outset, and exaggerated precision has always been the lesser evil compared with uncritical carelessness.

ii   I have discussed the theories of Darwin and Spencer at greater length in the essay 'Musikpsychologie in England. Betrachtungen über Herleitung der Musik aus der Sprache und aus dem Tierischen Entwicklungsprozeß, über Empirismus und Nativismus in der Musiktheorie', *Vierteljahrsschrift für Musikwissenschaft* 1 (1885): 261–349.

iii   Ancient authors are very fond of describing the effects of music on animals (elephants, spiders, etc.), and an appalling number of unbelievable anecdotes going right back to the Assyrian kings are dished up. Mario Pilo recently made quite uncritical use of these. That his book is regarded as important enough to be translated into German demonstrates how little our judgement has developed. Occasional comments about cats' and dogs' love of music by a researcher such as August Weismann (1834–1914) have more significance ('Gedanken über Musik bei Tieren und beim Menschen', *Deutsche Rundschau* 61 [1890]: 50–79, here 67). But the explanation of the respective behaviour of animals seems to me extremely difficult. If a dog sits howling along to music, what is actually going on in the animal? What purpose does howling with an upwardly stretched head serve? And what do we discover by stimulating a dog's sense of hearing, whether pleasantly or unpleasantly? Does it have something to do with intervals, chords, modulations, with rhythmic accompaniment? This seems out of the question to me. Conclusive observations about the actual quality of a dog's sensation of feeling [*Gefühlsempfindung*] are as yet unavailable.

   If we examine the phonation [*Tongebung*] of animals themselves, we generally only find clear intervals among birds, while when mammals yelp or roar individual notes are not usually differentiated sharply from each other and their pitches are not maintained precisely.

   To be sure, Athanasius Kircher would have us believe an American sloth sings the C major scale from c to a and back again, and a gibbon is even once supposed to have sung—as Waterhouse and Darwin always earnestly maintained—an entire chromatic scale up and down accurately, which is one of the hardest exercises for trained human singers. Indeed, a horse apparently tackled this task through its neighing and a cow through its mooing, if we want to believe the notation that an American observer wrote:

Example 3.4. Horse

Example 3.5. Cow

A. P. Camden Pratt in T. Wilson, *Prehistoric Art: Smithsonian Institution Annual Report 1896* (Washington: Govt. Print. Off., 1898), 516.

One can certainly put everything into notes like this, even the hee-haw of the donkey, the whistling of the storm, and the creaking of a boot. But we should not spoil scientific books with such childishness. That the vocal movement of a neighing horse runs from top to bottom may well be correct; it may relate to the same physiological conditions that allow a cry of joy and so many primitive melodies (see our examples) to begin high and end low. But such a beautiful chromatic scale—no!

Better to write out certain bird melodies. Alongside fairly fierce twittering and cawing we also find motifs that make an undeniably melodic impression on us, more melodic than some melodies sung by primitive peoples. The crowing of the cock, the call of the cuckoo— these are easy to transcribe (although different individuals intone differently). Occasionally one almost hears pure triads, especially in a rising sequence of pitches. Karl Sapper claims to have observed thirty bird melodies, among eighty-seven in the ancient forests of Guatemala, that move exclusively in triadic pitches; he thus connects this to the occurrence of numerous triadic melodies among

Indians (see the melodic examples). Anyhow, many sins have been committed while transcribing birds imaginatively. Thus the American Xenos Clark ('Animal music, its nature and origin', *American Naturalist* 13 [1879]: 209–223), for example, believed to have found the following C major scale with whole tones and semitones in a leaf warbler:

Example 3.6.

I have transcribed many bird melodies in field and forest, but never heard such an immaculate major scale. It is supposed to be impossible even for the birds in 'the land of boundless possibilities' [i.e. the USA]. One only has to appreciate what amount of mental work and historical development is tucked into a diatonic scale. In a different case by Clark, a forest sparrow singing in C minor (no. 25) even differentiates enharmonic differences between D♯ and E♭. The naivety with which the three flat signs are prescribed here—although the pitches B♭ and A♭ do not occur at all—proves once again that the author simply lent our awareness of tonality to the good sparrows. Similarly, in no. 14 three sharps are prescribed despite the fact that the song only consists of the single pitch A♯, and so forth. We may wonder why birds who have come so far, do not once sing in duets and trios, or at least in octaves or parallel fifths, as primitive peoples do. For the time being we must be wary of the thesis Clark extrapolates from his transcriptions [*Aufschreibungen*], and which is often expressed in any case—namely, that harmonic intervals predominate in birdsong—because we are disposed, as a result of becoming familiar with, and fond of, our intervals, to insert them into what we hear.

We must of course remember to be even more cautious when drawing conclusions about the *feelings* that the little musician wants to express. Wundt, who with astonishing gullibility simply accepts Clark's notation as canonical avian music, still thinks he is in fact able to hear the feelings of these little animals (*Völkerpsychologie* 1, part 1: 261). Indeed, he even discovers therein the three 'dimensions' of feelings that he differentiates in his theory, and which is so contested by humans:

Example 3.7. Joy

Example 3.8. Depression

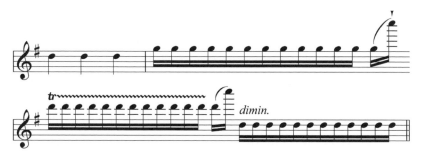

Example 3.9. Vigorous excitement

One may find it credible that a bird *can* be joyous, depressed, or vigorously excited. But why he *must* be depressed in the second melody, for example, and why he cannot in fact feel any of these three feelings (or others besides) in each of the melodies, is totally unclear. Not even if a human whistled, sang, or played these notes, would their feelings be clearly pronounced therein. With birds, whose entire inner life stands as far from ours as does their bodily organization, interpretation is literally plucked out of thin air. We may just as little ascribe our melodic feelings—even if they were quite definite—to the hearts of birds as we may, for instance, equate the impression we have of a cow or of a pasture with that which an ox would have.

We must not allow all of this to spoil our joy in these lovely forest musicians. It is only a matter of distinguishing science from arbitrary additions. Recent animal psychology is stricter in this respect than the old. But in life the right to imagination and to instinctive empathy should not be denied.

Aside from the transcriptions by Clark and others, which are useless theoretically and practically, there are also transcriptions with purely *practical* aims, namely the recognition and differentiation of bird types: they can genuinely be utilized for this purpose. I particularly want to recommend Alwin Voigt as an excellent guide in *Exkursionsbuch zum Studium der Vogelstimmen* (Dresden: Hans Schultze, 1906). Besides musical notes, he uses a number of different graphic signs precisely because many melodies cannot— or cannot adequately—be captured in notation.

As these comments went to press, von Hornbostel published a study of birdsong in response to a book by Bernard Hoffmann— *Kunst und Vogelgesang* (Leipzig: Quelle & Meyer, 1908)—in which rich material is again exploited in an uncritical or exuberant way; I draw attention to this response for further orientation: 'Musikpsychologische Bemerkungen über Vogelsang', *Zeitschrift der Internationalen Musikgesellschaft* 12 (1911): 117–128. Von Hornbostel has concerns regarding the question of transposition, as do I, in which he points to a case mentioned by Hoffmann in which a green woodpecker first sang his call between c^3 and a^2, but then gradually allowed it to sink in pitch so that it finally came to rest between a^2 and $f\sharp^2$. Hence, von Hornbostel locates the essential difference between avian and human music not so much in the ability to transpose as in the use of motives in melodic forms. This depends entirely on what one understands by transposition. If coordinated muscular contractions, whose outcome is vocal melody, become weaker and weaker, the pitch of the whole must sink. I would not call this transposition, however, even if the shift in pitch was greater still [than a minor third]. Rather, I would speak of a situation where the singer accommodates a given pitch (or one selected by himself), as primitive peoples do with small pitch pipes; that is, if he *transfers* particular [intervallic] relationships to pitches other than the usual. Even so, extensive experiments would still be necessary to prove that such an accommodation of given pitches is impossible among birds. (Otto Abraham's observations, mentioned in the text, occur in his essay, 'Das Absolute Tonbewußtsein', *Sammelbände der Internationalen Musikgesellschaft* 3 [1901]: 1–86, here 69.) But based on previous experience, I already regard a success in the positive sense as very unlikely.

I agree with von Hornbostel that it is the occurrence of particular forms that characterizes human song, and that this is in fact its more essential, deeply compelling property; but this may go hand in hand with the ability to transpose since grasping relationships as such is a condition of both acts. At any rate the occurrence of particular forms will not be so easy to define and not so easy to apply in observation and experiment. For that reason I feel that the question of animals' musical faculties should be focused on the capacity to transpose in the sense given above.

iv   Louis Laloy, *La musique Chinoise* (Paris: H. Laurens, 1910), 55, 120. Laloy differentiates the Chinese concept of melody from that of our own in that, with them, a sequence of particular absolute pitches—each of which has a fixed significance—constitutes melody; while with us the *function* of pitches in any desired transposable scale is decisive. The matter requires closer investigation, however.

v   Even August Weismann brushes over this in the above-mentioned article (endnote iii). There may be some truth to his basic idea that humans gained their finest and most developed sense of hearing through processes of selection because it was necessary in the struggle for existence, and that by chance this organ of hearing can also be applied when listening to music. That the ability to perceive and recognize intervals as such is rooted in the organ of hearing, in the cochlea of the ear (p. 68), seems provocative to me, however. This faculty can only be conditioned *cerebrally* in my opinion, like the entire higher psychological performance of humans. Similarly, the differences between musical and unmusical people (p. 70) are likely to lie only in the smallest degree in the hearing organs. The sensitivity to difference does not necessarily appear to be less in unmusical types.

vi   As the originator of this idea, it is customary to quote Lucretius, *De rerum natura* V 1379–1381:

> At liquidas avium voces imitarier ore
> Ante fuit multo quam laevia carmina cantu
> Concelebrare homines possent aureisque juvare.
> [But imitating the liquid song with their mouth
> Came much before men could perform songs
> Smooth in sound and delightful to their ears.]

But my colleague Hermann Diels pointed out to me that Lucretius took the idea from Democritus (via Epicurus), whose fragment 154 (Hermann Diel, *Fragmente der Vorsokratiker* 1:462, n. 15) said: 'humans have become students of animals in the most important matters by imitating their art: the spider in weaving and stitching; the swallow in construction; the songbird, the swan and the nightingale in singing'.

Apart from the mere urge to imitate, we see that practical purposes can also motivate the imitation of birds and animal voices even today, as Willi Pastor has correctly noted, in hunting. Primeval superstitions may also play into this: belief in the power of singing animals to bring warmth and rain (see Konrad Theodor Preuß

[*Religionen der Naturvölker* (Leipzig: B. G. Teubner, 1904)]), whose voices would then be imitated.

vii   Edward W. Scripture, *Researches in Experimental Phonetics. The Study of Speech Curves* (Washington, D. C.: Carnegie Institution, 1906), 63. Scripture enlarged the tiny curves of the gramophone in such an ingenious way that they become accessible to quantifiable comparison and analysis. Thanks to the goodwill of the founder, extensive equipment was set up during one winter at the Berlin Psychological Institute, as a result of which the investigation mentioned in the following note was possible. Admittedly, the transcription mechanism does not guarantee an exact reproduction in every respect, but the changes of wave length are precise enough to be extracted from the enlarged curves. The curves cited in the text are created by measuring a large number of successive wave lengths, from which the constituent pitches (number of vibrations) are calculated and then the pitches are plotted as ordinates.

Other methods for objective portrayal of speech melody are Felix Krueger's improved Rousselotean 'throat-tone writer' (cf. *Bericht über den II. Kongreß für experimentelle Psychologie* [Leipzig: J. A. Barth, 1905], 115) and the Marbean 'soot method' whereby a soot-producing flame writes out its sympathetic movements (*Zeitschrift für Psychologie* 49 [1908]: 206ff.).

Fluctuations in normal speech certainly encompass at least an octave or a twelfth among most civilized nations. But the range appears far narrower in certain cases, even ignoring intentional monotony, which we mention in the text. Scripture found in his own reading of the Lord's Prayer that his voice moved almost exclusively among the pitches: g♯, a, a♯ ('A record of the melody of the Lord's Prayer', *Die neueren Sprachen* [January 1903]: 1–36). This deeply monotonous recitation of the Lord's Prayer is, however, a special case, as he noted; Scripture's normal speech tone moves within far wider boundaries. Franz Saran's narrow range is highly conspicuous (admittedly only according to the ear); while declaiming a long poem he situates his speech melody almost entirely between c♯ and d♯ (*Melodie und Rhythmik der 'Zueignung'*

Goethes [Halle: M. Niemeyer, 1903]; *Deutsche Verselehre* [Munich: C. H. Beck, 1907], 216ff.). Undoubtedly there are individual peculiarities in this respect. But with such a tiny habitual range, I will only be able to believe it if it is substantiated by objective methods.

viii Wilhelm A. T. Effenberger, *Über den Satzakzent im Englischen*, Part 1 (Berlin: Mayer & Müller, 1908). The complete volume has not yet appeared; the curves that appear in the text were made available to me by the author.

ix I also owe this reference to my colleague Hermann Diels.

x Edward W. Scripture, 'How the Voice Looks', *Century Magazine* 64 (February 1902): 148–154, here 150.

xi Cf. My *Tonpsychologie*, 2 vols. (Leipzig: S. Hirzel, 1883–1890), 1: 164 (Klunder's measurement). The work of Otto Abraham, already mentioned, supplies further information about this.

xii One often finds among primitive peoples a dragging movement—especially during downward motion—in the voice, particularly at the beginning and end of songs. Yet in the course of such rapidly executed movements a note also occurs at the beginning or end. These are already given in older chronicles, e.g. in the first and third songs from New Zealand reproduced in George Grey's *Polynesian Mythology* (London: J. Murray, 1855), which hardly move from the spot (Grey thinks he hears quarter tones), but slide down an entire octave from the final note. In the first song the written scale certainly also signifies a sliding movement. Furthermore, compare my Bella Coola song (pp. 415, 421, 423; the range of the sliding motion is an octave or fifth), quoted above in endnote i [p. 68]; see also Baker's Indian songs, *Über die Musik der Nordamerikanischen Wilden* (Leipzig: Breitkopf & Härtel, 1882), 1: c: 17. Phonographic recordings offer frequent examples; some are given in our sample melodies. Among those still-unstudied Pawnee songs brought to us by the museum director George A. Dorsey (Chicago), is a doctor's song that commences with a frequently repeated constant tonal movement from top to bottom, whose start and end point is not easy to discern. It has something strangely threatening to our conception.

A very old Appenzell 'Löckler' (the call for driving home the cattle) forms an interesting counterpart, which ends just like Grey's songs from New Zealand:

Example 3.10. A. Tobler, *Kühreihen oder Kühreigen, Jodel und Jodellied in Appenzell* (Leipzig: Hug, 1890), 9. See also Tobler, *Das Volkslied im Appenzellerlande* (Zurich: Schweizerische Gesellschaft für Volkskunde, 1903), 119.

But among folk singers in modern Italy, one can also often hear a portamento extending over the space of a major third. I heard the following song constantly repeated this way in Venice, where the voice regularly descended at the end, gradually falling from e to c:

Example 3.11.

This practice is not considered to be in good taste within our art music, so this way of performing is only permitted exceptionally and in very narrow ranges (thus occasionally from the leading note to the tonic). In general, however, it is forbidden altogether because it blurs the boundary with speech, though also with elementary howling and other artless emotional settings. The same goes for other primitive ways of performing, like grunting or humming through closed teeth among Indians, which occurs for instance in a Dakota [Sioux] scalp dance, and, together with a sliding tonal shift, 'can have a really shiver-inducing effect.' (Baker, p. 17).

[xiii] The ethnologist Father Wilhelm Schmidt comments likewise against the derivation of music from language (in an article to which my attention was drawn by a lecture of von Hornbostel's after the publication of this script), whereby he points to the constant transitions of speech tone ('Über Wundts Völkerpsychologie',

Mitteilungen der Anthropologischen Gesellschaft in Wien 33 (1903): 361–389). He nevertheless declares a musical reproduction of ordinary speech tone to be necessary, and sets Wundt's notation alongside others that seem more accurate to him. There are absolutely no universal and exact rules here, however (cf. remarks in the treatise mentioned in endnote ii, p. 278ff.). It certainly also depends a lot on dialect. That a noticeably large number of attempts at speech notation emanate from a Saxon milieu is typical. I even believe that with Richard Wagner (a disciple of speech theory), who sought to imitate the intonation of speech in his recitatives, echoes of his Saxon accent are clearly discernible in his musical phrases.

Schmidt derives music positively, not from passionate speech, but from passionless yet loud *calls*, particularly from signalling calls like those we still hear today from street sellers. Musical intervals are abandoned, especially when a lot of people speak just a little loudly together, e.g. when praying together. In fact, the use of music in such cases deserves a statistical survey and an examination of causes. What comes to light today, however, is already under the influence of our music and cannot make the first emergence of fixed intervals comprehensible in general. Rather, we must try conversely to understand the musical qualities of these cries from those of already extant intervals (in which respect I attempted, for example, to derive the widespread preference for minor thirds—when calling out—from an integration of physiological factors with musical habits; see the treatise mentioned in endnote ii, p. 283ff.).

Schmidt's basic idea seems correct to me, however: that calling, and particularly concerted calling, was one of the starting points of music and led in particular to the discovery of consonant intervals. We will elucidate what it was that tipped the scales. I gladly emphasize that we agree in this important matter.

xiv As the brain has developed, these characteristics of sound perception, e.g. of underlying brain processes, have of course gradually evolved. I attempted to set out a hypothesis about the factors divided thereby (the relative frequency with which an interval occurs beneath the overtone, also the smaller ratio of difference tones to primary tones) in *Tonpsychologie* 2: 215ff. The calling out of signals by men and women simultaneously, however, is already alluded to in this context; see also 'Konsonanz und Dissonanz', *Beiträge zur Akustik und Musikwissenschaft* 1 (1898): 1–108, here 62. But in *Tonpsychologie* I took as a basis the view that in the primordial origins of the human race the differences of fusion had not yet been fully formed, a view I no longer regard as likely. The study of sense sensations [*Sinnesempfindungen*] among primitive peoples today shows increasingly that intrinsic differences with our own sense sensations do not exist. Almost everything is reduced to differences of faculty and route of conception [*Auffasungsfähigkeit und Auffassungsrichtung*]. Cf. von Hornbostel, Ph.-A. no. 23.

xv   *Tonpsychologie* 2: 145, 148. *Beiträge zur Akustik und Musikwissenschaft* 2 (1898): 1–24, here 20.

xvi   It remains contentious whether the concept of a tonal relationship may also be expanded to encompass simple tones. In spite of certain difficulties that I highlighted (*Tonpsychologie* 2: 198ff.; *Beiträge* 1 [1898]: 45ff.), Charles Lalo felt compelled to advocate this theory (*Esquisse d'une Esthétique Musicale* [Paris: F. Alcan, 1908], 146ff.). Von Hornbostel too tends towards it (Ph.-A. no. 23). The supposition would undoubtedly facilitate understanding of the development of a purely melodic music. But since the voice and instruments (flutes included) in fact possess overtones, we could also manage for this purpose with the relationship of *sounds* [*Klänge*] in Helmholtz's sense.

    Perhaps we should also consider whether a kind of 'coherency' (after G. E. Müller's expression) or 'attraction' (Gilman, *Hopi Songs*, 15) might not play a part between successive simple tones. The consistent simultaneous occurrence of consonant overtones in the sounds of the voice as well as instruments could—if purely physiologically—facilitate the progression from the one tone to the other. We have to leave the question undecided here.

xvii Both Abraham and von Hornbostel have conducted a long series of experiments in recent years on so-called distance judgements [*Distanzurteile*] between tones, i.e. on the problem of what distance between tones to regard as equal, if one sets aside as far as possible the adaptation of our intervals, or renders this harmless by the conditions of the experiment. They found that it is in fact possible to estimate small tonal distances [microtones] equally between themselves with a certain assurance no matter what the absolute pitches are. And admittedly the distances judged as equal exhibit the same ratio *relationships*, not the same difference. The same supposition was made earlier by Ernst H. Weber, Gustav T. Fechner, and not least Wilhelm Wundt ('that we possess a measure for qualitative gradation of tones in our perception, and that this measure accords to Weber's laws', see *Physiologische Psychologie* [Leipzig: W. Engelmann, 1874], 1: 394). Wundt later substituted this supposition because one of his students falsely interpreted experimental results arising from the assumption that we find equal distances there where equal *differences* of ratios are given, which leads to quite impossible consequences. The original supposition also agrees with the fact—to be elaborated below—that entire scales occur in which all neighbouring steps stand in one and the same unchanging frequency ratio to each other.

For these reasons I regard it as entirely possible and likely that one came across certain small transposable tonal steps by mere 'distance estimates' [*Distanzschätzungen*]. Only the formation of fixed and by a particular feature, perfect steps—i.e. the isolation of the consonant intervals of the octave, fifth, and fourth—would be inconceivable in this way.

xviii Ph.-A. no. 16, p. 248ff. The conclusion about causal context becomes almost irrefutable in cases where instruments with numerous notes show exact correspondences of absolute pitch (frequencies). So von Hornbostel's measurements of Melanesian panpipes (from New Ireland) accord quite strikingly with Javanese instruments in the absolute pitch of individual notes (Ph.-A. no. 12, p. 132ff.), and also Indian wind instruments in north-west

Brazil accord with excavated ancient Peruvian pipes (Ph.-A. no. 22, p. 388ff.).

xix   Alberto Vojtěch Frič found panpipes assembled according to this principle among Brazilian Indians (see von Hornbostel, 'Musikalisches vom XVI. Internationalen Amerikanischen-Kongress in Wien', *Zeitschrift der internationalen Musikgesellschaft* 10 [1908]: 4–7, here 4).

xx   Von Hornbostel studied this kind of panpipe from Indians in Peru and observed an interesting (unpublished) fact there. Open pipes are all slotted [*ausgekerbt*] at the end, namely open for tuning purposes. Open pipes do not produce the pure octave that covered pipes of an equal length do, rather it is somewhat deepened [*vertiefte*]. This was noticed and appropriate incisions were made to achieve the pure octave; a nice proof of our advancing sense of hearing. Even if one wanted to accept that the octave interval is first encountered in general through the pitch difference of an open and covered pipe (of equal length), one has to admit that the ear has set itself up as judge and has reconfigured intervals given by nature according to *its* requirements. This is all the more remarkable since the same phenomenon is not only found in modern Indian pipes, but also in those unearthed from the ancient Peruvian period.

xxi   One often hears of the derivation of consonant intervals from the first overtones, e.g. from Edward B. Tylor (*Anthropology* [London: Macmillan, 1881]), from Richard Wallaschek (*Anfänge der Tonkunst* [Leipzig: Barth, 1903]); just as, since Helmholtz, overtones must assist in all difficulties. (Willi Paster quite wrongly attributed this to me in *Geburt der Musik*, [Leipzig: Eckhardt, 1910], 52.) Aside from the problem mentioned in the text, there is still a lot that speaks against the conjecture that overblown notes would have been the only—or the main—source [for deriving consonant intervals]. For instance, often the higher, partly discordant overtones are easier to bring out than the fundamental ones.

I do not want to say, however, that overblown notes were without influence. That primitive peoples' sense of hearing occasionally adapts itself to the de-tuning [*Verstimmung*] of these pitches like-wise emerges from von Hornbostel's study of a Brazilian panpipe (Ph.-A. no. 22). An instrument consisting of eleven pipes—whose structure initially appeared entirely opaque—arose in all likeli-hood by the fact that, based on one pipe, another was carved in such a way that its third partial forms a double octave with the fundamental of the first. One obtained a fourth (somewhat too large) in this way, and proceeded according to the same principle from the second to a third pipe, and so forth. In doing so the fifth overtone of the first pipe finds itself equal with the fundamental of the seventh, which is acoustically possible only because the over-tones are all a little too low [*tief*]. A second set of pipes—formed in the same way—would then be interpolated into the pipe system thus formed, whose [additional] pitches always lie at the midpoint between any two [pitches] in the first set. This was done at any rate because the tonal step of a fourth seemed too large to use in a melody. The principle of overtones is utilized similarly in another exemplar [of panpipes].

In this case we see that overtones are certainly utilized, but that the method of mere mechanical transfer by preparing new pipes in accordance with the overtones of the first one did not lead to the pure intervals; not once did it lead to pure octaves, fifths, and fourths.

The fact that we do not use the seventh, eleventh, and thirteenth overtones (looking back to Debussy's six-note scale here would just be perverse) is indeed already evidence that overtones as such are not the crucial factor for our sense of hearing. We occasionally hear those overtones while overblowing, but they do not impress us, save for the enthusiasts who worship natural products as such: we cannot use them in connection with our well-grounded tonal system. On the other hand, we still find the seventh and eleventh overtones actually in use in elemental musical conditions. This is the case in the *Ranz des Vaches* [*Kühreien*] in Switzerland, which is doubtless traceable back to the influence of the alpenhorn. It migrated from this instrument over to song without being corrected by the ear. The Alpine herdsman who yodels with the augmented fourth (eleventh partial) while working in the barn, calls it 'chüadreckeler' and finds the non-scale tone pleasing, perhaps also more characteristic for this 'business'.

On the alpenhorn itself the following melody, for example, was blown at the beginning of the previous century (see Johann R. Wyß, *Sammlung von Schweizer Kühreien*, 3rd edn. [Bern: J. J. Bürgdorfer, 1818]; rpt in Alfred Tobler, *Kühreien oder Kühreigen, Jodel und Jodellied* [Leipzig: Hug, 1890], 46):

Example 3.12.

The oldest notation of a *Ranz des Vaches* is in Georg Rhaw's *Bicinia Germanica* from 1545 (the lower voice has the melody). We can clearly make out the alpenhorn model in the melody; see the section:

Example 3.13.

But the raised fourth here is corrected into a perfect fourth. Then again, a *Ranz des Vaches* notated in 1710 displays the raised fourth distinctly in different places (see August Glück, 'Der Kühreihen in J. Weigl's "Schweizerfamilie"', *Vierteljahrsschrift für Musikwissenschaft* 8 [1892]: 77–90). As I read in Hermann Berlepsch (*Die Alpen* [London: Longman *et al.*, 1861], 360), the singing of the *Ranz des Vaches* was accompanied by the alpenhorn. The raised fourth was thereby transferred to unaccompanied singing. These [intervals] are supposed to have been used much more frequently in the first decades of the nineteenth century (Heinrich Szadrowsky, 'Die Musik und die tonerzeugenden Instrumente der

Alpenbewohner', *Jahrbuch des Schweizer Alpenklubs* 4 (1868): 275–352, here 283).

As one of the vocal melodies (among many) arising from the same root we give here the oldest transcription of an Alpine song from the Appenzell region (from Johann G. Ebel, *Schilderung der Gebirgsvölker der Schweiz* [Leipzig: Wolfische, 1798–1802], rpt. in Tobler, *Kühreien*, 57):

Example 3.14.

The augmented fourth also survives in one of the oldest 'alpine blessings', as sung today in areas of the old Swiss Confederacy. See the notation of the Alpine blessing from Melchsee-Frutt (where I myself heard it) in Arnold Schering, 'Ein Schweizer Alpen-Bet-Ruf', *Sammelbände der Internationalen Musikgesellschaft* 2 (1901): 669–672. It begins:

Example 3.15.

whereby not b♭ but b is quite definitely intoned.

From modern Styria [south-east Austria], Josef Pommer gives the following example, among others, in his collection *444 Jodler und Juchezer aus Steiermark* (Vienna: F. Rörich, 1901), which was sung with exactly the same intonation every time (cf. Pommer,

'Juchzer, Rufe und Almschreie aus den Österreichischen Alpenländern', *Bericht über den III. Kongreß der Internationalen Musikgesellschaft* [Vienna: Artaria/Leipzig: Breitkopf & Härtel, 1909], 248–251, here 251):

Ju - hu   hu - hu - hu - hu!

Example 3.16.

In one case, this alpenhorn's F♯ had a profound effect on classical music: I, at least, regard it as very probable that the horn melody in the last movement of Brahms' C minor symphony—like a victory or salutary pronouncement from the mountain top, which is then taken up by the answering flute—arose as a consequence of such Swiss notes:

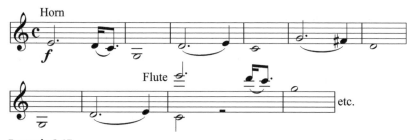

Example 3.17.

The twelve-year-old Mozart already used this overblown note with humorous intent—it intervenes unintentionally among clumsy brass players—in *Bastien und Bastienne* (see the little bagpipe number to which Colas enters [No. 3, interlude]), as had Mendelssohn in the sonorous funeral music for Pyramus' death [in his incidental music to *A Midsummer Night's Dream*, Op. 61]. Hence, occasional influences from non-harmonic overblown notes are also possible in our classical music, though not their systematic use.

We should not drag in the raised fourth of the so-called gypsy scale, oriental melodies or even of the fifth church mode here; they have nothing to do with the eleventh overtone.

In a similar way to the alpenhorn, the Nordic 'lur'—an ancient, large bronze horn, from which twelve or more overtones can be produced by overblowing—may have affected the development of local music. Since two lurs with the same tuning were almost always found together, it was suggested that they were blown as two voices (Angul Hammerich, 'Studien über die Altnordischen Luren im Nationalmuseum zu Kopenhagen', *Vierteljahrsschrift für Musikwissenschaft* 10 [1894]: 1–32, here 29ff.; Willi Pastor, *Die Geburt der Musik* [Leipzig: Eckhardt, 1910], 68ff.). But let us also consider other reasons for their appearance in pairs. Hammerich, the foremost expert on this instrument, expresses himself very cautiously about it. Yet in our music we are precisely in the habit of using instruments with *different* pitches for polyphonic playing. Furthermore, the precision with which the instruments found in pairs are tuned alike indicates that they were blown in unison.

xxii The differentiation between wind, string, and percussion instruments, as it appears in the text, may transpire in this short illustration. But it should not be considered exhaustive (e.g. grooved instruments occur, whose tone is produced by stroking over them). Neither is it logically flawless, if taken precisely. We can either classify according to the devices, whose immediate consequences are air vibrations (e.g. sharp rims past which a stream of air whistles, vibrations of strings or membranes, and so forth) or according to the activities that set these devices in motion (e.g. striking or depressing, then stroking, blowing, and so forth). According to this principle of classification, the organ and the piano belong in the first case to separate categories, in the second to the same category; string instruments are the other way around, first to the same categories, second to separate ones. But we are not concerned here with these logical refinements.

xxiii Recently, von Hornbostel studied phonograms of dance songs from the Admiralty Island of Baluan [Papau New Guinea] recorded by the explorer Richard Thurnwald. He found that these songs were all for two voices, and essentially move in parallel seconds in fact, even proceeding at the end from unison back to a second in order to close with this sonority (Ph-A. no. 24). Certainly for our taste this is the strangest item of all that has so far been found. And yet it is not without counterparts in other areas of the world, even in Europe, to which von Hornbostel alludes. For now I want to regard the explanation given in the text as the most probable. One clearly discerns the rawness of the pitch simultaneity and the twanging of [acoustic] beats in the phonogram cylinder.

xxiv   What Theodor Billroth adduced about the significance of rhythm in the instructive little essay 'Who is musical?' strikes me as very appropriate. [See Billroth, *Wer ist Musikalisch?* (Berlin: Gebruder Paetel, 1895).]

xxv   Charles Samuel Myers, 'The rhythm-sense of primitive peoples', *Bericht über den 5. Internationalen Psychologen-Kongreß in Rom* (1904), 287–289; 'A study of rhythm in primitive music', *British Journal of Psychology* 1 (1905): 397–406, here 397. (The results are gathered through graphic registration and by measuring the temporal gaps between the accents of gong strikes among the Sarawak Malays in Borneo.) For other matters about exotic rhythm and rhythmic polyphony, see particularly Franz Boas' work on the Kwakiutl Indians, and von Hornbostel, Ph-A, no. 14, p. 159ff.; no. 16, p. 252ff.; and no. 23, p. 266ff.

xxvi   In addition to the samples of rhythmic complications included in the musical supplement [this volume, Part II], here is another example of the simultaneous linking of dissimilar rhythms. According to Franz Boas' study, many songs among the Kwakiutl Indians that are accompanied by timpani exhibit the following form:

Example 3.18.

Each part, as Boas assures us, maintains its rhythm internally with the utmost precision. In one of the songs he notated, the voice is in 4/4, the timpani in 5/8, and in such a way that three bars of the voice equals four bars of the timpani; thus each 6/8 for the voice corresponds to 5/8 for the timpani; the timpani rhythm is once again the one given above, which generally appears to be very popular.

xxvii The first classic example given by Wundt (*Völkerpsychologie* 2: 1) would belong here. It is taken from Franz Boas' work on the Central Eskimos. Boas, however, differentiates sharply between the Eskimo *songs* that move in large intervals, partly in broken triads, even in octave leaps (see our melodic examples nos. 4.49 and 4.50), and the *recitations* [*Erzählungen*]. As he expressly remarks, what is reproduced in notation here is the reciting tone [*Erzählerton*] which is maintained at a constant pitch and only deviates by a semitone on accented syllables. There is no shadow of proof that this manner of performance and vocal movement which occur among Eskimos would have existed *previously*, and that it therefore represents the remnants of their actual primitive singing. Cf. endnote xxviii.

xxviii In John F. Rowbotham's great work, *History of Music*, 3 vols. (London: Trübner & Co., 1885–1887), the primeval history of music (vol. 1, 1885) is presented so that in the first stage, only one note would have been used, in the second, two, in the third, three (always only ever distinguished by a whole tone step). In a fourth stage we proceeded straight to a five-step scale, whereby the step from the third to the fifth, and that from the sixth to the octave of the fundamental appeared to primeval humans to be the same size as the preceding whole-tone steps.

It is of course easy to arrange the available musical examples from primitive peoples in such a way that one preserves these four classes, among others. But it is not possible to prove that they proceeded strictly in this chronological order. Up until the most recent times we find impassioned declamation on a single pitch, or on only a few pitches, among all peoples, *alongside* richly developed melodies (quite apart from cases of particular craftiness such as the famous one-note song by Peter Cornelius ['Ein Ton', Op. 3 no. 3]). If we are to accept that the first songs were relatively monotonous, it seems to me quite arbitrary and forced to regard absolute monotony as a starting point (and according to Rowbotham, these songs are strangely always on the note g). Besides, it remains quite unclear in Rowbotham's account why exactly these specific steps alone were chosen, steps that resulted in an octave when joined together, and why [the size of] both upper steps are supposed to have been estimated as being equal to those preceding. It always comes back to the old mistake: the emergence of consonant intervals remains unexplained.

In a similar way, François-Joseph Fétis, who utilized the available ethnological material of his time knowledgeably but uncritically, had already allowed the scale to emerge (but from semitones and still smaller steps instead of from whole-tone steps), whereby the stereotypical call of 'progressive brain organization' replaces for him the lack of a psychological means of explanation. Such an account appears far too deductive to me. Reality does not submit so easily to schematization.

^{xxix} These scales have been securely identified by Land, Ellis, and me (after collaborative studies with Otto Abraham; Ph.-A. no. 1). Following a written exchange, Myers too recorded songs by the islanders of the Torres Straits, which seem to adhere to an equally spaced scale of six steps (see our melodic examples nos. 4.9 and 4.10). Yet the frequencies observed do not equate very consistently and closely with those calculated, so much so that we cannot base a firm conclusion on them. In singing one simply never obtains such an exact agreement with any principle as one does by the use of pitched instruments such as the Siamese and Javanese xylophone and metallophone.

Wundt regards the supposition of forming such an equally spaced scale based on a mere sense of hearing as 'self-evidently invalid' since it contradicts the experimental studies conducted in his institute. (Wundt, *Völkerpsychologie* 3, part 2: 477.) He appears to seek a positive explanation in certain regular gradations of the sizes of wooden staffs [*Holzstäbe*] and bells, which make up Siamese instruments. I, at least, draw this conclusion from the fact that he specifies the dimensions of each instrument in my [published] descriptions. But he overlooks my remark (Ph.-A. no. 1, pp. 71, 72, and 80), that the staffs are grooved on the underside and that lumps of wax are stuck on top of them for subtler tuning; likewise on the inside of the bells. Hence there is nothing to be learned from even the most conscientious specification of dimensions. Incidentally, a stroll through the Leipzig museum [of ethnology] would be enough to rule out such ideas. The museum's collection contains is a twenty-two-note xylophone from Burma whose staffs are slotted by varying amounts underneath, and one can detect places in which lumps of wax may have sat. (Of course, one cannot conduct pitch measurements on instruments that have lost their tuning, as Wallaschek did).

But let us just assume that Siamese scales arose originally by mechanical means, in which staffs of fairly homogenous material and equal overall thickness were used, if only from different places: according to what law did the lengths have to be staggered in order to produce these scales? Since the frequencies of every two adjacent pitches are in the ratio $1 : \sqrt[7]{2}$, and since the lengths of the staffs—according to the named simplest premises—must have an inverse-quadratic relationship to the frequencies, one must divide a given staff length (L_1) by $\sqrt[14]{2}$ in order to obtain the next staff length, L_2. How are the Siamese supposed to get started without logarithm tables? I myself have [Ph.-A. no. 1, p. 101f.] envisaged a hypothesis according to which Siamese scales could have arisen mechanically from a peculiar string division, but I also proved this principle to be very unlikely. So it will probably have to remain that the equally spaced Siamese and Javanese scales arose from a sense of *hearing*. If this does not correspond with the experimental studies in Leipzig, I can only infer a new confirmation of the proven fundamental mistakes in the experiments (cf. Stumpf, 'Über Vergleichungen von Tondistanzen', *Zeitschrift für Psychologie und*

Physiologie der Sinnesorgane 1 [1890]: 419–485; and endnote xvii).

xxx Ph.-A. no. 1, p. 96ff.

xxxi Ph.-A. no. 21 (Fischer).

xxxii Guido Adler published an essay specifically about heterophony ('Über Heterophonie', *Jahrbuch der Musikbibliothek Peters* 15 [1908]: 17–27). Since he misses any mention of the term heterophony in Helmholtz, it seems to have escaped him that before my essay on Siamese music, nobody at all had spoken of heterophony as a particular stylistic form. I took the expression itself from a passage of Plato that provoked much discussion among philologists and which I believe already to have made more comprehensible by interpreting the word 'antiphony' in the sense of 'diaphony' (*Geschichte des Konsonanz-Begriffes* [Munich: Franz, 1897]). It seemed to me that by 'heterophony', Plato meant the simultaneous looped playing [*Umspielen*] of the same melody through variations, as occurs nowadays among oriental peoples, and thus I suggested the term for this kind of musical practice. But for me it had nothing to do with the name, of course, rather with the thing, i.e. with a summary of widespread and peculiar phenomena under one particular concept that is differentiated from that of polyphony and harmony just as from that of pure monophony [*Einstimmigkeit*]. That is what, in this case, issued from me, not that I want to see it as a great achievement. Long ago Max Müller and Kurt von Zedtwitz had published Chinese and Japanese scores; Jan P. N. Land and Isaac Groneman Javanese scores, from which the facts and circumstances could be gathered, and which I already mentioned in *Tonpsychologie* 2 (1890), 402. Daniel de Lang, who is cited by Land-Groneman and by me ('Tonsystem und Musik der Siamesen', *Beiträge zur Akustik und Musikwissenschaft* 3 [1901]: 131) had also already described this kind of music making quite correctly. But that is enough about the historical aspect.

Much more depends on whether the new concept retains its uniqueness and does not immediately become blended with others. In this respect I want to note that although parallel organum and the bagpipe can both occur in *connection* with heterophony, they are in no way themselves to be conceived as heterophony, as appeared to be the impression in Adler's study, if I have understood it correctly. Moreover, I should say that the musical examples Adler includes are only really heterophonic in the smallest degree, but otherwise are either just cases of forms of the early counterpoint, 'nota contra notam' [note against note], or, as in the Russian songs [transcribed by] Eugenie Lineff, essentially examples of popular, clumsy harmonization. (Even so, Lineff herself describes them entirely in the sense of heterophony on page xv of the introduction. But their scores indicate only that harmonic direction is pursued in the lower voices, particularly passages in thirds, and that this always falls back into parallel octaves in between. Sometimes, admittedly, melodic aberrations occur in these parallels, as in our village music when the clarinettist, say, performs his escapades. In general I cannot find heterophony carried out as a stylistic principle here, however; at the earliest, still only in the two-part songs of volume 2).

At the Viennese meeting of the International Music Society, Pfingsten 1908, von Hornbostel gave an overview of the manifold intermediate stages between pure unison and harmonic–polyphonic music. The extensive classification of forms that was distributed among the listeners in printed form was not included in the congressional report. But it can be found in an informative explanation of views, provided by the most expert researcher, about the development of exotic music in this respect (Hornbostel, 'Über Mehrstimmigkeit in der Aussereuropäischer Musik', *International Musical Society: Congress Report* 3 [1909]: 298–303. Cf. also Ph.-A. no. 19, p. 1038ff. about the comparison of exotic music with organum of the Middles Ages). In these things the exploration is still too much in a state of flux to be able to talk in terms of anything definite. In my own understanding, the different categories of music making present themselves in respect of monophony and polyphony in the following schema, about which one should note in advance, however, that the categories are in reality multiply linked to one another, and that continual transitions lead from the one to the other. Precisely for that reason, the boundaries can be drawn in different ways.

1. *Homophony* = monody [*Einstimmigkeit*]. We frequently use the term today for monophonic melody with chordal accompaniment. This usage is rooted in the prejudice that absolutely never and nowhere can there be melodies without a chordal basis. It seems useful to me to abandon this curious usage along with this prejudice, and—like Helmholtz—designate only purely melodic music as homophonic, which requires neither an objective nor a chordal basis even if just in the imagination of the listener. If an individual cannot imagine primitive melodies without chordal accompaniment, they must at least abstract their judgement from such subjective ingredients.

    Homophony, as we understand it here, can still be conceived in narrower and wider senses. In a wider sense, it encompasses doubling of the melody in octaves, insofar as one considers octaves as the same or at least equivalent notes.

2. *Organum* = singing or playing in parallel. If we do not recognize the identity of octaves, all octave-doubling then belongs here, as in the singing of a melody by men and women. But in any case, and above all, organum concerns realized parallel fifths and fourths. Parallel thirds, sixths, and seconds only strictly fall under this concept if major and minor thirds do not alternate, as is conditioned in our music by the diatonic scale. That such quasi-parallels occur in Africa appears to point to a European influence. Only in equal-tempered scales, i.e. in our chromatic scales for example, are there parallel thirds with a completely unchanged interval.

    Three or more voices can, of course, join together in this way by having two in octaves, the third going along between them at the fifth or fourth.

    For organum in the wider sense, we also count the cases in which the parallelism is not realized note for note without exception, but where other intervals are interpolated here and there. As when the voices proceed successively from a unity to a fourth, and then continue in parallel at this interval in order to blend again into unity at the close. (Cf. Hucbald's rambling organum, and the 'occursus' with Guido d'Arezzo, which likewise find analogies with exotic music.)

3. *Drone*—or in the manner of the bagpipe (pedal point) = holding a note while another voice states a melody. The fixed note can lie above or below the melody, even in between the other voices where there are two or more; it can be given unbroken or with pauses, roughly at the beginning of every bar; two or more notes can enter regularly in immediate succession, or alternate in short periods (ostinato), and other modifications can occur that do not alter the nature of the thing.

A particular form of Guidonian organum coincides with a primitive pedal point ('saepe autem ... organum sustensum tenemus', notation in *Oxford History of Music*, ed. H. E. Wooldridge [Oxford: Clarendon, 1901], 1: 69): an example of the transition of forms into one another through boundary cases.

4. *Heterophony* = the simultaneous performance of several variations of a theme. In its simplest form this is nothing but an easy form of homophony; it occurs when a more mobile instrument or a solitary singer introduces a little embellishment here and there, for example. One wants to say that heterophony is the inevitable consequence of the collaboration of several people who want to perform the same melody. Just as parallel octaves or parallel fifths inevitably result when singers or instruments with different ranges want to play the same tune together, and just like the pedal point that results when two sound sources combine where one source only actually possesses a single pitch. Like the remaining forms, heterophony initially occurred at all events by chance, then developed into an intentionally employed art form that was utilized without being reliant on its original causes.

5. *Polyphony* = the simultaneous performance of several different melodies that only occasionally meet on consonant intervals or at the unison. Here too examples or antecedents appear in exotic music. The early period of our musical epoch offers particular evidence of this. Our hearing finds it stimulating to follow several quite different melodies simultaneously (e.g. when rapidly shifting attention), and the more different the melodies in direction, tempo, and the entire character of pitch movement, the better. It does not principally concern the effect of the individual simultaneous pitches that arise. As soon as this point of view essentially becomes possible, and one strives for a frequent meeting of pitches in consonances and above all in consonant triads, this form turns into the next.

Polyphony, in the broadest sense of the word, encompasses all forms except the first, of course. We use it here in the specific sense is has obtained in music history: for the simultaneity of several melodies that are understood as essentially different. In this sense it stands *alongside* the remaining forms, if junctions everywhere are conceivable.

6. *Harmonic music* = the simultaneous resounding of several different pitches and the derivation of aesthetic pleasure and aversion in the succession of such tonal complexes.

I do not want to claim that primitive peoples everywhere take no joy whatsoever in multiple simultaneous sounds as such, i.e. a preliminary stage to our feeling for harmony (see figures 2 and 3, pp. 176–177). But our chordal system, as it gradually developed with its main triads in major and minor on the tonic, dominant, and subdominant; with scales derived from triads, in which each note is first obtained from the triads out of feeling and effect, and also first attains its exact tuning; with dissonant chords (discords) that turn into the main triads and finally into the tonic triad according to particular rational rules—that is something thoroughly new for which we find no equivalents before the last millennium or in present-day exotic music.

But harmonic music assimilated into itself all the earlier forms that it could. The great masters teach the art of counterpoint as it combines with polyphony. Heterophonic forms [*Bildungen*] occur thousands of times within harmonic space, even among each secondary voice ornamenting the melody with figures. A drone-like manner extends from an ostinato bass, from a pedal point, organum extends from peoples' parallel fifths, from the 'mixtures' of the organ, as in so much modern audacity, whereby a lot rests on the fact that one does not perceive the parallels clearly. Only strict homophony does not exist for our consciousness, in that even a melody performed entirely monophonically will instinctively be understood according to the harmonic schema if it lies within our major or minor scales and carries the other traits of our melodies (clear tonic, customary rhythm, and structure). Triads always vibrate with you, so to speak. Admittedly this is different if one retrains oneself through familiarization with exotic melodies.

But we also find this kind of insertion of other forms into a predominant principal form within exotic music. Thus extended parallel fourths are often inserted into the heterophonic music of the Siamese, Javanese, and Chinese. According to recently received recordings, there is in fact an interesting version of heterophony in China, where a theme is performed simultaneously in variations by two voices that are a fourth apart, i.e. a realized conjunction of principles two and four. (Ph.-A., no. 29.)

All previously known types of musical practice, regarding monophony and polyphony, ought to be soluble within the forms just given.

Chapter 4

Part II: Songs of primitive peoples

The following examples will, at least in part, elucidate and attest the remarks made in Part I and its endnotes. The majority of them are taken from the sources more closely specified in endnote i. 'Ph.-A. no. …' denotes the number of the relevant publication in the Berlin Phonogram Archive.[1]

Primitive peoples mostly have a tremendous passion for singing. They sing at every opportunity and for hours on end; the selfsame melody can be repeated indefinitely, if not always without changes. Where repeat signs refer in our notation to an entire song, they ordinarily mean this kind of multiple repetition. But equally, where we have no such signs before us in an author's original notation, it is to be assumed that such repetitions in fact took place.

If we call the following melodic specimens 'primitive', we must not take this label too literally, as compared with most products of so-called primitive art that belong to the present. There are even songs from non-literate peoples and those without a literature. If we delve into the structure of the melodies and simultaneously consider what must precede everything in order to make the emergence of such forms possible, we will have to regard them in the majority of cases as products of an artistic sense that is already fairly developed. The boundary between art inspired by theoretical reflection, and elemental, instinctive [*reflexionslos*] art always endures. Concepts of the 'exotic' and the

---

[1] See the endnotes to Part 1: endnote 1, section 3, pp. 69–71. In terms of recordings, the most recent catalogue of the complete archive was compiled in 2000. The most up-to-date inventory of the wax cylinders which Stumpf would have known is Susanne Ziegler, *Die Wachszylinder des Berliner Phonogramm-Archivs* (Berlin: Ethnologisches Museum, Staatliche Museen zu Berlin, 2006).

'primitive' can no longer be lumped together today—as August Wilhelm Ambros did, for instance, when he brought together Chinese, Indian, and Arabic music under the heading '[The First] Beginnings of Music'[2]—as happens even in a recent large work about this subject where examples of old Chinese Temple hymns are given between a song from a native of Papua New Guinea and that of a Fiji islander.

Generally this means that the impression of a primitive song is more or less inadequately reproduced by the notes. Intonation is already subject to characteristic deviations in many passages. Through particular signs (see below) we try to suggest these deviations and other characteristics of intonation in the more conspicuous passages. But the art of vocalization and numerous performance habits (of which our ornaments—appoggiaturas and the like—give only an attenuated picture) are often just as essential for the whole impression as the existing notes. If there were no phonographic recordings, our own songs, according to the mere notes, could only be reproduced very inadequately in later times. Neither would performance indications suffice, for we would argue over their performance as we already argue today over the performance of signs from two centuries ago. If we heard the actual sound of a plica or hocket (Schluchzer) from the thirteenth century, we would probably be surprised.[3] Indeed, singing is always permeated by performance practices, and it is precisely these vocal practices that are poorly conveyed by signs. These now outdated forms of vocal performance appear to have a certain similarity with those of primitive peoples. I explain about this in the commentary to our musical examples, as well as in endnote xii. Full particulars are given in Theodore Baker's Indian

---

[2] August Wilhelm Ambros (1816–1876) was an Austrian composer, music essayist, and historian. Stumpf refers to the first chapter ('Die Ersten Anfänge der Tonkunst') of Ambros' study, *Die Geschichte der Musik*, 5 vols. (Breslau: F. E. C. Leuckart, 1862–1882).

[3] In chant notations, a *plica* is a notational sign for liquescent neumes during the thirteenth and fourteenth century; the first note is fully vocalized, and the second is only semi-vocalized and is often sung on consonant letters as a passing pitch before the next main pitch. *Hocket*, from the same period, is a dovetailing of sounds and silences that alternate between different voices or instruments. Finally, a *Schluchzer* is a descending appoggiatura, imitative of a tear drop, known more commonly today as a seufzer or pianto.

songs,[4] in my work on the Bella Coola Indians,[5] in the articles from the Phonogram Archive, and in more recent descriptions from explorers (the oldest reports do not bother much with such detail).

The rhythm and division of the bar make for numerous difficulties. In many cases everything is immediately clear, in others one either does not arrive at a rhythm that fits our metrical forms, or one has constantly to change metres. And yet it is better to use this aid where it works: the division of accents given by the bar structure makes an overview of the whole structure easier, extraordinarily so.

The song texts are omitted in almost all cases since they would only have been comprehensible to a few who are well-informed. Only the purpose of a song is mentioned in the notes, where statements about it exist.

Frequently one has to think an octave lower than the notation as authors opted to use the treble clef even for songs by men, much as we use it for the tenor voice.

+ above the note means a raised pitch; − a lowered pitch; ⌐ ⌐ a sliding descent from an indistinct pitch to the pitch in question; and a descent from the latter, respectively; ⌐ ⌐ a sliding connection of two notes; ⌣ legatissimo; ♩ ♩ ♩ a repeated, distinct accentuation of a note without striking it anew (pulsando, a performance habit particularly among Indians, incidentally also practised in the Middle Ages as 'reverberatio' and until the eighteenth century as 'vocalisazione aspirata' or 'balancement'); ♪ the same as the previous sign, when the duration of a note does not exceed that of a crotchet; v a pause for breath without metrical value. The bracketing of a note (♪) means that its pitch is not quite recognizable. The prescription of two time signatures such as 3/4, 5/4 is to say that both alternate regularly with each other, bar on bar, throughout the whole song.

Most of the following songs are reproduced according to phonographic recordings, whereby the greatest reliability can be attained. In several cases I have inserted songs written down aurally that are

[4] Theodore Baker, *Über die Musik der Nordamerikanischen Wilden* (Leipzig: Breitkopf & Härtel, 1882).

[5] Carl Stumpf, 'Lieder der Bellakula-Indianer', *Vierteljahrsschrift für Musikwissenschaft* 2 (1886): 405–426.

particularly well certified or, if doubt remains about the details, offer something of particular interest through certain characteristics that we may regard as accurately reproduced. The notation originating from the Berlin Phonogram Archive (as far as it has been published) was reviewed closely by my partners Erich M. von Hornbostel and Erich Fischer, and we clarified small deviations from the earlier form [of notation]. Certainly one can notate the metre, the key signature, even individual notes that lie between our pitches in a number of different ways; moreover, the constant practice of both men led to growing security in the rapid capture of details. Several songs are reproduced more extensively than in their first publication, others are published for the first time.

We begin the series with the most primitive songs that are reliable and accurately known to us, those of the Vedda in Ceylon [modern-day Sri Lanka]; but we order the following songs not according to progressive melodic development, rather—at least in general—in a geographical direction eastwards from Ceylon, further on to the Pacific Ocean; thence to America, which we explore from south to north; onwards to the Eskimos; and finally to west and east Africa. At the same time, however, one often notices progress in melodic formation within smaller geographic groups anyway. It is currently impossible, and perhaps will remain so, to establish a clear progressive succession from the collected musical products of humankind because, from the outset, progress advances in very different directions. On the other hand, we will gradually find increasingly cohesive or related musical conditions within geographically contiguous or ethnologically coherent groups of people, and thereby achieve a large, unified picture of musical achievements. The following survey does not remotely make a claim for this; it only wishes to deliver quite fragmentary specimens from which certain characteristics emerge particularly clearly. There can be no doubt that within a short period of time these musical features will stand equally alongside others, teaching us to recognize the connections between the peoples of the world. Yet even now, in individual cases, the conclusions based on this can claim the weight of great probability; namely, when one considers the construction of instruments—and their precise tuning—at the same time as the construction of melody, whereby coincidences have been shown regarding absolute pitches, scales, etc., coincidences whose random occurrence would contradict all rules of probability.

But a prerequisite for such penetrating force is careful study of all the details, in melodies just as in instruments. The remarks appended to our examples may afford the general reader an idea of which points matter the most. Besides, all documents that can shed light on the primordial history and surviving deeper stages of civilization of our race deserve the closest analysis. We painstakingly examine prehistoric pots and shards and every edge of an eolith, we compare and analyse— rightly so—the most awful grimaces, the crudest attempts at drawing [*Zeichnungsversuche*]. So do we have to devote objective and penetrating study to the musical products of primitive peoples, instead of modernizing them to the point of unrecognizability, and performing them with piano accompaniment, passing them down as the 'USA National Music' of the sweetly singing ladies of the salon, or of composers devoid of invention. The harshest words with which von Hornbostel castigated this deplorable custom are unfortunately only too timely.

Example 4.1a. 🔊 1

Example 4.1b. 🔊 2

Example 4.2a.

Example 4.2b.

Examples 4.1a and 1b are two songs of the Vedda from Ceylon, reproduced from the phonographic recording by Margarethe L. Selenka
(Ph.-A. No. 20).[6] Three or two notes form the motif that is repeated
incessantly with slight variation. The interval between the lower notes in
1a is a whole tone according to Max Wertheimer's measurements and
that between the middle and upper notes is a semitone, so the melodic
range here amounts to a minor third. The highest note mainly occurs at
the beginning, never in the closing formulae. In the second song [4.1b]
the gaps between pitches are reduced, however. The lower two pitches

---

[6] Margarethe L. Selenka (1860–1922) was a zoologist and anthropologist, whose travels in
Ceylon with her husband Emil Selenka, a professor of zoology at Erlangen University,
were jointly written up as *Sonnige Welten. Ostäsiatische Reiseskizzen* (Wiesbaden: C. W.
Kreidel, 1896).

are just three quarters of a tone apart from each other, and a third, higher pitch that also occasionally occurs here lies just a quarter tone above the second note, so that the entire range only spans a whole tone. Perhaps the third note is not even intentional, and only arose through strong accentuation of the second note. Since the two songs were sung by different singers (one young, one old), we can perhaps regard the different gaps between pitches as individual characteristics of the singers.

The metronome markings have been added here according to statements by Selenka who still remembers the songs very clearly (the device mentioned in Chapter 3.1.1 [pitch pipe] also helps here). The tempo is strictly maintained. I have increased the number of bars compared with the original. We could reduce the frequent change of metre if we chose 2/4 as the main metre, but periodization becomes clearly noticeable in our form of notation. The insertion or omission of individual parts of the bar, whereby even bars become uneven, sounds strange to us [*widerstrebt unserem Gefühl*], but occurs frequently among primitive peoples. It may be related to the text or to the manner of performance.

From a musical standpoint we would regard both songs as almost identical, as barely different forms of the same melody. The Vedda probably regard them simply as varieties within a type. The texts are different (according to Charles G. Seligmann's note in *The Veddas*, the first is a song whose purpose is to entertain).[7]

Almost all of the songs Selenka brought back are of this kind. In a waltz (not reported on by Wertheimer) there is indeed a duet in which two voices unmistakably sing according to a certain rule, but in such a way that it is hard to work out what this is. They also only move within the range of a minor third.

These Vedda songs may present an example of that primordial or precursory stage of music that uses only small tonal steps. Neither consonance nor tonal relationships appear to have played a role in them. Nevertheless, they already have a certain structure, tuning, regular recurring phrases with variations, and finally particular,

---

[7] Charles Gabriel Seligmann and Brenda Zara Seligmann, *The Veddas. With a chapter by C. S. Myers and an appendix by A. Mendis Gunasekara* (Cambridge: Cambridge Univ. Press, 1911; rpt. Oosterhout: Anthrological Publications, 1969).

specially-formed closing formulae. The closing formula itself always follows an 'opening gambit' [*Vorbau*], whose last note is often the lowest, while the final closing note typically occurs on the middle note, for example:

Examples 4.2a and b are also Vedda songs from the book *The Veddas* by Charles G. and Brenda Z. Seligmann,[8] in which the psychologist Charles Samuel Myers (Cambridge) reproduces and analyses numerous songs recorded on phonographs. He divides them into three groups: those that use two notes; three notes; or four to five notes. Among the latter group, however, he already supposes outside influences. The songs in the first two groups are really very similar to Wertheimer's, for this narrow supply of notes, the small pitch gaps, and the simple rhythm can hardly be different. Both songs chosen here (from groups B and C)—which belong to the most primitive Vedda tribe, the Sitala Wanniya—are interesting for the regular recurring metrical sequence 3/4, 5/4 that also occurs in another song (a lullaby) from the same tribe. The division of accents in 4.2a prevents us from simply prescribing 4/4 time. Again, both songs, as Myers already noted, are varieties of a melodic type (or are melodically identical anyway).[9] In the second song both of the higher pitches are intoned slightly lower so that everything shifts together in a similar way to the second of Wertheimer's songs.

Incidentally, not all of Myer's songs are transcribed using metrical bars; many did not conform to them. The same tempo marking from

---

[8] Ibid.

[9] In the first song, Myer's notation sketches out a third sharp, for A♯, only in error; according to the tonometric statements on page 353 the interval of both higher pitches is actually a little smaller than a halftone. [SN]

both Myer and Wertheimer seems to be a coincidence; there are many other metronome markings.

The Vedda, or at least the primeval people not influenced by neighbouring tribes to whom these songs belong, have no instruments—not even one percussion instrument.

Example 4.3.

Example 4.4.

We now have two examples from the earliest inhabitants of the Andaman Islands (examples 4.3 and 4.4). Admittedly, they are not recorded on phonographs but for external and internal reasons are authorized as correctly notated. This goes particularly for the first song, which was transcribed by Maurice Videl Portman after eight further examples from the southerly tribes of the island group.[10] The precise,

---

[10] Maurice Videl Portman, 'Andamanese Music', *Journal of the Royal Asiatic Society* 20, (1888): 181–218, here part II. [SR]

detailed descriptions of Andaman music that Portman gives inspire trust. Regarding the intervals, Portman (who always writes E♯ instead of F) remarks that what is notated as a semitonal step was actually sung as quarter tones, but that they were probably intended as semitonal steps. They will certainly not correspond exactly to our intervallic steps, as with the Vedda, since our chromatic scale is a product of later development; but here only small steps (still differentiable through the voice) are sung, which of course do not always come off in quite the same way. It would be incorrect to deduce the use of quarter tones in the theoretical sense of the term from such notation and reports. Moreover Portman gives a damning verdict on the sense of hearing of the Andamanese. The best singers could hit a given note only approximately; the majority remain about a semitone above or below it. The less one can attribute an aural capacity to them, the more training of the voice and the ear would be demanded. The systematic use of quarter tones and still smaller differentiations of pitch, as reported, for example, by the Greeks, is a product of a refined culture.

(Some oft-quoted examples of allegedly quarter tone music can be examined here in passing. Four melodies from New Zealand have been passed down in the work of Governor George Grey (cf. endnote xii), which James A. Davies—who first gave a learned introduction to the Greeks' enharmonic system—transcribed with the help of a monochord, and which move not only in quarter tones but also in enharmonic intervals. A song, for instance, found without critical commentary in the collections of examples under discussion, consists almost entirely of the notes D, E♭♭, E, E♯, and F. A native should thus differentiate between D and E♭♭, E♯ and F. Someone else may believe that!

Those melodies of the Nukahiwa (on Washington Island in the Pacific Ocean),[11] transcribed in Georg H. von Langsdorff's old travel writings,[12]

---

[11] Also known as Teraina (Kiribati); formerly known as Prospect Island and New York Island.

[12] Georg Heinrich von Langsdorf, *Voyages and Travels in Various Parts of the World During the Years 1803–7*, 2 vols. (London: H. Colburn *et al.*, 1813–1814).

and very often cited and accepted without question, would also have been sung in quarter tones. They constantly go from E to G and back again. Only F and F♯ are given as intermediary steps in the notation; but the commentary on this (by Tilesius) mentions that it is a case of quarter-tone steps. It probably just amounted to pulling the note up and down, a 'droning pull' [*ein 'brummendes Ziehen'*] of the voice, as it is called in the report. Incidentally, the notation is deficient. It emerges from the commentary that the treble clef is erroneously used instead of the bass clef, which Fétis had already rectified.)

Portman's collected songs consist of solo and subsequent chorus, and all move in these small steps within three notes; only the absolute pitch is given differently. The final note is not always the middle one, however; sometimes it is the highest or lowest of the three. The solo is sung in free tempo, the chorus strictly in time.

The parallel octaves and fifths in the chorus, repeated alike with every song, are very striking. Concerning the fifths, Portman again remarks that he regards them as intentionally uniform, but that they are occasionally intoned as minor sixths. He remarks how intervals other than those notated came to light, which he understands simply as deviations from the intended unison of individual voices. All of this points to a keen observer.

By way of instruments, the Andaman people only have timpani that actively take part in choral songs, as example 4.3 shows.

Example 4.4 is taken from Edward Horace Man's book, *On the Aboriginal Inhabitants of the Andaman Islands*.[13] Jan L. A. Brandes transcribed it. The commentaries are scanty. The lower voice, appearing as the note D in the example, is certainly not to be understood as vocal song, but as a timpani rhythm. The song's restricted tonal range and the monotonous repetition (the piece is as long as desired; the author tells of hours of nightly songs) correspond so closely to the

---

[13] Edward Horace Man, *On the Aboriginal Inhabitants of the Andaman Islands* (London: Trübner, 1883), 172.

previously cited reliable examples that we may regard this too as basically authentic. Melodies with larger tonal ranges do not appear among Andaman aborigines, as with the earliest tribes of the Vedda. Hence, the use of the octave and the fifth is all the more important in choral singing.

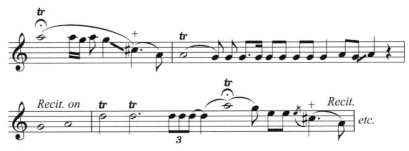

Example 4.5. ⏺ 3

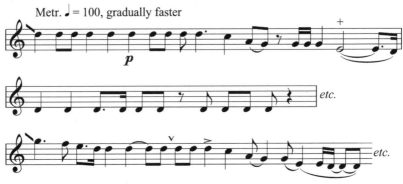

Example 4.6. ⏺ 4

Example 4.7. ⏺ 5

Examples 4.5–4.7 are Songs of the Kubu forest people on Sumatra, after phonographic recordings by the museum director Fritz Hagen in Frankfurt am Main. Ph-A. No. 16.

Here we encounter an entirely different [melodic] type. The large consonant intervals of the octave, fifth, and fourth dominate, and are struck quite purely despite the fact that the Kubu exist at a very low cultural level, and their songs do not conform to our forms, especially not to a metrical division of the bar. Where a drum beat exists, it appears essentially to be in seven but seems unconnected with the rhythmically intoned passages of singing. In fact, von Hornbostel believes a somewhat more fixed, seven-part rhythm is recognizable in only two songs (he examined and transcribed all of them), which are interrupted in different places anyway, by the use of pauses, by shortening or lengthening of tone.

Example 4.5, dubbed 'a love song of a teenager' but sung by an old man, begins with a trill or tremolo on the octave above the fundamental [*Grundtons*] (if we take a^1 as the fundamental), dips down to a raised major third ($c\sharp^2$) which is probably to be understood as the fourth of the fundamental, and lingers for a long time on it, with pitch deviations up and down a whole tone. There follows some declamation on both final notes, which von Hornbostel in no way wants to regard as intoned speech in the proper sense, since the tonal element always remains keenly developed. Thereafter the voice reintroduces the freely struck fifth more strongly, rises suddenly up to a sustained octave and drops down in a similar manner. Different repetitions then follow with exactly the same intonation.

Example 4.6, a magic spell for healing the sick, sung by a doctor, shows the same pitch movement but traverses all the notes of a five-step scale (in the repeat an f is interpolated as a passing note). In between the passages reproduced here, the voices move for a long time only between d, e, and g, in a similar way to the first piece (g, a) but in a distinct tempo.

Most of the remaining Kubu songs are of a similar type. Almost all deploy a high, long-sustained note with great strength, typically the octave above the principal note [*Hauptton*]. Its timbre is often more a cry than singing, but the intervals are musical in the strictest sense of the word. Consonant intervals stand out everywhere as resting points, sometimes even the minor seventh above the fundamental.

Nevertheless, the interval of a second—mostly major, sometimes minor—may be struck in the process simply as the result of splitting the difference between two notes. But with abruptly inserted, well-struck fourths, fifths and octaves, it is impossible to accept this. From time to time a note is reached by a rapid, constant glissando from above or below without thereby compromising the certainty of the intonation.

Obviously the whole tonal movement strongly recalls that of the Tyrolean herdsmen, and seems good evidence of the hypothesis, mentioned above, of music's origination from [vocal] signalling. One of the songs is even labelled 'call of the Kubu in the forest'. It proceeds from the first note directly down a twelfth, and essentially consists only of these two notes.

Example 4.7 is a duet sung by a witch-doctor and a woman. For a long time she sustains the higher octave above the fundamental—to which she steadily rises from an indistinctly intoned fifth—while the man recites on the fundamental and a fourth below it. And so it goes on. It is interesting as the most primitive kind of pedal point polyphony.

The Kubu have wind instruments, several kinds of flutes, though these seem to have been adopted from the neighbouring Javanese. These instruments have certainly contributed to the naturalization and consolidation of intervals in the singers' consciousness, but are not used in the songs above.

Example 4.8. Recorded phonographically on the west coast of Australia (Beagle Bay) by missionaries; previously unpublished.

In example 4.8 the song is repeated continuously; in the process the opening E frequently forestalls the final c so that the e occurs five times. It is sung in an exact tempo and is most simply notated as here, structured in two parts, each of twelve crotchets: the first in four 3/4 bars, the second in three 4/4 bars. Yet according to the accentuation, the first twelve crotchets would conform still better to the bar sequence 4/4, 5/4, 3/4. The song is accompanied by drumbeats on every crotchet and by rattles.

Beginning on a high, strong note and sinking to a lower, weaker one seems to be quite typical for Australian songs. Numerous correspondents from ancient and modern times, from Collins to Beckler, mention this feature. Even Father Wilhelm Schmidt reports that the melodic line mostly descends with the Karesau-Papua in German New Guinea; the end of the phrase always occurs on the lower tonic or with a leap from there up to its higher octave.[14]

Example 4.9.

Example 4.10.

[14] Wilhelm Schmidt, 'Über Musik und Gesänge der Karesau-Papuas, Deutsch-Neu-Guinea', *Haydn-Zentenarfeier: III. Kongreßbericht der Internationalen Musikgesellschaft* (Vienna: Artaria & Co, / Leipzig: Breitkopf & Härtel, 1909), 297. [SR]

Charles Samuel Myers[15] recorded Examples 4.9 and 4.10 phono-graphically on the Murray Islands in the Torres Strait, and kindly left me his transcriptions and measurements of them. The word 'semarer' is constantly repeated on the triplets of the first song.

Most remarkable in both songs is that they appear to indicate an endeavour to split the octave into six equal parts, as can be done using our tempered whole tone. According to Myers's appended tonometric determinations, the intervals—at least in the first song—correspond quite well to such a requirement. In the second song, the whole tone becomes ever smaller while descending, so that the last of the three [intervallic] steps only amounts to a good three quarter tone. In a third song—not reproduced here—whose structure resembles that of the first (rising stepwise with a rising octave leap in the middle), single steps become considerably larger than our whole tone. For the time being, then, it is not yet safe to believe that an equally spaced, six-tone scale is intended until we have further indications.

In any case, the overall descending pitch movement is again remark-able, likewise the occurrence of the octave leap which seems to be well struck to boot.

Example 4.11 (below) is a 'rain spell' from Lamassa, sung by a tribal chief. The rhythmicization—as simple as it now appears—presented von Hornbostel with enormous difficulties and turned the process of notation into a true ordeal. Although the chosen metrical scheme occa-sionally does not correspond to the melodic and dynamic accents, it appears to be the most suitable. The first note is introduced, as with other songs from the same region, with a downward glissando so skilfully carried into this first note that it is hard to make it out as the opening note. The close is formed by a kind of lip trilling, a simultaneous

---

15 Charles Samuel Myers (1873–1946) was an English psychologist, who co-founded the British Psychological Society and the National Institute of Industrial Psychology. In addition to such works on psychology as *Text-Book of Experimental Psychology* (1909), *Mind and Work* (1921), and *In the Realm of the Mind* (1937), he also published studies in the field of comparative musicology, such as 'A Study of Rhythm in Primitive Peoples', *British Journal of Psychology* 1 (1904): 397.

Example 4.11. ● 6

Example 4.12. ● 7

Example 4.12. *(continued).* ♩ 7

Examples 4.11-4.12 are two specimens from the southern part of New Ireland.[16]
Ph.-A. No. 12.

upward and downward sliding tonal movement on 'br'; von Hornbostel
supposes this to be a symbolic imitation of thunder.

Example 4.12 is sung by many singers simultaneously for sun dance
celebrations and is accompanied by dance movements; only one native
sang on the phonographs, however. The periodization [*Periodisierung*]
is clear; each strophe has a high and a low part, which always ends with
extended lingering on the lowest note. The melodic motion generally
remains the same in the repetition, though each strophe brings
variations (several more are published in von Hornbostel's essay). The
tempo is excellently maintained; but bars in our sense should not be
applied even if a 4/4 bar appears to emerge from time to time.

The consistent alteration between falsetto and chest voice (denoted by
F and C) in higher and lower sections is very striking here, as with other
songs of New Ireland, whereby falsetto sounds very soft and pleasant,
and the transition of registers into each other is skilfully accomplished.
The insertion of a twelfth in the repetition is also quite remarkable.

----

[16] When Stumpf published his book in 1911, the island was part of German New Guinea,
and bore the name Neu-Mecklenburg, which is how he denotes it in his text. At the out-
break of the First World War, however, the German protectorate fell to Australia, and the
island in question was renamed New Ireland (now part of Papua New Guinea).

The intonation of the intervals, which von Hornbostel measured exactly here, is sometimes only approximately rendered by our notes. In Example 4.11, which consists only of the notes a—d^1—e^1—g^1, the fourth a—d^1 is greatly enlarged. The fourth d^1—g^1 is pure. e^1 lies almost exactly in the middle between d^1 and g^1. Therefore one always has to regard a as substantially lower, and e^1 as substantially higher, than would be the case according to our intonation. In Example 4.12 the third e^2 measured from c^2 is somewhat raised. The octaves c^1—c^2, d^1—d^2, and e^1—e^2 are very pure; and a is a little too low against a^1, though only insignificantly. On average, the intonation of octaves is strikingly pure among primitive peoples.

In New Ireland there are well-cultivated panpipes on which melodies are played; thus, they have independent instrumental music. These pipes clearly indicate an earlier connection with Java, according to von Hornbostel's studies. Yet the songs do not appear to be closely interrelated with those melodies performed on the pipes.

Example 4.13.

Richard Thurnwald[17] brought this among many other melodies from Melanesia for our collection; to out ears example 4.13 is aptly labelled as 'threnody of a mother'. It originates from the small island of Nissan,

---

[17] Richard Thurnwald (1869–1945) was an Austrian ethnologist, whose magnum opus was the five-volume study of social behaviour: *Die Menschliche Gesellschaft in Ihren Ethno-Soziologischen Grundlagen*, 5 vols. (Berlin: W. de Gruyter, 1931–1935).

between New Ireland and the Solomon Islands. Von Hornbostel notated it meticulously from the phonogram and left it to me as a specimen of the entirely characteristic yodelling singing practices there. This art, which we already encountered in New Ireland and which is equally well known to African tribes, occurs here with a high degree of skill. The falsetto pitches are written in notes with the stems pointing upward, the chest notes pointing downward. The melody is continually repeated, though always with variations wherein one is not entirely bound by the division of the bar. Hopefully closer studies will soon throw light on how such a melodically and technically advanced art of singing arose in Melanesia. It seems to be connected with an often fully realized polyphony, which astonishes us, but we have no examples of this which can be communicated here.

The blatant expansion of the 3/4 bars by interpolation of a crotchet is noteworthy. But the exotic asserts itself in one melodic note within an otherwise very catchy tune: in the e^1 of the fourth bar. The constant fourth steps d^2—a^1—e^1—a^1—d^2 strike us as unmelodic and severe. Such melodic direction becomes necessary, however, if the third of the fundamental is avoided for whatever reason: is it that this note does not occur in the scale used in this region, i.e. the tonal material from which all the melodies are constructed; or is it that a particular expression is half excluded in a few melodies? The scales, insofar as they can be extracted from these melodies, would be: d—e—g—a—b—d^1, a five-step scale without a third, as occurs frequently among Indians. So the triad and dominant seventh chord that our inner hearing supplies in this melody would be illegitimate additions, and would thereby push the melody itself considerably further from us.

Example 4.14. ❶ 8

Example 4.15.

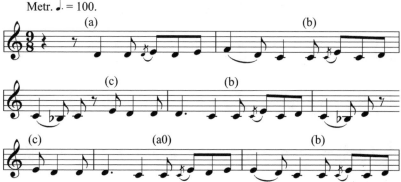

Example 4.16. ● 9

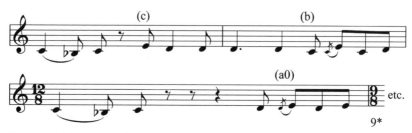

Example 4.16. *(continued).* ♩ 9

Example 4.17. ♩ 10

With these examples we turn towards America, to the Indians, and first to the South American Indians. The most primitive melodies that occur here may have been those of Tierra del Fuego,[18] specimens of which were recently sent by Charles Wellington Furlong.[19] They have a certain similarity to the Vedda songs. But I cannot share anything from them since they have not yet been closely examined.

Examples 4.14–4.17 are songs of the Tehuelche in Patagonia, recorded phonographically by Robert Lehmann-Nitsche.[20] Fischer transcribed fifty-one songs into musical notation (Ph.-A. No. 15). They are generally at a low [developmental] stage, consisting of small, short motifs within which those of the voice move almost entirely in whole tones or semitones and are endlessly repeated. In all, a tonal range of a fourth or fifth emerges most often, rarely anything larger. Nevertheless, these songs too offer their notable, indeed attractive sides to those who become engrossed in them, especially with regard to their structure.[21]

Example 4.14 rather resembles the Vedda songs, with a range of a minor third, and a fairly uniform melodic direction.

Example 4.15 is already a little richer, as though the melody were developed by elaborating the motif of the first (example 4.14). Part II is

---

[18] An archipelago off the southern tip of the mainland of South America, consisting of one large island (known in German as 'Feuerland') and several smaller islands. Stumpf's text refers to the group as a whole: 'Feuerländer'.

[19] Charles Wellington Furlong (1874–1967) was an American explorer, whose principal publications include *The Gateway to the Sahara: Observations and Experiences in Tripoli* (London: Chapman & Hall, 1909); and *Let 'er Buck, a Story of the Passing of the Old West* (New York: Putnam, 1921).

[20] Robert Lehmann-Nitsche (1872–1938) was a German doctor and ethnologist, who spent most of his life in Argentina, where he published the majority of his work.

[21] In Erich Fischer's essay our four songs are nos. 31, 21, 8 (p. 946), and 46. The form of notation [above], which because of the above mentioned revision was adjudged by us as the most applicable, differs from that given there. But the deviations concern either formality of writing (e.g. in the note value that is halved in no. 16) or other positioning of bar lines or longer continuation of the melodies. Only in no. 14 does the rhythmicization differ somewhat from that of Fischer, probably because we took as a basis not the beginning of the forever recurring tune but later repetitions that stood out particularly clearly. Even for this exceedingly simple tune the most fitting form of notation was hard to find because of the small intervals and the multiple blending of notes. [SN]

an abbreviated repetition of part I, whereby an enclave of three quavers, bounded by dotted brackets, is interpolated twice in the otherwise regular 3/2 bar; it seems to allude to an echo, similar to the beloved echoes of music in the eighteenth century. Several further repetitions then follow, of which the fifth is given here because an enclave of no less than nine quavers is interpolated in the otherwise unchanged repetition of the melody. These insertions, which in part II occur even between the two quavers of a crotchet, seem quite irrational to us, but are certainly not arbitrary. Indeed, they follow certain rules. We could say, furthermore, a normal 12/8 bar is expanded both times in part II to 15/8, and in part V to 21/8; all of which can be divided by three. And one could, were it not too reckless, also refer here to parallels with the early period of our own music: to the subdivisions of novenaria and duodenaria among the mensuralists of the fourteenth century.[22] Alteration of pauses also occurred at that time; we no longer use them in such a way, but we still encounter their use among Indians.

Example 4.16 is the most comprehensible of the songs to us. It is made up of three motifs that constantly supersede one another in different orders. Motif (a) appears one moment with the first crotchet, the next without it (a_0). Occasionally a pause of three quavers is interpolated, whereby the 9/8 bar spills over into a 12/8 bar, as in the last bar of our transcription. In later analogous passages these pauses are filled not with (a_0) but the (a) form resulting again in twelve quavers.

We have reproduced example 4.17 at greater length because it presents a particularly informative structure. One immediately notices the frequently interpolated 7/8 bars. Part II is an exact repetition of part I in this respect, as well as in its entire rhythmicization. Part III is enlarged,

---

[22] Johannes Wolf, *Geschichte der Mensural-Notation von 1250–1460,* 3 vols. (Leipzig: Breitkopf & Härtel, 1904), I: 28ff., 274ff. [SR]

More recent treatises on notation include Richard Rastall, *The Notation of Western Music: An Introduction* (New York: St Martin's Press, 1982); Carl Parrish, *The Notation of Medieval Music* (New York: Pendragon Press, 1978); and of course Willi Apel, *The Notation of Polyphonic Music 900–1600* (Cambridge, Mass.: Mediaeval Academy of America, 1942).

again by the insertion of two bars bounded by dotted brackets, that seem to repeat both preceding bars; and also by the last three bars which present themselves likewise as a reiterative affirmation of the close. Otherwise the bars are constructed identically. Right at the start of part IV, in the passage marked by an asterisk, the two first bars from part I are left out, and it then continues analogously. Many variations then follow on the same basic form.

No less remarkable is the pitch movement in these pieces, which could only be grasped using a variety of study techniques. The tonal steps have not yet been measured physically, but there is no doubt that on the whole the above notation broaches actual suspensions of pitches, and that at the end of part III the singer again arrives accurately on the note d, an octave lower than the initial note. He achieves this simply by whole-tone steps, and intervals of a fifth, and a fourth from one phrase to another; indeed, g♭—b is the habitual fourth interval for primitive singers.

Anyone who takes the trouble to analyse in more detail just one single song of this type from a very humble Indian tribe, will certainly no longer be able to share the widespread opinion that primitive peoples tend more towards formless howling than artistically formed products; nor will he even be able to accept Karl Bücher's view that they only valued rhythm in music and had 'no feeling for different pitches', and that their songs were 'monotonous, almost without melody'.[23]

Certainly we cannot regard the intonation of Patagonians as outstandingly precise. According to Fischer's observations, the thirds in one and the same piece, for example, become now large, now small, and now neutral. The tempo and rhythm, by contrast, are very evenly maintained, which is consistent with the fact that most songs are dance songs.

In addition to the drum, Patagonians have a musical bow on which pieces with an extremely limited range and similar uniformity to example 4.14 can be played.

---

[23] Karl Bücher, *Arbeit und Rhythmus* (Leipzig: S. Hirzel, 1897).

Example 4.18. The song of a Tobo Indian from Bolivia, recorded phonographically by Lehmann-Nitzsche in San Pedro, transcribed by von Hornbostel and Fischer, previously unpublished.

Nothing is mentioned about the content of the emotive performance of example 4.18. It is another example of a typical descending movement with decrescendo. After lingering for a long time in the depths, the repetition suddenly starts with the initial high note, very well struck, with full strength. The details of pitch movement and metre are reproduced here with particular diligence. They appear complicated enough, but recur in exactly the same way at the repetitions of the song, and within the three extant recordings of the whole song from the same individuals. We have counted, for example, how many crotchets fall on the note c^1 within bars 8–10: there are always precisely fifteen. After various attempts, the chosen way of transcribing the ornament of the c^2 in bars 2–4 should only be taken as approximate. An e^2 also seemed to occur here but these are embellishments that we can neither transcribe exactly nor replicate. Even the tonal space here is different from normal. The pitch movement too in both 7/4 bars is not easy to write out; seven crotchets result after counting in any case.

The song has an extraordinary range of two and a half octaves. It essentially employs a five-step scale that includes a third (sometimes major, sometimes minor); other notes are used only in passing.

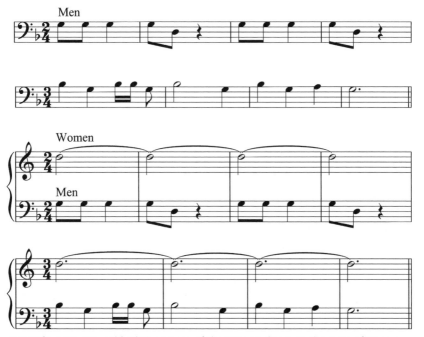

Example 4.19. 'Very old religious song of the Yaqui Indians', in the state of Sonora, on the northern border of Mexico.

This was the description of example 4.19 which John Comfort Fillmore shared with me, among a number of Indian songs.[24] It is not written by Fillmore himself, rather it was passed on to him by the brother of a man who lived for about thirty years as a prisoner among the Yaqui. I assume no guarantee here of the accuracy of the transcription, of course, and have only accepted it because, as Fillmore notes, it is unique among Indian songs in respect of the accompanying notes sustained above the male voices by the female voices. In this respect the transcription is certainly reliable. If one does not want to suppose that there is a European influence, we would have therein a nice case of the use of pedal points among primitive peoples, analogous to example 4.7. Both times the sustained note sits on top. But we will also find an example of the contrary position [of the sustained note] common today (see example 4.27).

Example 4.20.

Example 4.20 originates from the Zuñi Indians (Pueblos). It is transcribed by Benjamin Ives Gilman[25] from a phonographic recording by

---

[24] John Comfort Fillmore, 'Indianergesänge', *Beiträge zur Akustik und Musikwissenschaft* 3 (1901): 1–5. [SR]

[25] Benjamin Ives Gilman (1852–1933) was an American academic psychologist and curator of the Boston Museum of Fine Art. His main contribution to the field of comparative musicology was 'Hopi Songs' which formed the fifth and final issue of *Journal of American*

Walter Fewkes (the first that used this melody) and rewritten by me in a clear way, but without any material changes (see endnote i).[26] Here it is set a semitone lower. The lines that are introduced are supposed to denote the main passages. No bar structure is indicated but both main sections (which begin with *mf*) could each be divided into a 4/4 bar and a 5/4 bar (the final note only lengthened by 1/8), while the final passage is essentially suited to 3/8 metre.

The song, which is only a segment of a longer vocal piece, again shows the descending pitch movement and simultaneous diminuendo of so many primitive songs. With its fanfare-like introduction and its quietly disappearing coda it is a beautiful example of the emotive, impetuous manner that seems particularly distinctive to the singing of the Pueblo Indians. We would say that it consists of the descending melodic minor scale, with a close in the major. But we probably cannot take the major and minor third so seriously here; the intonation only approximates more the one or the other; Gilman selected the note lying nearest each time. Oddly, the introductory part and the main part both begin with the second of the fundamental, which appears to us as a tonic, and in this case it probably is for the Indians. To be sure, we too do not always begin on the tonic; but starting on the second is rare. With frequent listening we can become accustomed to the ethos of this melody at any rate, and gain an impression thereof; which I do not want to claim would be quite the same as that of the Indians.

North American Indians have extremely meagre instruments, and not many of them; other than timpani and rattles, they occasionally have flutes, and in some regions a xylophone that, however, appears to be imported from Africa. All the more astonishing is their unbounded wealth in various well-constructed songs.

Ethnology and Archeology, ed. J. Walter Fewkes (Boston: Houghton Mifflin Company, 1908). Rpt. *Hopi Songs* (New York: AMS Press, 1977).

[26] Only at + in the penultimate line does Gilman notate a semitone higher. But this is certainly a case of a chance gaffe by the singer. Besides, the notes mostly only approximate the note values, without fulfilling them entirely; moreover, such quiet, short, and low notes are often hard to identify. [SN]

Example 4.21. From Gilman's recently published religious songs of the Hopi (Moki) Indians—which also belong to the Pueblo—using Fewkes' recordings.

From his tonometric analyses, Gilman came to the view that Pueblo Indians have a tendency towards consonant intervals; to the octave and particularly to the fifth and fourth, which, however, allow the greatest freedom in intonation. What is more, each singer reproduced the intervals differently. It is only the general contour of the melody that is sketched out. He therefore calls these 'rote songs',[27] and devises a graphic scheme that better expresses them than our notes can.

Example 4.21 is the third of eight 'snake songs' that are strikingly similar to each other: all are simply constructed, with a simple rhythm and with ever-recurring descending intervals of (approximately) a fourth, third, or fifth. The notation here is not that given by Gilman himself, which is only supposed to present his general subjective impression; rather it has been traced according to his meticulous diagrams by von Hornbostel as a kind of average (not in a mathematical, but a psychological sense) of the numerous variations among the repetitions that Gilman recorded in his diagrams. In fact, the pitch of individual notes fluctuates not imperceptibly, though mostly within a semitone. Thus the principal note, e, to which the melody always returns, is frequently intoned as d♯, and the low g♯ as a, by the same token. The predominance of the *interval of a fourth* is the main characteristic feature of this song in any case. But some subjectivity remains even in von Hornbostel's 'averaging' notation; otherwise one would have to transcribe the collected repetitions in elaborate diacritical notation and new, small alterations would ultimately have occurred with each new repetition.

---

[27] A rote song is one that is learned by imitation, or by rote.

Equally, von Hornbostel proposes that—according to the diagrams—the metrical division is probably intentional; Gilman eschews metrical structure.

The remaining songs, besides the snake songs, are significantly more complicated. They show a structure similar to our next example, as well as a large range, e.g. a twelfth; likewise the descending pitch movement that gently dies away, then the sudden transition again to the higher, strongest vocal register, where the note is sometimes driven up about a semitone.[28]

Von Hornbostel tentatively transcribed all the songs with all repetitions in the same way as that above, from the diagrams; and we have the impression that, in spite of the undeniable irregularities of intonation, a fixed tonal and metrical framework underlies them, as Gilman is inclined to accept. There are singers among us too whose intonation is more accurate, others less so. But it seems that, among Indians also, certain notes of the scale are struck more securely, others less so, or rather these allow more latitude in intonation. Then there are the alterations in particular recurring parts of a melody; alterations conditioned by expression, so in no way haphazard, but rather quite consistent. We will find all this is readily confirmed by the next song.

Example 4.22.

----

[28] Benjamin Gilman, *Hopi Songs* (Boston: Houghton Mifflin company, 1908), 171, 181. [SR]

Example 4.22.

Example 4.22. Old 'death song' of a troop of Pueblo Indians who came to Berlin a few years ago.

[The Pueblo performers] were labelled as Hopi Indians, but it is not certain that they really belonged to this tribe. Example 4.22 was transcribed by Fischer from one the of the gramophone discs recorded by the Favorit-Gesellschaft; the notation was then reviewed many times by von Hornbostel and me since it caused great difficulties. The song resounds so vivaciously and atmospherically from the recording that we wanted to try to bring it as close as possible to the imagination and appreciation. The image is as faithful as it can ever be when produced with our signs. The sustained f♯ in the seventh line was pitched extremely impurely, differently by different singers, but much too high on the whole. In other places as well, the emphatic f♯ is struck somewhat higher; sometimes (at ⁓) it also sounds like a trill on e♯, where someone seems to have sung it too low.

The tonal material is essentially that of a five-note scale, though it is hard to determine a principal note. Most likely c♯; for us it would be a, of course. Very few notes fall outside of the five-note scale: apart from the indistinctly intoned introductory formula; g♯ occurs once, f a few times, and f^1 once, as well as b♯ (within section C1) in particular passages. These are surely not gaffes, but rather deviations for particular expressive purposes. There is nothing to note here about impurity within the voices; and f, like b♯, is struck in exactly the same way in the repetitions.

We note furthermore that the pitch is steadily pulled upwards during the song, altogether by about a quarter tone. This is not taken into account in the notation. The same pull [of intonation] frequently distinguishes Gilman's Zuñi songs. I notice the same among the Bella Coola songs; likewise, Hjalmar Thuren among the Eskimos (see examples 4.49 and 4.50).

The *structure* is distinct and very interesting. At the outset, as so often in Indian songs, there is a short introductory formula whose pitches emerge entirely indistinctly; which is why they are written here in small notes. They are almost barked more than sung. Thereafter follow the sections denoted by double bars and letters, among which those with the same letter obviously count melodically as repetitions. **B** occurs four times, though always with certain liberties; **C** appears twice; **A** and **D** just once each. **A** begins with the passages in fourths with which we are already familiar, and which sound severe to our ears; it then proceeds in a long sprawling mumble to the notes f♯, e, and c♯, which remain rhythmically strict, however. **B** is an intermediary phrase that prepares a new upsurge three times at **C$_1$**, **D**, and **C$_2$**. The *ff* passages are performed with great fervour. **B** proceeds parlando the second time, which some singers begin even while others are still holding the final c♯. It is performed rhythmically in exactly the manner given [in the transcription]. The conclusion of the whole is formed by a kind of yelling, all at the same time, but on different pitches which approximate to those given. The song probably goes on much longer still, and the singers have simply added an artistic close for their performance at that moment.

The metrical division is quite complicated in our view, and yet it is not random. The tempo is maintained extraordinarily strictly, although the song is neither supported by timpani nor clapping. On the whole a four-part bar seems to underpin the song, but in one or two places this is extended, sometimes shortened. Again, however, these alterations occur with a certain regularity. Compare the first three versions of **B**. Their bar groupings are:

$$1. \frac{4+6+5}{4}; \ 2. \frac{4+6+4+6}{4}; \ 3. \frac{4+6+5}{4}.$$

The first and third versions are divided in exactly the same way; the second is different but again consistent in itself. The division of **C** is almost exactly the same both times (in individual places the semiquaver pauses—which seem inconsistent to us—are added in brackets in order to permit the notation in 7/8; actually, one would have to notate in 13/16; this is a case of a very precisely held pause that cannot be reproduced in our normal bars). **D** breaks down into two sections with exactly the same metrical sequence:

$$\frac{4+5+6}{4}; \frac{4+5+6}{4}.$$

Example 4.23.

Example 4.24.

Examples 4.23-4.24 are from Natalie Curtis' large collection.[29]

I cannot vouch for complete accuracy here, but the technically adroit notation and structural analysis bespeaks such musical understanding that one may consider the tonal figures [*Tongestalten*] as mainly correct, if perhaps reproduced a little impressionistically. Example 4.23, from page 489 in Curtis' book, is a Hopi lullaby. The semiquaver triplets probably signify a sliding transition [between notes]. The song also sounds full of atmosphere; the descending diminished fourth is not insignificant in contributing to this if the f♯ is to be understood simply as a flatly intoned g. The song's structure merits attention. The first section has seven bars, which are repeated unchanged, the second section presents a new, five-bar theme that is repeated twice with minor variations, and the final repetition is shortened by a bar. Thereupon the reprise of the first section begins (which I separate with double bars), initially in seven bars with an altered opening, making it similar to the theme of the second section. Then the next seven bars copy the first section exactly. Hence, the scheme is: 2 × 7, 3 × 5, 2 × 7 (disregarding the excised bar in the second section).

Example 4.24 (p. 120 in Curtis' book) is an Iruskan dance, of the Pawnee tribe in Oklahoma; again proceeding from high to low, and resting for a long time on the final note. It uses the five-step scale without a third.

---

[29] Natalie Curtis, *The Indians' Book* (New York and London: Harper and Bros., 1907).

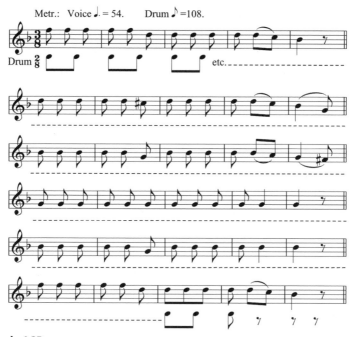

Example 4.25.

Example 4.26.

Examples 4.25-4.26 are from the work of Alice Fletcher on the Hako ceremony, a religious celebration of the Pawnee Indians.[30]

The songs were transcribed by Edwin S. Tracy from phonographic recordings, who then also compared his transcriptions with the singing of the Kurahus (the leader of the ceremony) on one occasion.

Example 4.25 (p. 171 of Fletcher's book, where it is notated an octave lower, and should be read there in the tenor clef) was described as a very old song. It refers to the wren[31] which the Pawnee consider to be an ever-laughing, happy bird. One easily sees that the song consists of six phrases, each of five bars. We have separated them with double bars. The same syllables recur in the three final bars of each phrase: *whe ke re we chi,* which ostensibly imitate bird calls. The melodic motion is also interesting: the five-bar phrases first set off from f¹, then from d¹, then from b♭; which must count as the principal note. Then they drop a third below this and stay entirely on g [in the fourth phrase]. The next, the fifth[32] section, again starts on the principal note. The final section repeats the first. Conspicuous for us, though by no means rare, is the dissimilar rhythm of the timpani and singing.

Example 4.26 (p. 251 of Fletcher's book) is sung during another episode of the celebration, and is accompanied by steady, rapid drum strokes (tremolo) as well as by the noise of rattles and pipes. It contains an invitation to children to come forward and bring their gifts. All quavers are sung with a slight tremolo and with 'pulsation'. After the descending main theme, in which a three-bar motif repeats once and a two-bar supplement is appended, a five-bar intermediate theme follows at a lower register. Then the main theme comes again and a two-bar closing formula that recreates the earlier supplement. Again, this uses a five-step scale without the third.

---

[30] Alice C. Fletcher, *The Hako: a Pawnee Ceremony*, Bureau of American Ethnology annual report 22 (Washington: Govt. Print. Off., 1904). Rpt. *The Hako: Song, Pipe, and Unity in a Pawnee Calumet Ceremony*, ed. James Murie (Lincoln and London: Univ. of Nebraska Press, 1996).

[31] Stumpf's term 'Laubvogel' is an unusual translation of Fletcher's 'wren' (which Stumpf also cites in English). The more common German name for the bird is 'Zaunköni', but in the context of his discussion of Fletcher, there can be no mistake about the bird to which he refers.

[32] Stumpf mistakenly calls this the fourth section.

Example 4.27.

repeated 5 times

Example 4.28.

Example 4.29.

Example 4.30.

Example 4.31.

These songs—among many others—were transcribed by Theodore Baker[33] before the phonographic era, but with very conscientious observance and illustration of details.[34]

Example 4.27 is a war song of the Iroquois (text: I go). It appears to be divided into phrases of six or three bars. For a continuation, a bar's pause comes to mind initially. The song is remarkable for its second voice, which marks each bar with the fundamental; perhaps in lieu of timpani. Here the pedal point lies below [the first voice], in contrast to the examples just mentioned.

Example 4.28 is an ancient Iroquois religious song of thanksgiving, sung by men who trotted around wooden benches in the middle of the dance hall.[35] Besides the main accents, every graceless step brought a weaker accent on the corresponding note. Instead of our [metrical] division (Baker abandons barring), one can piece the song together from one 4/4 bar and one 5/4 bar (2/4 + 3/4), if the main accents are to coincide consistently with the bar accents. After a fivefold repetition it closes with a slide [*Schleifer*][36] that 'is performed like a shout of glee'

[33] Theodore Baker (1851–1934) was an American music scholar and lexicographer. His doctoral dissertation at Leipzig University was on North American Indian music (1882) though he is better known for *A Dictionary of Musical Terms* (New York: G. Schirmer, 1895) and *A Biographical Dictionary of Musicians* (New York: G. Schirmer, 1900).

[34] Theodore Baker, *Über die Musik der Nordamerikanischen Wilden* (Leipzig: Breitkopf & Härtel, 1882). [SR]

[35] Ibid., 37 [SR]

[36] A conjunct double appoggiatura.

and at any rate consists of a steady downward slide of the voice.[37] What is most remarkable about the song is its range, which, aside from the ending, consists of one single note. Such songs—which many regard as the most primordial [*uranfänglichsten*]—really occur; and this one probably is very old. But who knows whether or not it was an exception when it first appeared, and whether the monotony was chosen deliberately because of its solemn effect?

Example 4.29, the 'Omaha dance', is a favourite dance of various Indian tribes among the Dakota (Sioux). Baker writes it in 2/4. With the time signature $\frac{(4+6)}{4}$, the structure seems to me to become very clear. The section after the double bar (added by me) is obviously a repeat of the first section. One only has to assume that in the first bar of this second section the singers shortened the pause by a crotchet (interpolated here above the stave), a slip that also occurs with us; and that, conversely, Baker inserts a surplus crotchet pause, perhaps a pause for breath, in the antepenultimate bar.

We can easily see that the second part of each bar, with its six crotchets, is only an extended repetition of the four crotchets of the first part, in terms of the rhythm. The whole appears very attractive to me, rhythmically speaking.

The song's opening is also curious: on the second of the principal note.

Example 4.30 is the first song of the Iroquois harvest festival, a dance song whose dramatic performance is described by Baker (p. 39). It is accompanied by the striking of rattles on a wooden bench. Text: 'he came down from heaven to us and gave us these words'. Baker transcribed the song without metrical divisions, but it appears to me to become quite clear in 7/4. One only has to imagine a crotchet pause interpolated before the repeat. The pitches belong exclusively to the [major] triad. The ending is made up of interjections.

Example 4.31, a love song of the Kiowa in Arkansas, is again only built from pitches of the major triad. I indicate the structure with double bars.

---

[37] Baker, *Über die Musik*, 17. See also endnote xii [SR].

Such *triadic melodies* seem to support a view held by Fillmore and Fletcher that ascribes a latent feeling for harmony to Indians.[38] But the experiments with Indians that Fillmore considers proof thereof, whereby Indians are supposed to have recognized particular chordal accompaniments as corresponding to their intonation, are subject to serious misgivings. Suggestion seems to have contributed after all, as a real expert, Franz Boas, told me. All the same, the frequent occurrence of Indian melodies that are formed entirely or almost entirely from the pitches of proximate triads demands an explanation. Perhaps the answer lies simply in that, within a particular type of melody, one loves to be restricted to the three notes of the customary five-step scale that are set apart by more than the smallest step of this scale. Von Hornbostel, who had the opportunity of undertaking intonation studies among the Pawnee in Oklahoma, supposes that the use of fragmented triads was achieved when a note was inserted approximately in the middle of the interval of a fifth, i.e. by estimating distance. Supporting this is the fact that it is precisely the thirds that are often intoned in an unstable way. They remain a softer part of the musical skeleton, so to speak, long after the fundamental consonances solidified.

It was also earlier claimed—frequently—that primitive peoples sang in the *minor*. Such a generalization is entirely unsupported. If anything, the major is better represented, but in truth neither of our two tonalities is very pronounced in most cases. (A case where a given song was transcribed by Boas in the minor, by Fillmore in the major, is typical.)[39] The distinction between major and minor only becomes clear when you have the systematic *simultaneous* use of at least three notes, which, as is well known, occurred very late in the history of music.

---

[38] Cf. Stumpf, 'Konsonanz und Dissonanz', *Beiträge zur Akustik und Musikwissenschaft* 1 (1898): 1–108, here 63ff.; and Stumpf, 'Neueres über Tonverschmelzung', *Beiträge zur Akustik und Musikwissenschaft* 2 (1898): 1–24. [SR]

[39] See Franz Boas, 'Songs of the Kwakiutl-Indians', *Internationales Archiv für Ethnographie* 9 (1896): 1–9, here 2. [SR]

Example 4.32.

Example 4.33.

Example 4.34.

Examples 4.32-4.34 are samples from Frances Densmore's 200 songs of the Chippewa (Ojibwa) Indians in north Minnesota, recently published from phonographic recordings and accompanied by explanations and analyses.[40]

The author did not attempt any tonometric measurements, but highlights characteristic deviations of intonation in particular passages and observes that they recur with great consistency. Two singers who had repeated around twenty songs after seven months showed the same deviations in the same places. The tempo of the timpani accompaniment frequently displays the strangest incongruence with that of the singing in these songs; so much so that it was impossible aurally to perceive the rhythmic relationship of both, and that even the metronome marks given separately to the voice and timpani did not, as intended, uncover a simple relationship. The assumption arises that in such cases both parts execute a particular absolute tempo irrespective of each other.

Example 4.32, an initiation song at the main religious ceremony, immediately offers an example of this. The timpani perform regular

---

40 Frances Densmore, *Chippewa Music*, 2 vols. (Washington: Govt. Print. Off., 1910–1913).

strikes without accent, of which approximately—but not exactly—
every two coincide with three quavers of the song. Only in the final
section do the strikes fall together exactly with the quavers of the song.
The song itself grants us a very clear picture; the theme from I commences a fourth lower in II, and is expanded and leads down to the
depths. After a short intermediary phrase (III) that begins with a daring
leap, an exact repeat of II (IV) ensues, and finally a short closing formula (V). The whole habitus of this song, the falling movement, the
imitative repetition at lower intervals, the large range, all are typical for
the majority of these Chippewa songs.

In example 4.33, also an initiation song (recorded without timpani
accompaniment), II is an exact imitation of I at the lower third. III leads
back to the principal note with a kind of contrary motion. The whole
song is then repeated exactly, except that in two places 4/4 is switched
to 3/4 and vice versa. The lengthening or shortening [of notes] around
a unison is considered to be inessential in such cases, as we have found
so often already.

Example 4.34, a healing song (also without timpani accompaniment),
performed by an old woman with a rasping voice but very secure
intonation, again shows a perfectly clear structure. The rhythmically
compelling motif from I is repeated at the lower third in II according to
all the rules of art; III is somewhat freer with respect to pitch, but leads
the melody again in exactly the same rhythm and in the same direction;
IV goes down to the lower fundamental with a phrase copied from the
opening. The scale, like example 4.32, is built of five steps.

The vast majority of these songs have the range of a twelfth, and are
particularly fond of starting with the twelfth above the principal note
and gradually sinking downwards in order to finish on the latter. Several
even extend over two octaves. There are also distinctly triadic melodies
in this collection, within which other notes (of the five-step scale) occur,
mostly as occasional passing notes (e.g. nos. 115 and 128). Yet the sixth
above the fundamental joins in occasionally as a component of the
triadic pitches that is not inessential for the melody (e.g. no. 129).

Example 4.35.

Example 4.36.

Example 4.37.

Examples 4.35-4.37 are from the songs of the Bella Coola Indians in British Columbia, which I transcribed before the phonographic era, albeit as meticulously as possible (see endnote i, part I). Stumpf, 'Lieder der Bellakula-Indianer', *Vierteljahrsschrift für Musikwissenschaft* 2 (1886): 405–426.

Only the metrical forms remain doubtful to me at some points, since I did not know at that time that 5/4 and similar metres are quite common among Indians. The second of the songs I transcribed, which I wrote in 12/8, is suited to 5/8 according to a message from Franz Boas, who later heard it himself in the homeland of the troupe. Quite how it is to be set in this metre is not at all clear to me. I wrote down two other songs in 5/4 at that time following Boas' suggestion (a medical song and a cannibal song).

Example 4.35 is a love song ('This is my brother, he has made my heart sick, he has taken my beloved: so I cry on this day'). The choral refrain, which is made up of interjections, was sung as an independent piece at the 'communal dance', and was taken slightly faster there ♩ = 80. The grace notes—preceding and following—signify a pulling up or down of the note; they recurred at the relevant places with complete regularity. The scale has five steps, the overall melodic motion again proceeds from high to low, likewise there is a decrescendo in the chorus, and at the close there is almost more droning than singing. It is striking that the final phrases lead to the third [degree of the scale]. The timpani strikes always occur on the quaver offbeat. The melody of the solo singer is reshaped by the chorus (or vice versa) in an amazing manner. The first six bars of the soloist correspond to the first three of the chorus; the last five of the soloist to the last five of the chorus. The reshaping is loose [*frei*] and yet the correspondence is unmistakable, as we require of a good—I want to say stylish—variation of a theme in our music.

Example 4.36, a dance song performed over interjections, again with consistent timpani strikes on the quaver offbeat, again from high to low and with decrescendo, again with a final phrase closing on the third. In two places e is intoned in a strangely unstable way, the first time apparently slightly raised, the second time apparently slightly lowered, and at the same time quieter than the adjacent notes. And this hesitant, tentative intonation in very particular places—as though one did not want to appear fixed—seems absolutely to belong to the expressive means of primitive music. Incidentally, in no way does this note play the same role for Indians as the principal note does for us, which means we would harmonize the song in E minor. In fact, B is certainly the principal note.

Example 4.37 is a dirge that is performed at cremations, and may not be sung to outsiders. The text appears to consist of interjections (Uai, etc.). The process of notation was particularly tricky here. A number of notes were altered in the way indicated by the signs. We can perhaps best conceive of the structure by regarding the first two bars as an introduction [*Vorbau*], as the Indians love to; then comes the main theme in three bars, which is repeated in the following bars alongside an initial melodic gesture reminiscent of the introduction and with a lengthened close. At the end, there was actually no longer any metre governing the performance; the last three notes were almost held as minims.

Example 4.38.

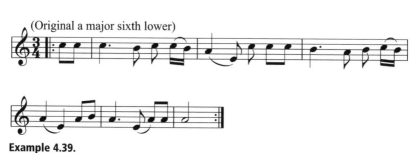

Example 4.39.

Examples 4.38-4.39 are from the songs of the Nootka Indians, who also live on the coast of British Columbia, transcribed directly by Boas.[41]

The first is a chief's song for a potlach festival.[42] Every chief has his own song, which is also sung after his death at the funeral reception. It stands here as a further example of a monotone song (cf. example 4.28). Here too, the monotony is supposed to express the highest dignity and solemnity. The second song from the same tribe (a lullaby strongly reminiscent of that of the Hopi, example 4.23) teaches us that this [example 4.38] is not a product of the most primitive musical conditions. It [the lullaby, example 4.39] probably did not actually sound as European as it now appears in notation; but is a long way from monotony, in spite of its soporific purpose.

---

[41] Franz Boas, *Report of the British Association for the Advancement of Science: Sixth Report on the Northwest Tribes of Canada* (London: Burlington House, 1890).

[42] A gift-giving festival practiced by indigenous peoples on the Pacific north-west coast of America.

Example 4.40. A song of the Kwakiutl during a game of lehal,[43] also notated by Boas.[44]

Example 4.40 is written in 5/8, but with the use of two 3/4 bars. The five-step scale with a major seventh is striking (the entire pitch movement of bars 3–5 corresponds to that of the Alpine blessing from Melchtal [see endnote xxi] but the b here can hardly have the same origin; it is probably intended simply as a flat c, analogous to the f♯ in example 4.23). The ending on the second is typical.

According to Boas, the Kwakiutl are very keen on accurate performances of songs and dances; each mistake is taken as an insult. Indeed, on certain occasions the dancer is put to death in such cases. Their flutes are unusually well and artistically made (see the illustrations in Boas' great study.)[45]

---

[43] An ancient guessing game played with hands or sticks by some North American Indian tribes.

[44] Franz Boas, *Journal of American Folklore* 1 (1888): 51. [SR]

[45] Franz Boas, *The Social Organisation and the Secret Societies of the Kwakiutl Indians*, USA National Museum, Report for 1895 (Washington: Govt. Print. Off., 1897), 445. [SR]

Example 4.41.

Example 4.41 is a dance song from the same tribe, recorded phonographically by Boas (from his book just mentioned), which I include here because of its rhythmic oddity. One can of course adopt 3/4 time throughout the voice part by allowing bars 2, 4, and 6 to be syncopated. In this, however, the impression of the whole, which conflicts with our rhythmic customs, is not neutralized; particularly when the quaver off-beats are accentuated by the drum. Furthermore, with the conversion from 6/8 time to 3/4 time, the third quaver—respectively—in these bars receives an accent that it often does not have from the singer's mouth. Later on, the otherwise regular drum rhythm is interrupted in several places by 5/8 time, which is why Boas prescribes 12/8 and 5/8 for the drum. The melodic line of the voice is strongly reminiscent of one of my Bella Coola songs (no. 2, not among those reproduced here). On this stretch of coast a strong economy of musical exchanges takes place according to the Indians' own statements.

Example 4.42. ❶ 11

Example 4.43. ⏺ 12

Example 4.44. ⏺ 13

Example 4.45. ⏺ 14

Metr. ♩ = 198.

Drum: etc.

Example 4.46. ● 15

Metr. ♩ = 164.

(Falsetto)

mf Drum: etc.

Example 4.47. ● 16

Examples 4.42-4.47 are from the forty-three songs of the Thompson River Indians in British Columbia, transcribed and determined tonometrically throughout by Abraham and von Hornbostel from Boas' phonograms (Ph.A., no. 10).

The majority of these have only a small amount of tonal matter [*Tonbestand*] and a narrow range. Some are even similar to the Vedda songs. Yet there are also triadic melodies among them (one is particularly striking through the pitches of the pure, descending minor triad, no. 16), and individual songs extend to the range of an octave or a ninth. The extraordinarily intricate rhythmicization of the majority of the songs was only ever made possible, in part, by the accompanying drum strikes. The metronome markings are only added here as a rough guide (based on the register of the male or female voices), since no pitch pipes were present at the recording.

Example 4.42, a singing game (written here in shorter than normal note values), makes a very spirited impression, and is sung with rhythmic verve and precision. The whole is sung with decreasing force, which is then reasserted at the (arbitrarily frequent) repeat. The descending fourth steps are reminiscent of those mentioned earlier.

Example 4.43, a melodically dull dance song built from three notes, is still interesting because of its rhythmicization, indeed also because of its structure. The uniformly barred drum that plays on the second quaver of every crotchet allows the crotchets to be distinguished and counted as notes of equal duration. The chosen bar structure, alternating between 5/4 and 7/4, is justified by the regularity that results for the whole. Bars 1, 3, 5, 7, etc. have the same or a related tonal inflection between them; likewise, bars 2, 4, 6, 8, etc. between them. Besides, all of the sections separated by a double bar are evidently melodically identical, and the deviations only variants. A continuation only brings further repetitions of these four bars with further variations. The first bar of the piece is an introduction, as we have often found it to be in other songs.

Taking cues from the lines above the stave, one could nevertheless write the whole in a regular alternation of 6/4 and 3/2 time. We must leave undecided which barring corresponds more to the sense of the Indians; both forms are very unusual for us, and yet both show strict consistency in their implementation.

The next two examples have religious contents. Example 4.44 is a religious dance song. Both are in triple metre, as the drum accompaniment again makes clear. The melodic direction of the first song [example 4.44] adds some exoticism through the syncopation, the five-bar phrases, and the flat seventh, which is foreign to us. The second song [example 4.45], uses a five-step scale, whose principal note, b♭, would also be the principal note in our sense.

Example 4.46 forms a contrast to this, a dance song with somewhat wayward melodic direction, because it shows particularly clearly how different our feeling for the tonic can be from that of the Indians. We would probably still harmonize the piece in F major. For the Indians, however, c appears to be the principal note, as both Abraham and von Hornbostel accept. That an adjacent note still emerges at the end, after the principal note has been held a long time, is something we have occasionally noted before.

Example 4.47, labelled as a 'lyrical song', starts with a short introduction on the first note, which is left out for the repeat (cf. example 4.42). It is nicely constructed in its two sections (one notes the imitation of the second and third bars up a fourth at the beginning of the second section), it is sung in a clear falsetto, and could also be pleasing to us. Only slight variations occur in the later repetitions. The intonation differs from ours particularly with f♯, which is taken a quarter tone too sharp. The high e[2] is also raised by the same amount.

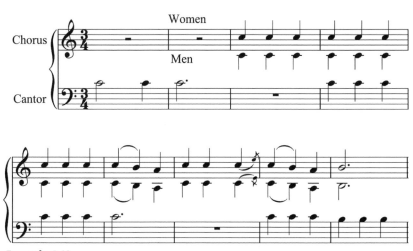

Example 4.48.

Example 4.48. *(continued).*

Exceptionally, we refer back here to a rather old transcription [Example 4.48] from the same coastal region. It was made in 1787, was printed 100 years later in the reports of the Smithsonian Institution for 1888, and has never been mentioned in recent literature as far as I know, but is well worth noting for its own reasons. It is in George Dixon's *Voyage Round the World*,[46] as a song of the Sitka Indians north of Vancouver before trading began (Dixon wanted to bargain for furs). The compiler of the report, one of Dixon's companions, does not think highly of his own musical skills and does not want to vouch for the accuracy of the transcription; but he heard the song often and describes its features in exact agreement with the notation, especially highlighting how the chorus and voice of the chief came apart. The song was always repeated without pause for almost half an hour; and was accompanied at regular intervals by clapping and drum strikes, shaking of a rattle, and multiple gesticulations by the chief. There is a corresponding description in the book of Dixon's travelling companion, Nathaniel

....

[46] George Dixon and William Beresford, *A Voyage Round the World* (London: G. Gouling, 1789), 243. Cf. German trans. by Johann R. Forster, *Der Kapitaine Portlock's und Dixon's Reise um die Welt* (Berlin: Voss, 1790), 219. [SR]

Portlock, from the same year.[47] He emphasizes 'the most exact manner' of the singing.

Since the technique of notation is impeccable (the tenor clef is used in the original), I want to regard the author's self-reproach more as a sign that he listened well; for few musical ears do not care to mention directly the difficulties of migrating exotic intonation into our system of notation. Whether the individual tonal steps corresponded exactly to those given here is of course uncertain, but the general form of melodic motion will be captured correctly. It deserves attention in two respects: first because of the historic period from which it comes, and from which hardly anything credible on primitive music has been transmitted in notation; but then secondly, particularly because of the idiosyncratic kind of polyphony. The chief's melody—repeatedly interrupted by fermatas—is introduced on c^1 and then drops down to a. The melody of the chorus, entering later but then with no further interruptions, proceeds partly in unison with the chief's melody, and partly by playing around one of his sustained notes, it drops down similarly, and at the end even proceeds to the lower dominant and from there back again to the tonic. But each of the two tunes, the simpler one of the chief, the richer one of the chorus, conveys the same general character. With good reason, then, this way of singing is marshalled under the concept of heterophony, of which we no longer find any examples among Indians of the present day. One could actually find the faint beginnings of contrapuntal voice leading in it, however.

Adagio non troppo

Example 4.49.

---

[47] Nathanial Portlock captained one ship (*King George*), George Dixon the other (*Queen Charlotte*) in a voyage undertaken between 1785–1788 for the purpose of commerce, specifically for the fur trade on the north-west coast of America.

Example 4.50.

Examples 4.49-4.50 are songs of the central Eskimos in the extreme north-easterly parts of the American continent and the neighbouring islands (north of Hudson Bay); aurally transcribed on site by Boas in 1883 or 1884 (see endnote i).

Here too [in the outermost regions] simpler tunes appear to be sung than among Indians of the middle regions. Both examples 4.49 and 4.50 begin and end with the interjection 'Aja' on the fermatas. They seem to fit excellently into our tonal system; the second song sounds almost like an arpeggiated four-note major chord. Other chords stand next to it that are less palatable to us, however. Boas has not shared any more details about the intervals.

In example 4.51 the major third is pure, the fifth is substantially lowered. The authors are of the view that no fixed tonal system developed in east Greenland. They have the impression that each singer owns their own individual scale (cf. Gilman regarding the Hopi). They praise the wondrous technique, however, regarding the complicated rhythm, which was performed with the greatest consistency. The rhythm of the drum (the east Greenlanders' only instrument) appears to be out of sync with that of the singers; only occasionally a singer's ritardando gives the impression that he wants to be together with the drum strikes; whereupon both then come apart again. The whole manner of performance gives evidence of an ancient tradition. The pitch movement (after the first ascent) is always downwards; the normal range is a fifth or a sixth.

Example 4.51. Kayak song from east Greenland, from samples recently published by William Thalbitzer and Hjalmar Thuren, transcribed by Thuren himself from phonographic recordings following the principles set out by Abraham and von Horbostel; studied tonometrically for the most part.[48]

Just as we went to press, the complete collection of both researchers appeared: *The Eskimo Music.*[49] It encompasses 129 songs from east Greenland together with a few from west Greenland; most were recorded phonographically. A large number show very similar pitch movement to the song above (no. 121 in the book): rising to the fifth and dropping from there by a third (and second) or by a fourth. Semitone steps only occasionally occur in passages. In one song a chorus accompanied the soloist in such a way that it repeatedly stated the note a while the soloist climbs up from f via a (very sharp) or directly to c; then came unison. Frequently, some musically indeterminable, strongly aspirated [vocal] sounds make up the songs' endings; as they also do among Indians, whose songs find several analogies here (e.g. the small gradual raising of absolute pitch—there was talk of that above in example 4.22, which admittedly also occurs with us). Music plays such a significant role

48 William Thalbitzer and Hjalmar Thuren, *Musik aus Ostgrönland; Eskomoische Phonogramme* (Leipzig: Breitkopf & Härtel, 1910).

49 William Thalbitzer and Hjalmar Thuren, *On the Eskimo Music in Greenland* (København: B. Luno, 1911).

among east Greenlanders that even at court trials prosecutor and defendant sing (juridical drum songs), from which arises—understandably—a particularly vigorous type of music.

According to Thalbitzer, music is strongly Europeanized in north-west and south-west Greenland. In recent years the Norwegian Christian Leden made phonographic recordings of the Polar Eskimos, which he will publish himself,[50] thirty-nine songs of which Robert Stein transcribed aurally in 1902.[51] Leden's recordings promise further gains for our understanding of relations between Eskimos and Indians.

Example 4.52.

Example 4.53.

[50] Christian Leden, *Über Kiwatins Eisfelder: Drei Jahre unter kanadischen Eskimos 1913–1916* (Leipzig: F. A. Brockhaus, 1927). Eng. trans. Leslie Neatby, *Across the Keewatin Icefields: Three Years Among the Canadian Eskimos 1913–1916*, ed. Shirlee Anne Smith (Winnipeg: Watson & Dwyer, 1990).

[51] Robert Stein, 'Eskimo Music', in Rudolf Kersting (ed.), *The White World: Life and Adventures within the Arctic Portrayed by Famous Living Explorers* (New York: Lewis, Scribner & Co., 1902), 333–356.

We now move on to a few more melodies from Africa. To be sure, a lot of phonographic material already exists from this part of the world, but it has not yet been thoroughly studied. In the coastal regions of Africa, and even in several inner regions, European influences are likely to have contributed; including influences from an earlier period. That the natives today regard a melody as their sole property and product is not sufficient proof that it really is.

Examples 4.52 and 4.53, which we can probably regard as authentic, were recorded phonographically by Father Witte in Atakpamé, Togo, and notated by Father Wilhelm Schmidt from these recordings.[52] They belong to the Ewe people, and indeed to the Ge or Aneho people. They are accompanied by drums. Regarding the particular significance of inflection in the Ewe language, Witte thinks it possible that the intonation of the melody partly interrelates with that of the text, but a strict dependency certainly does not exist. Indeed, the melodies have a character that is thoroughly comprehensible in purely musical terms.

The first song refers to an old shaman ban on planting yams twice a year. The structure is clear: after the two-bar theme is an intermediary bar, then a repetition of the theme at the lower fourth. The quintuple division of the bar is beyond doubt according to Schmidt. One of the attached little songs (sung by children to the white visitors) is analogous, and may already have a strong European influence; a G major tonality emerges still more clearly in it, but it also begins with d^2 and ends with d^1 all the same.

Example 4.53 is a girl's song that expresses sympathy for a young man. If it appears to us to be in D minor, d is hardly the principal note for the natives. The c♯ is flattened in several stressed places (I added the tie after the pauses, and the glissando line, according to Schmidt's statements). The song is sung in a fairly tight, almost stiff rhythm. Here the metre is also quintuple without a doubt; only once does a sixth quaver supervene at the end of the bar, where an (untranslated) exclamation seems to be inserted in the text.

---

[52] P. Fr. Witte, 'Lieder und Gesänge der Ewhe (Ge-Dialekt)', in P. W. Schmidt (ed.), *Anthropos: Internationale Zeitschrift für Völker- und Sprachenkunde* 1 (1906): 65–91, 194–210, here 71, 76. [SR]

Example 4.54.

Example 4.55.

Example 4.56.

These examples are taken from government instructor Josef Schönhärl's book *The Folklore of Togo*.[53] They too originate from the Aneho people. Schönhärl transcribed them aurally. His explanations and meticulous attention to rhythmic intricacies indicate that he is a good observer. He himself practiced performing the rhythms on indigenous instruments. Thus, one may generally regard the notation as authentic. The melodies are supposed to be very old, but they are always receiving new lyrics. The third melody is described as being just fifteen years old, however, and seems of decidedly European origin. It is incorporated here only because of the rhythmic accompaniment that the natives added. Schönhärl assures us that the majority of

---

[53] Josef Schönhärl, *Volkskundliches aus Togo. Märchen und Fabeln, Sprichwörter und Rätsel, Lieder und Spiele, Sagen und Täuschungspiele der Ew'e-Neger von Togo* (Dresden, Leipzig: C. A. Koch, 1909).

Ewe songs can be divided into duple rhythms, which explains why most of the twenty songs he shared are in 2/4 time. But songs were also sung without any drum accompaniment—particularly during the breaks between dances—which have very varied rhythms and cannot be divided into any metre. No metronome markings have been given, but Schönhärl mentioned that the dance songs are always sung throughout in a very buoyant, fast tempo, becoming ever more spirited.

Our tonalities can be transferred to these songs on the whole, indeed some (cf. the song included on p. 124 as a parable) even consist exclusively of pitches from the major triad, similar to many Indian songs. But we would still have to consider exact intonation, and besides, rigidities [Härten] would occur almost everywhere that teach us that an awareness of tonality is not simply to be equated with our own.

Example 4.54 can serve as an example of this notion. We could conceive of it in E minor, without the raised seventh (which, for us, was also introduced later). But even in doing so—and particularly with the ending on the second—it appears severe and disconcerting to us. According to the author, Ewe songs often end on the second, forth, or seventh (some note is of course already adopted as the principal note in these interval names). We encountered something similar among Indians. The accompaniment by percussion instruments, not included here, is still simple.

By contrast, examples 4.55 and 4.56 show a distinctly polyrhythmic accompaniment. The use of the right and left hand is signified by r. and l. African music is distinguished by its rhythmic polyphony and is undoubtedly original therein, frequently surpassing European music. The Ewe have a whole system of different types of drums, which participate in different ways in the song accompaniment. Certain rules govern the tuning of individual drum classes and the rhythm in which each is struck. Songs are always accompanied by a small drum orchestra as well as by striking small wooden or metal boards and by clapping in various rhythms.

Example 4.57. ◑ 17

Example 4.58. ◑ 18

Example 4.59. ♪ 19

Examples 4.57–4.59 are three instances of primitive polyphony from German East Africa [now partly Tanzania]; authenticated by phonograph.

The first, example 4.57, taken from Karl Weule's recording, belongs to the Wanyamwezi tribe from the Bantu family (Ph.-A. no. 19). It is part of a longer dance song in which chorus and solo alternate in like manner. The lower voice of the chorus comes across significantly louder on the cylinder so that the upper one seems like a discrete accompanying voice, and the whole becomes more palatable for our ears than it looks. In reality both voices could have been as loud as each other, however, and the differences of volume are due only to the different distances from the recording horn. Weule explains in his travel writings that the impression had been quite pleasant when, from a distance, he heard people singing such songs at twilight. He describes himself as unmusical even so. But other travellers too praise the Wanyamwezi singing as particularly impressive. In view of the whole structure, pieces like this have long since ceased to belong to music that is actually primitive.

In the remaining Wanyamwezi songs too (transcribed by von Hornbostel) the unison towards the end repeatedly proceeds to parallel fifths, fourths, and octaves.

Regarding the metre, the bars given in 6/4 admittedly fit very accurately according to the number of crotchets in this time signature (as they do in other recordings that exist of this song), yet the distribution of accents gives the impression of beginning a new metre in the places marked by small lines above the system. In this case, one would initially have a 7/4 bar before the first 6/4, and conversely a 5/4 bar before the resumption of a 3/2 metre. Imagining the [metrical] division in this way in fact gives us a better picture of the actual performance, as von Hornbostel noted. And we know well that lengthening or shortening bars within an otherwise securely maintained metrical scheme (i.e. 7/4 and 5/4 in an otherwise securely maintained 6/4) is not an unusual occurrence.

Example 4.58, described as a dance song for a wedding, shows the same characteristics. It consists of an ever-recurring motif that is always the same length. In the second section of the solo part, the song is modified melodically at first, but gives way to the same closing formula. The lower voice resumes the melody in the chorus, the upper one accompanies it in organum fourths [*Quartenorganum*].

The Wanyamwezi have a musical bow, a harp, horns, bells, and (again) many types of drum. Flutes rarely appear. Only drums and occasionally the musical bow serve to support the songs' rhythm. With this tribe too, new lyrics are always being adapted to the old melodies.

Example 4.59 offers a counterpart, recorded phonographically by Jan Czekanowski (Ph.-A. No. 25).[54] It belongs to the neighbouring tribe of the Wasukuma, who also display close linguistic relations with the Wanyamwezi. Reproduced here is the beginning and ending of a longer piece, transcribed by von Hornbostel (but not the ending of the whole piece, since the cylinder ran out). Here again the song is chiefly concerned with parallel fourths. Yet it is interesting how it always closes with the consonant fifth.

---

[54] Jan Czekanowski (1882–1965) was a Polish anthropologist and linguist.

Example 4.60.

Finally, I attach for comparison a cheerful little piece with passages in fourths that I heard among some other pieces by a Sinhalese troupe in 1887, and about whose performance I made extensive notes [example 4.60]. Even the pitches of the timpani were those that are notated here, if perhaps an octave lower. Here again it is the lower voice in the chorus' passages in fourths that continues in the pitches of the cantor [*Vorsänger*]. This is now no longer music of purely primitive peoples, but music that at least stands below that of the neighbouring Asiatic cultural nations, at any rate where the same parallel passages occur. Perhaps the parallel fourths and fifths in East Africa are not without a historical connection to these Asiatic fourths.

Thus we have returned to our point of departure, Ceylon, and conclude therewith our musical journey around the Earth.

Appendix

Images of primitive instruments

(see p. 51 ff.)

A few examples illustrating the principal types of primitive instruments and how they are played. Both cruder and more developed forms of each type are shown.

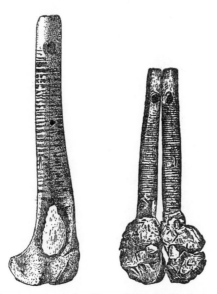

Fig. 1. Bone pipes from graves on the Channel Islands, Southern California.[1] The pipes are constructed according to the flageolet principle. Opposite the side hole— on the inside—are the remnants of a fillet made of rubber or bitumen, extending up to the open end, that creates the narrow fissure of the flageolet. The blowing aperture is well constructed. The second exemplar is a double pipe. Both pipe sections were held together at the lower end by a lump of bitumen that has now cracked; they were tied with raffia as well. Bone flutes with four holes were also found in other graves on the same islands.

---

[1] See Thomas Wilson, 'Prehistoric Art', in *Smithsonian Institute Annual Report* (1896), 325-664. [SR]

Fig. 2. An orchestra of panpipers on the Solomon Islands.[2] The image gives an idea
of the different sizes of panpipes. In fact, all those pictured here have two rows. Our
phonogram archive [the Berlin Phonogram Archive] also contains recordings of
polyphonic pieces played by such orchestras. They sound extremely amusing to our
ears (Ph.-A. No. 30).

---

[2] Adolf Bernhard Meyer and Richard Parkinson, *Album von Papua-Typen. Neu Guinea
und Bismark Archipel*, 2 Albums (Dresden: Stendel, 1894–1900), here album I. [SR]

Fig. 3. As a counterpoint to this, a Cameroonian orchestra with pumpkin trumpets, whose sounds were brought to us on cylinders by Bernhard Ankermann, director of the Berlin Museum of Ethnology.[3] It is the music of the 'Voma federation', a Balinese religious brotherhood in north-west Cameroon.

---

[3] Bernhard Ankermann, *Die afrikanischen Musikinstrumente* (Berlin: Haack, 1901).

Fig. 4. A musician playing on a musical bow from the forest lands of the upper Congo, west of Lake Albert.[4] The string is held by the teeth (though not by the tongue); it is shortened by the left hand.

4 Harry Hamilton Johnston, *The Uganda Protectorate: an attempt to give some description of the physical geography, botany, zoology, anthropology, languages and history of the territories under British protection in East Central Africa, between the Congo Free State and the Rift Valley and between the first degree of south latitude and the fifth degree of north latitude* (London: Hutchinson & Co., 1902). [SR]

Fig. 5. A Basuto[5] girl (South Africa) playing on a musical bow.[6] Here a pumpkin resonator is attached to the wood (frequently the strap is also looped around the string). One hand holds the bow and simultaneously shortens the string while the other strikes the string with a small rod.

---

5 Also known as the Sotho or Basotho.

6 Henry Balfour, *The Natural History of the Musical Bow: a chapter in the developmental history of stringed instruments of music. Primitive Types* (Oxford: Clarendon, 1899). Rpt. (Portland, ME: Longwood Press, 1976). Stumpf gives the source of this image as Frédéric Christol, *Au sud de l'Afrique* (Paris [etc.]: Berger-Levault et cie, 1897). [SR]

Fig. 6. A lyre from the Winam Gulf[7] area, north-east of Lake Victoria.[8] A tortoise shell (with a stretched animal fur on the inner side) serves as a resonator, through which the string passes.

---

[7] Stumpf's term, 'Kavirondo', refers to the former Kavirondo Gulf, encompassing two distinct native ethnic groups living under the British East Africa regime: Bantu speakers and Nilotic speakers.

[8] Johnston, *The Uganda Protectorate*. [SR]

Fig. 7. A harp of the Pangwe (Fang) in West Africa. The resonance box is a hollowed-out piece of wood with a small aperture at the side. The picture was kindly lent to me by Günter Tessmann, director of the Museum of Ethnology in Lübeck, whose work on the Pangwe is about to appear.[9]

....

[9] Günter Tessmann, *Die Pangwe; völkerkundliche Monographie eines westafrikanischen Negerstammes; Ergebnisse der Lübecker Pangwe-Expedition 1907-1909 und früherer Forschungen 1904-1907* (Berlin: E. Wasmuth, A.-G., 1913)

Fig. 8. Wood blocks from the Gazelle Peninsula in New Britain (Papua New Guinea).[10]

---

[10] Heinrich Schnee, *Bilder aus der Südsee. Unter den kannibalischen Stämmen des Bismark-Archipels* (Berlin: D. Reimer, 1904). [SR] New Pomerania (Stumpf's *Neupommern*) was the name of the island when it was under the protectorate of the German colonial empire within German New Guinea (1884–1914).

Fig. 9. West African signalling drums alongside a timpani drum, played during dancing. From the catalogue of the Crosby-Brown Collection in the Metropolitan Museum, New York.[11]

---

[11] Mary Elizabeth Brown, *Catalogue of the Crosby Brown Collection of Musical Instruments of All Nations*, 4 vols. (New York: Metropolitan Museum of Art, 1902–1907), here 3: 'Instruments of savage tribes and semi-civilized peoples. Pt 1. Africa'.

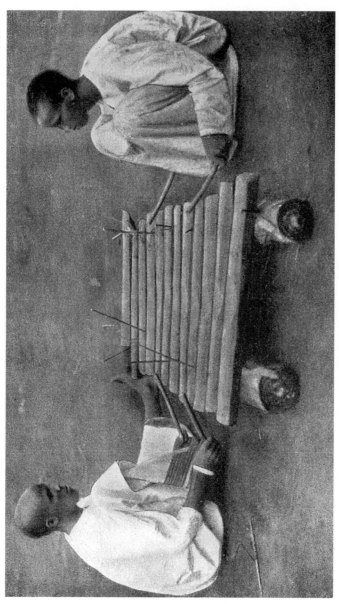

Fig. 10. A xylophone (called an amadinda) among the Bagunda tribe in East Africa.[12] Here two people play simultaneously on the same instrument. The mallets are resting on the same keys. One can see places in the wooden bars where notches have been cut for precise tuning. In most other examples the notches are carved on the underside.

12 Johnston, *The Uganda Protectorate*. [SR]

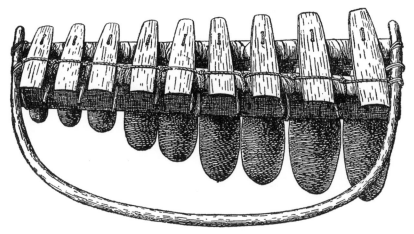

Fig. 11. A xylophone (marimba) of the Yaunde in Cameroon.[13] The numerous images and descriptions in [Bernhard Ankermann's book on African musical instruments] give the reader who wishes to find out more a notion of the diversity of the instruments that exist in Africa, particularly when combined with personal observation of the instruments, which every major museum of ethnology possesses in abundance.

---

[13] Bernhard Ankermann, 'Die afrikanischen Musikinstrumente', *Ethnologisches Notizblatt* 3(1901), bk 1. [SR]

Carl Stumpf: Life and work

Chapter 5

Carl Stumpf: A Self-Portrait (1924)

We spurn construction, love investigation, show
scepticism towards the mechanism of a system . . . we
are content at the end of a long life to have delved into
various lines of scientific enquiry, which lead to the
bottom of things; we are content to die on the journey.
(Wilhelm Dilthey, 1865)

I consented to the following self-portrait—whose length I beg to excuse
in view of the length of my scientific career—after some initial hesitation, when I noticed on various occasions how hard it was, even for my
scientific colleagues and students, to find the thread unifying my very
diverse writings and to find the roots of my life's work. Hopefully the
following text will be more successful in this regard.

5.1. Biography

I was born on Good Friday, 21 April 1848, in the market town of
Wiesentheid in Lower Franconia, and was baptized on Easter Sunday
according to Catholic rites. My parents were the county court physician
Eugen Stumpf and Marie Stumpf, *née* Adelmann. Three brothers have
been, and three sisters remain, my tried and tested fellow companions
in good times and in bad. My parents, who devoted their lives and cares
entirely to the welfare of their children, were still alive when I took up
my appointment in Munich. My grandfather, Andreas Sebastian
Stumpf, who died long before I was born, was a famous Bavarian historian and a member of several academies. My father's two brothers were
also active as academics, publishing work on statistics, biography, and
forestry. My great grandfather Adelmann (b. 1770), a forensic physician in Gerolzhofen, had studied eighteenth-century French literature

as well as Kant and Schelling, whose various works were found in his library along with extracts and marginalia. He spent the years of his retirement in our house, introducing me to the rudiments of Latin, and followed my progress almost up to university. The Adelmann family, who moved from Oldenburg to Fulda and Würzburg, included a remarkable number of doctors. I knew five of them personally—three of whom were university professors, in Dorpat, Löwen, and Würzburg—and four others by name only. It may well be, then, that a love of medicine and natural science was in my blood. Both of my parents were musical: my father an excellent singer, my mother a good pianist. I inherited from them a love of music.

Following a year at the Latin school in Kitzingen, I attended the grammar school in Bamberg (1859–63), and for the next two years the school in Aschaffenburg where my father was transferred in 1863. This charming little city became our second home.

Slight and feeble in physique, but with a vivacious and ambitious nature, at once religious and anxiously conscientious, I developed faster mentally than might have been good for my nerves. But I was able to spend my first ten years in the country where not only a large garden, but some farm work stimulated physical activity. Other exercise had an invigorating effect too, such as gymnastics, swimming, and particularly walks with my siblings through the lovely Franconian countryside, subsequently from Aschaffenburg through the Rhineland and the central German uplands, and later still cross-country across Tyrol and Switzerland. Walking and mountain climbing in good company seemed to me one of the most valuable aims in life—it broadens the mind and sets it free—while the school semester was only a purgatory compared to the heaven of the holiday. Many young people in southern Germany probably feel the same way. This passion for walking has remained with me into old age, and has certainly helped me attain the latter.

I do not have the fondest memories of my studies at grammar school, in the main. I progressed very quickly, but only with difficulty, for I was a year ahead of my age and did not have a good memory for history and geography. I only recall two tutors fondly, especially old Hocheder in Aschaffenburg, senior professor of the graduating class (and a passionate astronomer, incidentally), who first awoke in me a love of philosophy and of the divine Plato with his lectures on *Phaedo*. I have essentially remained a Platonist throughout my life. The lessons were generally anything but inspiring, even technically deficient. In Aschaffenburg mathematics in particular was taught in the most wretched manner. I had no particular aptitude for it, but with a proficient grounding at school I would probably have taken it further.

There were, by contrast, excellent opportunities for training in music at institutions of higher education in Franconia. Even in Kitsingen I had become acquainted with the old-fashioned notes of the four-line stave by singing from missals, and could soon sightsing in any key. We had a full orchestra in Bamberg that held regular rehearsals in the assembly hall[1] under the excellent leadership of Andreas Dietz the conductor. One could learn to play any instrument free of charge. I had already started the violin by the age of seven and had several opportunities to play in public during my school years. Besides this I was driven to learn five other instruments without lessons to varying degrees of success. Since it fell to me to lead during our domestic chamber music and singing, I became used to listening analytically to music while following the individual voices. I cannot objectively understand, incidentally, how is at all possible to appreciate the niceties of voice leading in polyphonic music—composition in its authentic sense—without this ability. The copying out of music, which I did extensively to save money, also gave me some insight into the mysterious craftsmanship of music, as it had done for Rousseau. I began to compose aged ten (my very first work was an oratorio for three male voices entitled 'The Walk to Emmaus') and this grew into a dominant passion by the last years of grammar school as I taught myself the theory of harmony and of counterpoint from treatises by Friedrich Silcher, Johann Christian Lobe, and Gottfried Weber. I wrote string quartets among other works, although inspiration admittedly did not keep pace with laborious reflection. The only original thing was a scherzo in 5/4 time.

---

[1] The Old Town Hall, a freestanding building in the middle of the Regnitz river, now belonging to the University of Bamberg.

Thus I arrived at university as a seventeen-year-old with more love for music than scholarship. In Würzburg I initially followed the normal Bavarian custom of attending lectures on general subjects. Among these, the philologist Professor Urlichs' course on aesthetics prompted me to study the *Critique of Judgement* from my grandfather's library. Hence Kant became another of my guiding lights in philosophy. In the second semester I chose to study law, not out of inclination but in order to have a job that would leave me some free time for music. I diligently attended seminars on institutions and pandects, on the history of Roman and German law. Towards the end of the semester, however, a great change came in the form of Franz Brentano's appointment to the faculty. I have already described elsewhere the transformation that his appearance, personality, and manner of thinking and teaching brought about in me.[2] Everything else receded before the great task of renewing philosophy and religion. Keen thinking had not come naturally to me up to this point, on the contrary I found it awkward. Brentano's iron discipline turned the need for logical clarity and consistency into second nature for me. All emotional life now had to submit to the imperative of reason. This was not to impoverish it, but rather to direct it towards those aims that quite simply seemed the highest to us. I was prepared to forego all worldly happiness in order to see the moral-religious ideas of Christianity realized in fellow human beings and in myself. This was my frame of mind for four years.

Alongside Brentano's lectures, I also took courses in natural science, as he considered both their content and their methods important for philosophy. The thesis of his postdoctoral dissertation [*Habilitationsthese*], that true philosophical methods are none other than those of the natural sciences, was and remains a guiding star for me. In order to become practically acquainted with this, I worked in the chemistry laboratory,

2 Carl Stumpf, 'Erinnerungen an Franz Brentano', in O. Kraus (ed.), *Franz Brentano. Zur Kenntnis seines Lebens und seiner Lehre* (Munich: O. Beck, 1919), 87–149; Eng. trans. L. Mcalister, 'Reminiscences of Brentano', in L. McAlister (ed.), *The Philosophy of Franz Brentano* (London: Duckworth, 1976), 10–46. See also Stumpf, 'Franz Brentano, Philosoph', *Deutsches biographisches Jahrbuch* 2 (1920): 54–61; 'Franz Brentano, Professor der Philosophie, 1838-1917', in A. Chroust (ed.), *Lebensläufe aus Franken* (Würzburg: Kabitzsch & Mönnich, 1922), 2: 67–85.

admittedly with the end result that, because of a careless reaction, I created a small fire that could easily have engulfed the whole building were it not for an attendant coming to the rescue. Manual dexterity was and is not one of my traits.

In my fifth semester, I travelled on Brentano's advice to Göttingen to study with Lotze, and to obtain my doctorate there.[3] Quite how he became a fatherly friend to me, I have also already explained elsewhere.[4] His way of thinking exerted a greater influence on mine than Brentano wished, even though I always retained the epistemological fundamentals that Brentano impressed upon me. Aside from Lotze's lectures, I attended those of the physiologist Georg Meißner and the physicist Wilhelm Weber. I must cite the latter, alongside Brentano and Lotze, as one of the formative influences on my scientific thought. The modest old man, whose entire presence in the lecture hall seemed bumbling, even comical, had by the most severe mental efforts devised a system of physics that introduced the method of inductive thinking to students better than any lecture on logic. I transcribed his lectures almost word for word for two semesters. Since then, physics has always seemed to me the ideal inductive science. Friedrich Kohlrausch's tutorials introduced me to investigative techniques. Such preparations are taken as read nowadays, at least for physiologists. At that time a philosopher attending chemistry and physics courses was still a rare bird.

I drafted my dissertation with particular attention to its logical form, and this may have been what brought Lotze round, as he was initially sceptical about the topic and dissuaded me from it. The procedure I derived from Brentano and—more distantly—Aristotle, namely, to carry out preliminary work by a complete disjunction of possible views, and to refute all but one with direct evidence, is to be found frequently in my later writings. To prepare for my doctoral viva, I read—if very cursorily—the whole canon of philosophical works, as well as reading the entire Platonic literature for my dissertation. I was of course already

---

[3] Brentano had not yet received his *Habilitation* in 1867, and was therefore not allowed to supervise dissertations.

[4] Carl Stumpf, 'Zum Gedächnis Lotzes', *Kant-Studien* 22 (1917): 1–26.

well informed about Aristotle through Brentano's writings and tutorials. Quite how much I was tormented by the difficulties of the doctrine of ideas—which even gave Aristotle some trouble and which is repeated *mutatis mutandis* in modern German idealism—is evident in the distress call of my first disputation thesis: '*Ideae nomen e metaphysica expellendum esse censea.*'[5] This cannot have pleased Lotze very much. In the same vein, the opening question of a somewhat arrogant [unpublished] paper I wrote in Würzburg on the psychology of the present asked: 'Are we still idealists?'

After gaining my doctorate in August 1868, I returned to Würzburg to resume philosophical studies with Brentano, but also to begin studying theology at the same time. In the autumn of 1869 I entered the seminary at Würzburg, where I also became familiar with liturgical practices of the church, the ascetic precepts which I followed most strictly, and with every detail of the religious exercises. I took no pleasure in the lectures on theology, with the exception of those by Schegg, a genial old exegete, who had himself travelled around the holy land and could describe it vividly. I diligently studied Thomas Aquinas and other scholastics besides, as well as Hebrew, for the sake of the Bible. The fact that the first letter of the alphabet is all I now know of this language is a striking example of the effect of disuse on memory.

Within the walls of the seminary, my second, more total conversion followed as soon as early 1870, again under Brentano's influence. The entire edifice of the doctrine of Catholic Christian theology and its worldview disintegrated before my eyes. In terrible spiritual agony, I had to give up my chosen ideals, my career, once again. In July I took off the black gown. I had not yet taken holy orders, so there were no complications for my later life. But I had to find my way back into the world again, and some consequences of this year, favourable as well as unfavourable, had a far-reaching effect on my life.

I was soon firmly resolved, however, to gain my postdoctoral qualification in philosophy at Göttingen. Lotze had written me a letter on 1 December 1869 acknowledging and justifying my entry into

---

5 'I think the name "Idea" [or "Form"] should be expelled from metaphysics.'

the seminary. I have quoted his religious views from this letter in my article on him,[6] but will cite its conclusion here:

> Lastly, I come to the most weighty point. I am not at all happy with the condition of the Protestant church and theology and will let your displays pass without approving of them. I suppose that you too are far from satisfied with everything that your church brings forth these days (its infallibility). Of course I cannot argue with you about the principle, since, like you, I regard the living faith as its only foundation. Your decision to become a priest is one I can only accept with deep respect for your conscientious conviction, and although one of my dear hopes has come to nothing, I recognize only too well the full extent of the blessing that your spiritual strength can bring to this appointment. I recognize this too well to want to oppose your firm conviction. Nevertheless, forgive me—as one to whom you are dear—one imperative, rather serious request: do not take the final, irrevocable decision too rashly in early youth, which you are still so happily enjoying! Everything else I leave up to your own expertise and consideration, but on this one matter I beg you!

I kept these words—which reveal his respect of each person's individuality as well as his personal affection for me (he wanted to visit me even during the vacations in Aschaffenburg or Würzburg)—like a treasure enshrined in my heart, but only now felt how right he had been with his 'rather serious' warning. When he heard of my change of heart he wrote in the same vein that he would regard it as indelicate to come to the aid of my inner struggles with views that originated from quite different starting points; that I would have to content with them myself.[7] 'I have only one thought to mention here: life is long and yours, I hope, especially so; is it necessary to settle all of your doubts about the most important matters now at this moment? But perhaps you torment yourself too much by ruminating incessantly on things, which—now that you have refused to tie a binding knot—can remain undecided for a while longer, until some intervening rest and refection allows you to return to these problems with greater calm, unselfconsciousness, and receptivity.'

---

[6] Stumpf, 'Zum Gedächtnis Lotzes', *Kant-Studien* 22 (1917): 1–26.

[7] Details of Lotze's correspondence are given in Ernst W. Orth (ed.), *Hermann Lotze: Briefe und Dokumente* (Würzburg: Konigshausen & Neumann, 2003). Stumpf gives the date of the letter in question as 22 July 1870, though there is no record of this in *Briefe*.

He approved of my decision. Even in the holidays I worked on a dissertation on mathematical axioms and at the end of October 1870, I obtained my Habilitation at Göttingen University. I have not published the text because the non-Euclidean perspective introduced to me by Felix Klein proved a little too much for me.[8]

The transition from the seclusion of the cloisters to this city of muses, which had produced the 'philosophers of the world' in the eighteenth century and where even today sociability blossomed in spite of the war, was extremely sudden and abrupt. But I had enough of the elasticity of youth soon to feel at home in the new milieu. Lotze's house was always open to me, as was Josef Baumann's and Friedrich Henle's, at whose weekly string quartet soirées I played the cello. Henle had the most genial sense of humour and showed the greatest goodwill to his friends. I even received a conversational letter from him shortly before his death in 1885. His 'Lectures on Anthropology' are famously full of keen psychological observations.[9] During these years I got to know, besides Göttingen's famous circle, two veterans of psychophysics in Leipzig, Ernst H. Weber and Gustav T. Fechner, the former at his brother's home, where he showed me various sensory fields on my own body, and the latter on a field-trip with Felix Klein. With Fechner I discussed the difficulties of atomism caused by the unity of consciousness, which he thought to resolve by analogy with the unity of concept. We then served as subjects for his experiments on the golden ratio. The personalities of these men, true scientific researchers, made a lasting impression on me. But in Göttingen there was also good collaboration among the many young minds. Besides Klein, my closest friend was William Robertson Smith, a Scot who had to endure serious persecution later in his homeland as a liberal investigator of the Bible.[10] Klein, who already

---

[8] Stumpf's text 'On the Foundation of Mathematics' has, nevertheless, been published. See W. Ewen (ed.), *Über die Grundsätze der Mathematik* (Würzburg: Konigshausen & Neumann, 2008).

[9] Friedrich Jakob Henle (1809–1885), *Anthropologische Vorträge*, 2 vols. (Braunschweig: Friedrich Vieweg und Sohn, 1876).

[10] William Robertson Smith (1846–1894) held professorships in Arabic (Cambridge) and Hebrew (Aberdeen), where he was tried for heresy in 1876. His text *Religion of the Semites*

showed a pronounced urge to organize, founded the 'Eskimo' with me; this was an association of young natural scientists, with lectures and friendly discussions, where I was to represent philosophical matters. Professors were excluded. The club still exists, as far as I know, with slightly more moderate rules.

I began lecturing on ancient philosophy, especially on Aristotle, who had preoccupied me for an entire year. For my first serious project I undertook a critical history of the concept of substance, which caused me no end of trouble, until I abandoned it and in Easter 1872 sought to tackle the psychological theme of the origin of spatial conception. I believed (and still believe) there is a manifest example or analogy of relationships to be seen in the relation between colour and extension, a relation which metaphysics assumes to exist between the characteristics of a substance. For me, then, the new work was connected to the old.

My work progressed quickly this time, and the book was published as early as the autumn of that year.[11] It appeared at a particularly propitious time for my professional advancement, as there were vacancies in philosophy at five universities. I was considered as a second choice in Vienna; in Würzburg, where Brentano and Lotze campaigned on my behalf, I was offered the position and was able to relocate there in autumn 1873 as full professor.

This early appointment at a significant university seemed to me like a great stroke of luck, of course, particularly for the sake of my parents. But it also had its downside: I had neither the experience nor the academic maturity for this difficult position. Since Brentano had stepped down and almost nobody turned up to listen to Franz Hoffman, an elderly disciple of Baader,[12] I had to represent the philosophy department virtually by myself. With the courage of youth I lectured on the gamut of great philosophical topics except for ethics. I was to feel the consequent overexertion for many years.

(London: Black, 1889) is credited with helping to establish the field of comparaitive religious studies.

[11] Stumpf, *Über den psychologischen Ursprung der Raumvorstellung* (Leipzig: Hirzel, 1873).

[12] Franz Xaver von Baader (1765–1841), a philosopher and theologian.

On a trip to Italy in 1874, I met—as well as Bonatelli and Barzelotti—the elderly leader of Italian philosophy, the remarkable Count Terenzio Mamiani[13] and his student Luigi Ferri, who enquired after the state of German philosophy. In the same year I took a trip with William R. Smith across the channel and was able to deepen my knowledge of English philosophy *en passant* in the British Museum; Smith had already given me an understanding of much of it in connection with my book on spatiality.[14] Like Brentano, I had a predilection for this lucid and logical, if not always so profound, philosophizing, and for keenly working out oppositions, as classically presented in Mills' book on Hamilton.[15] Only Herbert Spencer's constructive manner remained unpalatable to me.

For my first scholarly project I undertook a history of the physiology of association, which went together with the above-mentioned studies, but I gave this up again—just like my work on the concept of substance—and resolved to develop the field connecting my musical experiences and studies with the interests of psychology, which seemed most fruitful to me personally. I began working on *Psychology of Tone* around 1875. I had unrestricted access to the excellent acoustic facilities at the Institute of Physics through the goodwill of Friedrich Kohlrausch, my former professor at Göttingen. In addition, I often spent days in Hanau with Georg Appunn the organ builder, who had worked for Helmholtz, and vied with him over observations. I knew only too well that this kind of immersion in all the details of a field of sensation sharply contradicted the general conception of a philosopher's mission, although Fechner had been a famous example. But when I considered the bleak condition of current philosophy as it appeared in Ueberweg's survey[16] always new systems without any connection with each other, each

---

[13] Count Terenzio Mamiani della Rovere (1799-1885), an Italian statesman and writer, who worked for Italian unification.

[14] Stumpf, *Über den psychologischen Ursprung der Raumvorstellung* (Leipzig: Hirzel, 1873)

[15] John Stuart Mill, *The Collected Works of John Stuart Mill, Volume IX - An Examination of William Hamilton's Philosophy and of The Principal Philosophical Questions Discussed in his Writings*, ed. John M. Robson (Toronto: Univ. of Toronto Press/London: Routledge and Kegan Paul, 1979).

[16] Friedrich Ueberweg, *Grundriß der Geschichte der Philosophie: von Thales bis auf die Gegenwart*, 3 vols. (Berlin: E. S. Mittler, 1863-66).

mindful of originality, at least of its own terminology, none of them of really persuasive—when I compared this with the path of development in physics, what a vast difference! Surely it should be possible for specialists to work together as such, at least within a particular field? And if this were to be done in other fields, would it not lead to a result that was mutually beneficial for philosophy and the individual sciences?

Thus my time in Würzburg was for me the beginning of a line of work to which I remain committed even today; it stems from a conviction that, admittedly, has made me an outsider to the vast majority of my colleagues. My work in observation and experimentation has absorbed my time and energy even more than is the case with most experimental psychologists. But although I rate highly Aristotle's words that theory is the sweetest of all, I must also confess that it has always been reassuring and a kind of solace to switch from theories to observation, from reflection to facts, from the writing desk to the laboratory. And in the end I neglected my writing desk, producing not a single textbook or compendium, which ought to have been an obligation, even when I was an associate professor [*Privatdozent*]. Incidentally, I had not the slightest inkling that I would spend so much of my life on studies into acoustics and music psychology, as was the case later on. I reckoned on a few years. But it is not musicology but philosophy that has always remained mistress of the house, although—it is true—she has granted plenty of free access to her handmaiden.

In this cheerful Franconian city one did not live only to work. There was a large circle of friends and plenty of fun, tales of which would be out of place here. Among the oldest, Kohlrausch and Johannes Wislicenus[17] were closest to me; among the younger scientists there was Erich Schmidt,[18] who attended my lectures on metaphysics, and the

---

[17] Johannes Wislicenus (1835-1902) was a chemist with appointments at the Universities of Zurich, Würzburg, and Leipzig.

[18] Erich Schmidt (1853-1913) was a literary historian who held numerous academic appoints, including at the Universities of Würzburg, Strasbourg, Vienna, Weimar, and Berlin.

lively archaeologist Adam Flasch,[19] as well as the Romanist Eduard Mall, a man from the Palatinate who had imbibed the unsettled Berlin air during the 1860s, a sort of Mephistopheles Merk,[20] who was not without influence in my withdrawal from Brentano's unconditional optimism. After five years I was thoroughly weary of the bachelor's life and it was clear to me that an attachment from my time in Göttingen had put down deeper roots than I previously wanted to admit. Music, Beethoven's wonderful great trio in B-flat major, had brought us together.[21] In the meantime, Hermine Biedermann had been appointed to the Hochschule in Berlin. She followed the call and we secured our association for life. The great B flat major trio has now become our family trio.

In 1879 I received an appointment in Prague to succeed Wilhelm F. R. von Volkmann. The faculty wanted initially to hire Otto Liebmann; but Brentano (who had been teaching in Vienna since 1874) recommended me, without my knowledge, in order to strengthen the hold of our theories in Austria. I hesitated over these circumstances, but finally accepted, partly because the unfamiliar, romantic city on the Moldau appealed to my congenital wanderlust, but partly and indeed principally because my influence in Würzburg had declined sharply in recent years for local reasons. A philosopher who does not concentrate on popular lectures can count on a sizable audience in Würzburg only if theology students attend his courses. This had been the case during my first semester. But since I in no way concealed my independence of mind regarding the church, the theologists gradually dropped my courses almost entirely. A religious Protestant like Oswald Külpe is more desirable to a Catholic theological faculty than a heretical Catholic.

Thus my work in Prague commenced in the autumn of 1879. A year later, Anton Marty, my best friend from my student days in Würzburg,

---

[19] Adam Flasch (1844–1902) studied philology, history, and Archeology in Würzburg and Munich before being appointed the first professor of classical archeology at the University of Erlangen in 1882.

[20] Goethe's autobiographical term for a friend whose presence does one no good.

[21] Beethoven's piano trio Op. 97, the 'Archduke'.

arrived from Czernowitz.[22] My interaction and professional collaboration with this man, notable for his sharp mind and character, whose studies into the philosophy of language led him deep into cognitive psychology, was a huge bonus for me. It is perhaps not entirely right to assemble a faculty of philosophers who belong to orientations as different as possible, indeed opposed to each other. If the orientation itself is not too one-sided, both students and teachers will gain significantly from the harmonious cooperation of like-minded individuals.

Every winter in Prague I had to give a long course for law students in practical philosophy, which had concerned me little until then. I immediately developed the course systematically and explicitly in the most comprehensive way, simultaneously incorporating the philosophy of law and of the state. I was able to pick up several threads from my brief stint as a law student, and became particularly preoccupied with problems of penal law. I later gave many courses on practical philosophy and theories of voluntary action, most recently in Berlin in 1896.

The exertions of that first winter, in tandem with difficult domestic events and the unhygienic conditions of the city, adversely affected my health. Yet I was able to resume work on *Psychology of Tone* in the next year, despite the fact that I lacked almost all the necessary apparatus. Building on my investigations into extremely unmusical subjects—already begun in Würzburg—I now began studying music theory from antiquity and the Middle Ages, as well as examining ethnological music literature, such as it existed back then. The first volume of *Psychology of Tone* appeared in 1883, and despite its long gestation period, it was finished—like my book on spatiality—only after it went to press, and bears traces of this process.[23]

Among my colleagues, the closest to me scientifically, aside from Marty, were Ernst Mach and Ewald Hering. I did not become personally close to Mach in spite of my veneration of him, but I enjoyed lifelong friendly relations with Hering. These two were also leaders of

---

[22] Czernowitz, a city then on the extreme eastern edge of Austria-Hungary, is now Chernivtsi (southwestern Ukraine).

[23] Stumpf, *Tonpsychologie*, vol. 1 (Leipzig: Hirzel, 1883).

German culture in the university. During the struggle for our national-
ity which grew to a great intensity under the Taaffe administration,[24]
I myself first became a good German, and learned to hold the Germans
in Bohemia in high esteem as a serious, industrious branch of our people steeled by centuries of struggle.[25] I was delighted when, in 1882,
I received a visit from William James, who had approved of my book on
spatiality, and with whom I was soon on friendly terms. Later we saw
each other again in Munich, and we have remained in constant correspondence, even if I could not accompany him in his conversion to
pragmatism. The lively, warm-hearted nature of this brilliant man is
particularly clear in the letters published by his son.[26]

In the summer of 1884 I was called to succeed Hermann Ulrici[27] at
Halle, and work alongside Rudolph Haym and Johann E. Erdmann. My
longing for the German fatherland had grown so great that I accepted
the call with gladness. In the tranquil town of Halle I met Georg Cantor,
who was deeply interested in philosophy, and from 1886 Edmund
Husserl grew closer to me scientifically and as a friend, first as my student (recommended by Brentano) then as an instructor. There was
nothing to interfere with my work except the lively social scene, which
I always tolerated poorly, but I made good progress with the second
volume of *Psychology of Tone*. That I had to carry out the basic fusion
experiments [*Verschmelzungsversuche*] on the cathedral organ instead
of in a psychological laboratory was no disadvantage in itself, for there

---

[24] Eduard Taaffe (1833–1895) was a prominent Austrian statesman who twice served as
prime minister of Austria (1868–1870, 1879–1893).

[25] Stumpf refers here to the so-called Sudeten Germans, a population of ethnic Germans
then living within northern Bohemia, which became annexed as part of the Czechoslovak
Republic when this was declared on 28 October 1918. Following annexation, this population protested their right to self-determination, coming to wider notice in the late
1930s as a site of tension between Czech Social Democrats and the Sudeten German
Party (sympathetic to policies of Nazi expansion). See Meixner Rudolf, *Geschichte der
Sudetendeutschen* (Nuremberg: Helmut Preußler Verlag, 1988); and Karl Cordell and
Stefan Wolff, *Germany's Foreign Policy towards Poland and the Czech Republic: Ostpolitik
revisited* (Abingdon: Routledge, 2005).

[26] Henry James (ed.), *The Letters of William James* (Boston: Atlantic Monthly Press, 1920).

[27] Hermann Ulrici (1806-1884) was a German philosopher and champion of Shakespeare
who spent the whole of his professional life at the University of Halle (1834–1884).

is no greater source of constant tone in all possible timbres than a good organ. Then again, I felt the lack of necessary apparatus very keenly, but was able to carry out experiments directly on primitive subjects for the first time: on the Bella Coola Indians and other tribes, who honoured the city with their visit as a result of Alfred Kirchhoff's zealous efforts.

In 1889 came the offer to succeed Carl Prantl in Munich. Again I did not hesitate long at the prospect of being closer to home, and even in my beloved Munich. I relocated in the autumn of that year. Georg von Hertling—also a student of Brentano's—championed Catholic philosophy there. He was a loyal colleague to me, but we never became closer on account of our divergent views. My dearest friend here was Rudolf Schöll, an aesthetically minded philologist who sadly died too young. Using faculty funding, I gradually accrued a small collection of apparatus for experimental psychology and especially for my acoustic research. It was located partly in a cupboard in a university corridor from which I took the instruments on Sundays to a lecture room for observation and experiment, and partly on the upper floor of the high tower which still stands among the rear buildings of the university. The assistant at the physics institute had purchased for next to nothing a tuning-fork piano that must have dated from Ernst Chaladni's time; he took it apart and sold me the old tuning forks, a 'continuous row of tones' on which I was able to make many observations for the second volume of *Psychology of Tone*. This was how I made do in those days.

In Munich, in view of my appointment to the academy, I began writing a host of academic treatises—occasional writings after a fashion, since the choice of subject had to fit into the allotted space, to which philosophical topics yield less easily than those of the natural sciences, history, or philology. Many manuscripts remain from the lectures I gave later in Berlin, but I have added short summaries (customary in the session reports) to the index of my writings, for that can at least suggest my views on the various topics for those that are interested.[28]

---

[28] Stumpf included a selective list of publications when he brought out 'Self-Portrait' in 1924 (pp. 58–61). The present volume expands on this to provide a complete list of Stumpf's publications (see pp. 253–259).

My sharp criticism of work carried out at the Leipzig Institute embroiled me in an argument with Wilhelm Wundt, which he, for his part, peppered with the most extreme invective. That I was objectively right followed from the fact that the results of the experiments in question—allegedly overturning Fechner's law—were to my knowledge never and nowhere mentioned again, except in Wundt's textbook. But I was not deterred from taking issue with the later acoustic research at the Leipzig school, almost all of which was misguided, I felt; I hope, however, that I never overstepped the boundaries of objective criticism. Wundt's own methods had inwardly repelled me since his Heidelberg days, and still do today, although I wonder at the extraordinary breadth of his vision and his prolific literary productivity right up into old age.

I never imagined that I would be able to leave Munich again. But after five years, as in Prague and Halle, temptation sought me out. Friedrich Althoff conveyed a call to Berlin, where an experimental psychologist was wanted after Eduard Zeller resigned and Wilhelm Dilthey took over the historical approach. As great an honour as this call was, I have never felt any love for Berlin, and feared above all not being able to carry out my life's work as I planned there, so I declined. But after a few weeks I began to realize that Munich was not the right place to realize my aspirations after all. It was not possible to establish an institute. I had asked the minister, who had accommodated me so far, to grant 500 marks annually for experimental psychology. He answered that such a sum might indeed be possible but that he must put the matter before the state legislature, and that there might be objections that he was facilitating materialism. I therefore declared that I would have to leave. Shortly thereafter Theodor Lipps received an endowed seminary and later on, Oswald Külpe obtained a large institute. The real reason for the minister's behaviour most probably lay elsewhere, namely in my pronounced opposition to certain clerical wishes, shared by the court, regarding the Academy.

Thus I relocated to Berlin in the Easter of 1894 and now, after thirty years, I still believe my decision was for the best. My concern about not being able to complete *Psychology of Tone* and other planned works, sadly proved to be well founded. But the department of psychology has grown up from small beginnings—three dark back rooms—into a large institute; and it has been possible for me to pursue multifaceted activities, indeed often too much so, in any direction that interested me. Berlin's *genius loci*, the all-pervasive spirit of work, appealed to me. A wealth of stimuli came my way, and there was no arcane question on which one could not obtain an expert opinion. Moreover, Berlin was the greatest city in the world for music, and Joseph Joachim, the noblest of performing artists whom I had known for some time as a friend, was still at the height of his powers. I cannot even name here all the distinguished men with whom I came in close contact officially and personally, often socially, during this long period. But I do want to mention the fact that I could associate personally with Hermann von Helmholtz for at least one semester, and with Theodor Mommsen for a decade, that I had the best amicable relations with Dithey as with Paulsen and their successors, and could renew old friendships with Erich Schmidt and Kohlrausch. The personal interactions among Berlin colleagues were continually sustained—in spite of long distances—by the weekly faculty and academy meetings in addition to social life, and I always felt it a blessing in this respect that the large philosophy faculty, irrespective of its heavy administrative load, remained undivided. Among the many points of contact between psychology and modern thought and life, I found that, in addition to the sincerely scientifically minded, the metropolis contains many dubious careerists, who, under the cloak of science or the arts, even social endeavours, pursue only business or vain ends. Several uncomfortable and time-consuming tensions arose from this.

Since I feared not merely being distracted from my own work, but also the dangers of large-scale operations for such a young field of research, I wanted to begin quite modestly with my experimental set-up and accommodation. Soon, however, the needs of students prompted an extension, which was now harder to obtain of course. In 1900 the department was vastly expanded into an institute, though there were always fresh requirements, petitions, memoranda. In 1920 we were given twenty-five rooms in the former imperial castle, whose management alongside generally strained circumstances caused me great stress until I could delegate them to younger hands. In the course of the year four smaller institutes developed out of the original institute, serving medical, musicological, and military purposes, all led by students. Far more involved than I in the development of facilities were the assistants, first Friedrich Schumann, later Hans Rupp, an expert and enthusiastic technician.[29] They also led the experimental tutorials while I took care of those based around theory, in which we discussed psychological problems related to recent treatises and, in the spirit of Brentano, inculcated the necessity of logical thought alongside the need for psychological observation. I set great store by these meetings, for I do not in any way view experiments (the external type, at least) as a cure-all for psychology. We were particularly preoccupied with the theory of will and forensic psychology for a long time, and participants in our discussion such as Wilhelm Kantorowicz and Gustav Radbruch later became prominent specialists. This highly fertile area should, in my view, be explored much more thoroughly by psychologists. At that time the theory of will formed the subject of several of my academic lectures, which I have not published.

My research into acoustics in Berlin, which was aided early on by Otto Abraham, Karl Schaefer, Max Meyer, Oskar Pfungst, and later by Erich von Hornbostel, Johannes von Allesch and many others, was initially of a purely physical nature; it was published in the *Annalen der Physik*.[30] By examining sound sources for their harmonics and by producing entirely simple tones using the interference method, the ground was laid for all later acoustic study at the institute. This work has been collected since 1898 in my *Beiträge*, whose first volume, containing my theory of consonance, was conceived as the kernel of the third volume

---

[29] More information about the development of the Institute up to 1910 is given in Max Lenz, *Geschichte der Königlichen Friedrich-Wilhelms-universität zu Berlin*, 3 vols. (Halle: Buchhandlung des Waisenhauses, 1910-18), and in the University's annual chronicles. [SN]

[30] This journal, established in 1799, is available open source up to 1940. See: http://gallica.bnf. fr/ark:/12148/cb34462944f/date.r=Annalen+der+Physic.langEN [accessed 8 May 2012].

of *Psychology of Tone*, but had to appear independently.[31] Our acoustic equipment gradually attained a greater state of completeness, but only according to our research needs; not a single item was purely for demonstration.

In 1896, together with Albert von Schrenck-Notzing, I had to prepare for the Third International Congress of Psychology in Munich, and then to lead it. There were a huge number of international participants and the correspondence took up a considerable amount of my time. As the theme of my inaugural address I chose the central question of the relationship between mind and body. In particular, I tried not to allow hypnotic and occult phenomena to come to the fore as they had at previous meetings. Related disciplines were also represented by leading researchers such as Ewald Hering, Paul Flechsig, Franz von Liszt, Pierre Janet, Charles Richet, Auguste Forel, Théodor Flournoy, and Henry Sidgwick. There were sharp encounters, doubtless many of them stimulating. Nevertheless, no International Congress of Psychology has been held in Germany since, for we found it more beneficial to discuss such moot questions in the domestic circle of the '[German] Society for Experimental Psychology', where foreigners could also take part.

In 1900, with phonographic recordings of a Siamese troupe then performing in Berlin, I laid the foundation for a Phonogram Archive, which was further developed by Abraham and von Hornbostel, and later directed by the latter alone.

At the same time, the project established by Philipp Spitta, *Denkmäler deutscher Tonkunst*, which stagnated after his death in 1894, was reorganized by Rochus von Liliencron.[32] I had belonged to the committee since moving to Berlin and now, at the behest of Liliencron and Althoff, became deputy to the deaf, eighty-year-old president until his death in 1912. The friendship of this venerable and learned man, a nobleman in the best sense, was a great privilege for me. As for the rest, I dwelt now and then on Mommsen's saying that in every committee there should

---

[31] Stumpf (ed.), *Beiträge zur Akustik und Musikwissenschaft*, 9 vols. (Leipzig: J. A. Barth, 1898-1924).

[32] Philipp Spitta, Max Seiffert (et al.), *Denkmäler deutscher Tonkunst* (Leipzig: Breitkopf & Härtel, 1891-).

be one who does not understand the matter in question. That said, I was able to assume the merely formal direction of the discussions in good conscience and could thereby increase my knowledge of the old composers in a most desirable way.

That same year I founded the Berlin Society for Child Psychology [*Verein für Kinderpsychologie*] together with the headmaster Ferdinand Kemsies. I hoped thereby to draw teaching staff, particularly from middle school, but also people in medical circles and educated parents, into active participation in psychological studies and observation of the mental life of children. This had already been of manifold importance for the *Psychology of Tone*, and I had kept a detailed record about my own children. These efforts flourished for a few years, during which the excellent paediatrician, Otto Heubner, participated in particular from among the doctors. Two of my later lectures grew out of these studies, of which that published on the peculiar linguistic development of a child found particular recognition in the literature.[33] It gradually became apparent, however, that the teachers kept away because of their professional duties, but perhaps in part also through mistrust of suspiciously reformist psychologists. At the same time, so many troubles over applied psychology and school reform came to the fore that there was no longer any place for a society with expressly theoretical aims. Other commitments forced me to relinquish the leadership, and the society quietly died a death during the First World War.

I have frequently been able to study prodigies. For example, Georg Placzek, a neurologist, induced me to examine a four-year-old boy with an extraordinary memory in 1897, one who from his second year had been exhibited before scientific associations in various countries, indeed even at the Berlin Panoptikum. As a result of my extensive report in the *Vossische Zeitung*,[34] and with the assistance of well-to-do benefactors, a governess was appointed who helped him through the most difficult years. At school, his miraculous talent gradually wore off,

---

[33] Stumpf, 'Zur Methodik der Kinderpsychologie,' *Zeitschrift für pädagogische Psychologie und Pathologie* 2 (1900): 1–21.

[34] A prominent daily newspaper, published in Berlin between 1721-1934. Stumpf's article appeared on 10 January 1897.

for it was hardly compatible with normal development. To my great satisfaction, he has since become a capable head teacher. In 1903 I studied the early signs of musical talent in Pepito Arriola, a musical prodigy whom Charles Richet had already presented at the Paris Congress. He became a significant piano virtuoso during his time in America, though not an outstanding composer, as Arthur Nikisch and I had hoped after his childhood achievements. Similarly I studied the young Hungarian Ervin Nyíregyházi—about whom Géza Révécz later wrote an entire book—and others besides.[35]

With the pedagogical-didactic applications of child psychology and the experimental research into memory, applied psychology was born at the beginning of this century. In the Institute for Psychology, Hans Rupp dedicated himself to it, and now he runs an entire department of applied psychology. This remained far from my own personal interests, but I supported these daring endeavours wherever their execution did not lack the necessary prudence.

In 1903 I began an experimental examination of combination tones, occasioned by Krueger's studies in this field on which he based a new theory of consonance; this occupied me, with some lengthy interruptions, until 1909. One may wonder at the fact that I could dedicate so much time and effort to such a relatively small and remote field of phenomena, to which I myself attribute more physiological than psychological importance. But whoever reads the treatise will admit that questions of methodological principals needed to be settled here, and a wealth of individual questions of fact emerged that could be answered with the help of the newly developed process. Still it is true here, as so often, that had I known in advance how long it would last, the work would certainly have never been undertaken.[36]

---

[35] Géza Révész, *Erwin Nyiregyházy: Psychologische Analyse eines musikalisch hervorragenden Kindes* (Leipzig: Verlag von Veit, 1916); English translation, as *The Psychology of a Musical Prodigy*, International Library of Psychology, Philosophy, and Scientific Method (London: Kegan Paul, Trench, Trubner & Co., Ltd.; New York, Harcourt, Brace & Company, Inc., 1925).

[36] Stumpf's work on consonance between 1898-1909 spread over a variety of acoustic topics, and appeared in numerous issues of his journal *Beiträge zu Akustik und Musikwissenschaft*, including: 'Konsonanz und Dissonanz', 1 (1898): 1-108; 'Neueres

The year 1903 brought a distraction, to which in the interests of concentration I really ought to have been less susceptible. Two Berlin researchers arranged for Emanuel Cervenka, a Prague-based engineer, to give a demonstration of an allegedly highly significant phonographic discovery in the university's assembly hall; most senior members of the professoriate and the entire teaching body of the university had been invited. Photographs of sound waves were supposed to be transformed back into sound. At the Institute of Psychology we harboured the suspicion, like the members of the Gramophone Society, that here in this hallowed place a bold fraud had been perpetrated. I wrote one defiant, sarcastic article, then another in conjunction with the physiologist Wilhelm Engelmann.[37] The explanatory work was made difficult for us; but finally we produced the proof, and not a single word has been spoken of the great invention since. But the affair had positive consequences. One of these was a revolution in, and complete reorganization of, the International Music Society.

Shortly thereafter I became embroiled in another matter that concerned psychology more directly: the case of 'clever Hans'. Returning fresh from the Königsberg Kant centenary festival in 1904, I was asked by a ministry official to investigate claims made in a lecture by Wilhelm von Osten, since the ministry of education, to which von Osten had appealed, was in a quandary about what position to take on the matter.[38]

über Tonverschmelzung', 2 (1898): 1-24; with Max Meyer, 'Maaßbestimmungen über die Reinheit consonanter Intervalle', 2 (1898): 84–167; 'Zum Einfluß der Klangfarbe auf die Analyse von Zusammenklängen', 2 (1898): 168-170; 'Beobachtungen über subjective Töne und über Doppelthören', 3 (1901): 30–51; 'Tonsystem und Musik der Siamesen', 3 (1901): 69-138; with Karl L. Schaefer, 'Tontabellen', 3 (1901): 139-146; 'Über das Erkennen von Intervallen und Akkorden bei sehr kurzer Dauer', 4 (1909): 1-39; 'Über zusammengesetzte Wellenformen', 4 (1909): 62-89; 'Differenztöne und Konsonanz', 4 (1909): 90-104; 'Akustische Versuche mit Pepito Arriola', 4 (1909): 105–116.

[37] Stumpf, 'Grammophon und Photophonograph. Eine Betrachtung zur angewandten Logik', *Tag* (1 March 1903); Stumpf and Wilhelm Engelmann, 'Zur Demonstration in der Aula am 6. Februar', *Tag* (31 March 1903); Stumpf, 'Die Demonstration in der Aula der Berliner Universität am 6. II 1903'. *Zeitschrift der Internationalen Musikgesellschaft* 5 (1904): 431–443.

[38] Wilhelm von Osten argued that his horse was able to perform mental arithmetic, and believed he had thereby proved the existence of animal intelligence. An investigation by Oskar Pfungst disproved Osten's claims, however. This was published with an

That this was not a case of intentional deception, as in thousands of similar cases, but resulted from the fact that the horse responded to the famous African explorer Karl Schillings just as it did to von Osten. And so a study seemed appropriate after all. I made no secret of the extraordinary difficulties caused by the excitement in the city and even further afield, aroused by the daily newspaper reports about the strange case, the throng of curious observers, the wonderment over von Osten, the unfavourable location, and so on. But the inexorable desire to clarify the matter induced me to take up the investigation, and we were finally able to clarify what had happened, thanks principally to the sharp eyes and iron patience of my young collaborator, Oskar Pfungst. On this occasion there were several interesting, more general results to record. Unintentionally von Osten had, in grand style, confirmed by experiment the Aristotelian doctrine that animals lack a faculty of abstract thought. If a pedagogical method prepared so carefully as that which this former teacher of mathematics had used with unspeakable patience on his horse, if this had led only to the recognition of arbitrary movements of the trainer's head, the fault must surely lie with the pupil's limited faculties. The conclusion, admittedly, was not accepted everywhere. There were the horses from Elberfeld and the dog from Mannheim with whom professors of zoology and psychiatry actually entered into correspondence.[39] The same people still defend the existence of higher animal faculties in the pages of the *Zeitschrift für Tierpsychologie* (Journal for Animal Psychology). But I had no desire to investigate such cases any further. Later, when the Samson Stiftung enabled the Academy of Sciences to establish a research station on Tenerife, which would—at Max Rothmann's suggestion—systematically

introduction by Carl Stumpf as: *Das Pferd des Herrn von Osten; der kluge Hans. Ein Beitrag zur experimentellen Tier- und Menschen-Psychologie* (Leipzig: Barth, 1907); Eng. trans. Carl L. Rahn, *Clever Hans (the Horse of Mr Von Osten). A Contribution to Experimental Animal and Human Psychology* (New York: Rinehart and Wilson, 1911).

[39] Stumpf is referring to the correspondence of the *Gesellschaft für Tierpsychologie*, alongside such contributions as Maurice Maeterlinck, 'Die Pferde von Elberfeld. Ein Beitrag zur Tierpsychologie', *Die neue Rundschau* 25 (1914) 6: 782–820. A selection of contemporary publications for download is available here: www.denkende-tiere.de/ [accessed 8 May 2012].

study anthropoid apes imported directly from our colonies, I suggested Wolfgang Köhler for this task, and we all know how successfully this turned out.[40] Köhler did not aim at biologically useless stunts of arithmetic, but rather at the vital activities of animals, and provided proof that his chimpanzees' use of tools and ways of getting around problems significantly exceeded the previously accepted limits of animal intelligence, and showed, in a certain sense, 'intelligent' behaviour; that is, only demonstratively intelligent, not presupposing any general concepts, as arithmetic does.

In 1905 I was invited by the Kaiser Wilhelm Academy for Military Physicians (Pepinière) to give short annual lecture courses on anything I liked within philosophy. I gladly seized this opportunity to interest young medics in philosophy and its history. It may have been around the same time that the assistants of the Institute of Physiology teamed up with those of the Institute of Psychology to found the 'Cerebral Cortex' [*Hirnrinde*] in order to discuss problems in common; its purpose was much like the old 'Eskimo' in Göttingen. Medics soon became involved, among them Hugo Liepmann, who took over the chair. The society still exists and has proved fruitful.

I served as Rector of the university in 1907–08. In my inaugural speech I expressed my conception of philosophy's current position and purpose. The office provided me with many interesting experiences, such as contact with leading figures of all circles; representation of the university at scientific conferences; a forty-five minute conversation with the Kaiser during my official appointment, where he did almost all of the talking and was astonishingly frank; great satisfaction over the daily occupation with curricular and student issues; and, in the second semester, some unexpected excitement from a conflict with the 'Free Students' [*freie Studentenschaft*], whom I had initially received with

---

40 Wolfgang Köhler studied for his doctorate under Stumpf at Berlin. He then spent six years in Tenerife studying animal behaviour and problem solving capabilities. See Köhler, *Intelligenzprüfungen an Menschenaffen* [1917], 2nd ed. (Berlin: Julius Springer, 1921); Eng. trans. Ella Winter, *The Mentality of Apes* (London: K. Paul, Trench, Truebner & co., 1925).

particular fondness.[41] This body did not represent the entire number of non-incorporated students (*Finkenschaft*), but was rather only a relatively small group who had assumed the right to take care of the interests and cultural aspirations of all the non-incorporated students. On every occasion, however, they confused their representation with that of the *Finkenschaft* itself, and a small cohort of second- or third semester students, or rather their leaders, made demands that amounted to parallel government. So the war was on. There were general student assemblies, in which radical left-wing politicians like Rudolph Breitscheid and Hellmut von Gerlach raised the temperature. They spoke of the murder of academic freedom, of being under the Russian knout. I dissolved the Free Students, and the year ended on this note of discord. The senate had always supported me. The following semester, the board of education approved the association of the student body under new statues, which avoided the above-mentioned confusion. During the following years a general student board was established, which meant true representation of the student body, while the Free Students continued its otherwise entirely laudable work. It is possible that I took too much of a principled position with regard to details that I could have overlooked, and thereby fanned the flames of the conflict, which incidentally had already flared up elsewhere (Marburg, Halle). But sooner or later it had to come to an altercation. I deeply regretted that it fell to me in that year, otherwise so uplifting, for I love students. The words of warning in my second speech as Rector to the student body mixed an echo thereof with a premonition of the difficult times that lay before our fatherland, signs of which were already clearly apparent.

In 1909 the Berlin Philosophical Seminar—towards which Alois Riehl and I had been working for some time—was established with Benno Erdmann's appointment, and organized by him in exemplary fashion.

---

[41] The 'Free Students' was an explicitly liberal organization that called for reform of all aspects of student life. Its constituents were not members of the more tradition 'dueling' societies, and so were more likely to adopt a politically liberal stance. From 1900, the Free Students put increasing pressure on student societies to live up to time-honoured ideals of equality, tolerance, and academic freedom. See Lisa Fetheringill Zwicker, *Dueling Students: Conflict, Masculinity, and Politics in German Universities, 1890–1914* (Ann Arbor: Univ. of Michigan Press, 2011), esp. 78–102.

I was nominally one of the directors, but could only participate in an advisory capacity, and once gave a seminar on Aristotle's metaphysics. I would dearly have wished to establish some cooperation between psychology and philosophy in this manner, but the institute would not permit it. Occasionally Kant and Hume were also the basis of philosophical discussion.

The summer semester was pleasantly interrupted in 1909 by a request to represent the university at the Darwin centenary celebration in Cambridge. I had witnessed the rise and fall of Darwinism in its original form, but the theory of evolution had become ingrained in me, as it had for everyone; furthermore I admired Darwin's personality as a researcher so highly that I felt justified in accepting the mission. I voiced this appreciation in my address, published in the university's annual chronicles.

On the occasion of the university's centenary celebration in 1910 I was awarded an honorary doctorate by the medical faculty and felt grateful for the recognition of my efforts towards establishing closer relations between philosophy, psychology, and medicine. Less enjoyable was that, in the course of the year, I had to make use of such relations as a patient and experimental subject through three life-endangering abscesses of the ear, two trepanations of the right petrous bone, and twice as a *casus rarissimus* of ophthalmology. But my ear passed its rigorous examinations *magna cum laude*: it always recovered its hearing, and I was able to continue with the vowel studies I had begun just before the last operation. My eye, however, just about passed.

At the Sixth Congress for Experimental Psychology in 1914 I reported on recent experiments regarding the theory of tone.[42] Here I commented on Wolfgang Köhler's compelling study of vowels at the Berlin institute, which had first been reported at the Fourth Congress in 1910.[43] This led me to pursue more closely the nature of vowels and

---

[42] Stumpf, 'Über neuere Untersuchungen zur Tonlehre', *Bericht über den VI. Kongreß für experimentelle Psychologie in Göttingen vom 15. Bis 18. April 1914* (Leipzig: J. A. Barth, 1914), 305–48. Reprinted in *Beiträge zu Akustik und Musikwissenschaft* 8 (1915): 17–56.

[43] Wolfgang Köhler, 'Über akustische Prinzipalqualitäten', in *Bericht über den IV. Kongress für experimentelle Psychologie in Innsbruck vom 19 bis 22 April 1910* (Leipzig: J. A. Barth, 1910), 129–223.

speech sounds generally, i.e. more thoroughly than I had in the final paragraphs of *Psychology of Tone*. The experimental results fascinated me so much that I could not tear myself away from the study before this important field of phenomenology had been sufficiently cleared up. Since the institute had become deserted during the first years of the war, I was able to utilize the silence for the most intense exertion of my hearing capacity for analyses of tone. On the other hand, of course, very great difficulties and delays arose with the construction and maintenance of the apparatus. In the later years of the war younger minds made use of the institute in the interests of military psycho-technology (sound measuring systems, etc.), so of course my peaceful experiments had to take second place. Hence, they were only really finished by 1918.

During the war all the large nations involved in the conflict called upon experimental psychologists to collaborate. As the representative of psychology in the capital I was heavily involved in organizing this. Admittedly, however, we did not quite achieve the systematic and broad-based cooperation found in America.

In another enterprise, also occasioned by the war but eminently peaceful in itself, we have without a doubt surpassed other nations. At the behest of Wilhelm Doegen, a head teacher, a large number of philologists came together in 1915, with me serving as the music researcher; our object was make phonograph recording of the strange dialects, songs, and other musical performances of the prisoners-of-war who streamed towards us from all possible countries of the Earth, often even from inaccessible and still unstudied regions. The minister of culture appointed a commission to call on specialist collaborators from all over Germany in order to make technically excellent recordings in thirty-two prison camps, at the same time collecting the necessary material for the scientific study and classification of the records. Besides the commission's gramophone recordings, Georg Schünemann was asked to undertake numerous recordings with the more convenient Edison apparatus. I was entrusted with directing this work, and it took up a great deal of time, even consuming my lecture time for an entire semester. But it was worthwhile to be able personally to observe the manner of performance and the general bearing of the exotic singers, for their presence greatly enhanced my impression of the recordings, bringing them to life. After the revolution of the commission, however, the collection of gramophone recordings was transferred without a word of thanks to the Staatsbibliothek, where, in my view, it was not adequately cared for.

Our old phonogram archive,[44] assembled over twenty years, and containing roughly ten thousand recordings, has a quite inestimable value given that many primitive peoples have died out and foreign parts of the world are being Europeanized; initially, the archive was not taken over by the state and remained unfinanced. After the state lawyers had decided that the ownership of the archive—a question that had never crossed our minds—lay with von Hornbostel and myself, we handed it over to the state on condition that the state would provide for its maintenance and continuation. This was agreed, and the collection was incorporated into the Hochschule für Musik in 1923. Sadly this was not the end of the matter, for the state cannot sufficiently meet its obligations at the moment because of general cutbacks, which naturally fall first of all on matters not pertaining to everyday life. On a happier note, in 1922 it was possible, in spite of the difficult times, to found the *Sammelbänden für vergleichende Musikwissenschaft*, and thus establish an organ of publication for this field; with the promotion of Schünemann, Sachs, and von Hornbostel at Berlin University, furthermore, we were better equipped than anywhere else for this line of research.

My official duties at the university came to an end during the Easter of 1921, as a result of recent regulations over the retirement age, but I only stopped lecturing in the summer of 1923. In Berlin, where numerous professors represent the various branches of philosophy, my lectures had no longer covered the whole gamut of philosophy, but focused essentially on psychology, the history of philosophy, and logic. In more recent years I frequently gave a course on a kind of system of philosophy under the heading 'questions of world view' [*Weltanschauungsfragen*]. Until a few years ago the lectures caused me a great deal of work, for individual sections, particularly unsatisfactory ones, had to be redrafted

---

44 The Berlin Phonogram Archive, see this volume pp. xff.

each time. I was anxious to give an overview of the subject, and to trace the history of philosophy up to the present, illuminating research methods through more detailed sections along the way. I was never passionate about lecturing, however, and found it irksome as it drew me away from my scientific research, which was my primary concern and which always penetrated far deeper into the subject material than lectures; indeed, in view of my particular specialism, my lecturing traced some quite different threads. I have never lectured, for instance, on the psychology of tone or on musicological topics. Yet I do not underestimate the extraordinary advantages that arise from an alliance between teaching activities and research, particularly in the need always to keep the subject as a whole in mind.

Since I learned shorthand in my grammar school days, I made much use of it in lectures. Only in later years have my eyes forced me into full emancipation from notes, and I must say that I preferred this kind of 'reading' far more, precisely because it was no longer reading as such. I also had the feeling of entering into closer, livelier contact with my listeners. Constantly using shorthand has the general disadvantage, however, that one is used to thinking through writing, and one loses the ability to speak extempore. Nevertheless the advantages are so great, particularly for collecting material, for excerpting, for registering observations and attempts in every detail, that I heartily recommend it in general.

By about 1907 I had already resigned from the examinations committee for head tutors because the often dreadful preparation of candidates absorbed in their main subject troubled me, and because the recording of results, particularly of examinations in education, was unedifying and a waste of time. Another heavy burden in Berlin was the postdoctoral qualifying examinations, where philosophy is required as a secondary subject for lecturers in all subjects in the arts and sciences. But here the results were on the whole much more gratifying. I had a general policy of not limiting my questions to single topics, but probing here and there until I hit the solid ground. I often found that candidates had developed a real interest in philosophy, not just for the purposes of the examination.

I belonged to the committee for editing the works of Kant and Leibniz from the beginning of these projects, and occasionally had to serve as chair after the death of Dilthey, then Erdmann. I had the good fortune that Kant's correspondence was finished during these years—bringing to an end the long and difficult birth of the Kant edition[45]—and an effective start was made on the Leibniz edition, which was possible against all our expectations. In the preface I recalled the enthusiastic words of Émile Boutroux, the former director of the French Leibniz commission, which stand in stark contrast to the present exclusion of Germany from international scholarly enterprises, and I expressed the hope that the spirit of Leibniz would once again be all-pervasive. It gave me great pleasure that at the end of my term I got to mention my little native town of Wiesenthein, where copious Leibniz documents were found in the archives of the counts of Schönborn.

I cannot close this sketch of my life without mentioning that I left the Catholic Church in 1921. Although I had been estranged from it for fifty years, I had not hitherto severed my connection formally in view of the church's many beneficial functions, nor had I any inclination to take up a new creed. But the conduct of the officiating priest at the burial of one of my brothers caused me finally to take this decisive step (he deemed it necessary to excuse himself for standing above this grave, since the deceased, whose noble human goodness he felt obliged to praise, had not upheld the church's precepts). Although I am now technically non-denominational, I still profess Christianity from my soul as the religion of love and mercy—which requires not so much a revaluation as an appreciation—and I hope that in the course of time the divided denominations may come together under these emblems, if not in total reunion, at least by way of rapprochement and reconciliation.

---

[45] *Kants Gesammelte Schriften. Ausgabe der Berliner Akademie der Wissenschaften*, 29 vols. (Berlin: Reimer, 1900-). This edition was divided into 'Works' (vols. 1–9), 'Correspondence' (vols. 10–13), 'Manuscripts' (vols. 14–23), and 'Lectures' (vols. 24–29). The first section was completed under Stumpf's editorship in 1923; the fourth is ongoing.

5.2. Views and research

The following section has the double purpose of making my published writings more comprehensible in view of their intentions, methodologies, and results, while at the same time expanding on certain aspects of them so that the reader sees a coherent whole, not merely scattered fragments, which makes the component parts all the more intelligible. This form of presentation may seem dogmatic, if not quite superficial, but the reader should appreciate it is not my usual approach, and more detailed evidence can be found in my writings.

It must be said in advance that my views rest broadly on the impulses I received from Brentano. It would take us far afield to record the points of agreement and disagreement in every detail. In general it should be emphasized that the agreements pertain more to the earlier than to the later form of his teaching.

The Austrian philosopher Friedrich Ueberweg claims in his paragraphs on Husserl that I began with Brentano, but now display greater affinity to Husserl.[46] This makes it sounds as if Husserl's accomplishments had been decisive for me in some respects. That is simply not the case. My deviations from Brentano's teaching are the result of an entirely intrinsic, gradual development of ideas. There are of course many points of overlap among Brentano's students owing to their common point of departure, but also because of the necessity of changes, elaborations, and further development felt by those proceeding in the same direction.

5.2.1. Towards a definition of philosophy

However we formulate the difference between mind and nature, each individual will differentiate them somehow. The philosopher, though, wants to find the common ground. So philosophy is in the first instance the most general form of science or metaphysics, to which epistemology forms the entry point. That philosophers since ancient times mostly

---

[46] Friedrich Ueberweg, *Grundriss der Geschichte der Philosophie* (Berlin: E. S. Mittler, 1863-66); Stumpf is probably referring to 11th edition, expanded and updated by Max Heinze (Berlin: E. S. Mittler und Sohn, 1920).

regarded psychology as belonging to their field of study is objectively explained by the fact that the mental realm has been significantly more important than the physical in forming basic metaphysical concepts. It is therefore expedient to define philosophy principally as a science according to the most general laws of the mind and of the actual (or vice versa). Only in this way can we justify classifying logic, ethics, aesthetics, philosophy of law, pedagogy, and other branches under the umbrella of the philosophical sciences. The connecting link is always essentially psychology, from which arises the obligation not to forget the higher aspects of the soul (not scrutable in this manner) and the large general questions amid all the details of the experiments.

5.2.2. On the history of philosophy

Brentano described a schema of four phases in which each of the three periods of philosophy since Thales has so far run its course—a phase of growth with predominantly theoretical interests and empirical methods, a decline through the unchecked encroachment of some popular philosophy of life, followed by a sceptical and finally a mystical reaction. This has always appeared to me to be a good key for understanding the development of philosophy, at least for antiquity and for modern times. The path was intrinsically modified in the Middles Ages by the influence of the church and authorized religion. Historical similarities or analogies are not laws of nature. To be sure, the schema cannot be applied blindly to every detail (how are the sophists to be incorporated, for instance?), and we should not take the 'decline' to mean that brilliant, profound, momentous achievements are precluded in such phases. Finally, we must not forget that classifications are possible according to many other points of view, though I regard their methodology as the most important point.

My first project pertained to the history of philosophy: work on Plato's idea of the Good and his conception of God.[47] It sought to eradicate the contradiction that Eduard Zeller allowed to persist between the personal religious convictions of philosophers and their scientific

---

[47] Stumpf, *Verhältnis des platonischen Gottes zur Idee des Guten* (Halle: Pfeffer, 1869).

system, in order to restore the Aristotelian conception of ideas as entities intrinsically different from real, different essences, and at the same time prove that God is identical with the idea of the Good. The latter theory—also shared by Zeller, incidentally—is almost universally acknowledged nowadays; the debate over the correct conception of ideas continues unabated. I still regard the realistic conception as correct (as do Theodor Gomperz, Wilhelm Windelband, Otto Apelt) and find the attempts at evasion brilliant but unhistorical. Admittedly my description was too attuned to a system that was closed in itself and took too little heed of the changes induced by Plato's course of development, especially the deviations in his later writings, about which our philological methods have given us a fuller understanding.

Among my later articles, the two about ancient music theory (in 1897) contain many detailed remarks about passages of text that also concern the history of philosophy but have hardly been noticed by my colleagues.[48]

Two decades later, after much experimental work, I chose Spinoza as the subject of a treatise, not out of any particular sympathy for his philosophy, but because I believed I was able to say something new about a central point of his, the parallelism of attributes.[49] I believe I showed that this doctrine is fundamentally different in both form and rationale from modern psychophysical parallelism and is only an outflow of the old Aristotelian scholastic doctrine of parallelism of acts and contents of consciousness. The second study concerns the infinite number of attributes and seeks, hypothetically at least, to explain the terse suggestions of philosophers and make them comprehensible on the basis of the theory of parallelism at least; and to explain how I, in spite of the multiplicity of objective attributes out of which substance consists,

---

[48] Stumpf, 'Die Pseudo-aristotelischen Probleme über Musik', *Abhandlungen der Königlich-Preußischen Akademie der Wissenschaften, Philosophisch-historische Abhandlungen* (Berlin: Reimer, 1897), 1-85; and Stumpf, 'Geschichte des Consonanzbegriffs. Erster Teil. Die Definition der Consonanz in Altertum', *Abhandlungen der Königlich bayerischen Akademie der Wissenschaften*, 1. Classe 21, 1. Abteilung (Munich, Franz, 1897), 1–78.

[49] Stumpf, 'Spinozastudien', *Abhandlungen der Königlich-Preußischen Akademie der Wissenschaften* (Berlin: Verlag der Königlich Akademie der Wissenschaften, 1919), 1–57.

could maintain their unity.[50] A third study pertained to the 'geometric method' and was to find for the first theorems of ethics and their proofs, which Leibniz justly condemned, the silent preconditions that made them appear formally necessary for Spinoza himself.[51] Hitherto we have approached criticism from without. The task of clarifying Spinoza's extreme conceptual realism alongside his dependency on scholasticism I recommend to lovers of logic.

I find the achievements of post-Cartesian philosophy that are most worthy of emulation, methodologically speaking, to be those not of Kant or Hegel, but (in agreement with Brentano) of Locke and Leibniz, to whom I would add Berkeley. Even though phenomenalism and the polemics against general concepts rest on misconceptions, there are also mistakes of this kind among the greatest minds. But Berkeley's clear and precise exposition and the energy of his thinking place him even above Locke, who exceeds him only in versatility. Nobody will deny today that Leibniz far surpasses his forebears. Among the direct precursors to Kantian critiques, I was particularly gripped by Johann Tetens, whose *Philosophische Versuche* is very rightly described as the German counterpart to Locke's *Essay*.[52] During my Halle days I recommended to Schlegtendahl and even to Störing that they work on Tetens, and myself dedicated a later study to his theory of relations.[53] The spirit of impartial and painstaking investigation was perhaps never as vitally effective in any other German philosopher before Lotze.

For me, Kant's intellectual and ethical greatness consists above all in that he redeveloped with full force the idea of necessity and its ethical counterpart, the concept of duty. But while he stands with one foot still

---

[50] Stumpf, 'Die Attribute der Gesichtsempfindungen', *Abhandlungen der Königlich-Preußischen Akademie der Wissenschaften, Philosophisch-historische Klasse* 8 (1917): 1–88.

[51] Stumpf, 'Vom ethischen Skeptizismus', *Internationale Wochenschrift für Wissenschaft, Kunst und Technik* 2 (1908): 993–1008.

[52] Johann Nicolaus Tetens, *Philosophische Versuche über die menschliche Natur und ihre Entwicklung* (Leipzig: M. G. Weidmanns Erben und Reich, 1777); John Locke, *An Essay Concerning Humane Understanding* [1690]. rpt (London and New York: Penguin, 1997).

[53] Stumpf, 'Psychologie und Erkenntnistheorie,' *Abhandlungen der Königlich Bayerischen Akademie der Wissenschaften* (Munich: Franz, 1891), 19, pt 2: 465–516. [SR]

in Hume's hypercritical way of thinking, the other is firmly planted in the later speculative-dogmatic period. I cannot in good faith regard either path as an ideal worth emulating for philosophers, particularly not the second with its obsession with construction. I dealt repeatedly with Kant and critical philosophy in the constructive philosophy of *Rebirth of Philosophy*.[54] But whether we are already in a decisive and widespread period of ascendancy is doubtful to me, as it was for Brentano in his final period. The rich multiplicity of approaches, none of which are built on each other, has never borne any real resemblance to the systematic progress of true science. Even in psychology the disintegration has assumed worrying forms, but we can always still comfort ourselves with Heraclitus' dictum that struggle is the father of all things, for the ground of facts is steadily expanding.

The *Table for the History of Philosophy* (to whose third edition Paul Menzer contributed) is intended for pedagogical purposes rather than as a tool for historical research.[55] It originated in Munich as I introduced Prince Friedrich Karl of Hesse—who diligently attended my lectures on logic—to the history of philosophy while walking in the Englischer Garten. I believe the linear schema did not go down too well with my colleagues, but they should not forget that it is intended for a novice.

5.2.3. On epistemology and logic

These two disciplines are distinguished by the fact that epistemology is theoretical, whereas logic is practical, in their directives for testing and uncovering cognitions. Psychology—which addresses the processes of thought and cognition as such, among other processes—is the foundation for neither discipline, but it is also indispensable for both. With Kant's fundamental theses I showed how the neglect of psychology avenges itself, but at the same time denounced the attempt to use

---

[54] Stumpf, *Die Wiedergeburt der Philosophie*, [speech on the Rector's installation at the königlichen Friedrich-Wilhelms-Universität Berlin, 15 October 1907] (Berlin: Francke, 1907).

[55] Stumpf, *Tafeln zur Geschichte der Philosophie* [1896], 3rd ed., ed. P. Menzer (Berlin: Speyer & Peters, 1910).

methodologies of psychology to deduce truth criteria from the mechanism of mental functions.

5.2.3.1. On the origin of fundamental concepts (categories)

To consider these a priori would simply mean cutting the Gordian knot. We should always keep trying to find the original phenomena forming the foundation of their perception. Thus, in view of the conception of things or substances, let me point out that in certain apperceptions we discern [*wahrnehmen*] the interpenetration of parts of the whole directly. In every sensory perception [*Sinnesempfindung*], the attributes—quality, intensity, expansiveness, etc.—form not a sum but a whole; indeed, the parts are merely later abstractions. In the domain of mental functions, intellectual and emotional functions, as well as all simultaneous conscious conditions, are related to each other in the most integrated way (unity of consciousness) and are perceived directly as a unity. So Hume's research principle was not wrong, but he did not observe carefully enough, otherwise he would not have had to define substance as a cluster, but rather a whole made up of properties or conditions.[56]

He also abandoned the concept of causality too soon. There are in fact circumstances that can be perceived not merely as a sequence but as an inner nexus. Whoever pursues a train of thought attentively is in a certain fundamental frame of mind (interest), and this is causal and we are aware of it as such: it accounts for the retention of ideas and everything bound up with these, their comparison, combination, etc. It is not the case that we are interested in something, and only *then*, after the interest has passed, are its effects felt; rather it is an intrinsic, permanent, and inwardly observable causality. It cannot only be about a transference [*Übertragung*] within natural processes, and, while

---

[56] David Hume's statement on substance reads: 'When we gradually follow an object in its successive changes, the smooth progress of the thought makes us ascribe an identity to the succession. . . . When we compare its situation after a considerable change the progress of the thought it broken; and consequently we are presented with the idea of diversity: In order to reconcile which contradictions, the imagination is apt to feign something unknown and invisible, which it supposes to continue the same under all these variations; and this unintelligible something it calls a *substance, or original and first matter*.' Hume, *A Treatise of Human Nature* [1739-40], ed. P. H. Nidditch (Oxford: Clarendon Press, 1978), 220.

unavoidable, this is no use to the investigator who is interested only in the strictly lawful succession of events.

The concept of necessity or lawfulness[57] [*Gesetzlichkeit*] may be grasped in its full rigour by realizing the contents (facts of the case) of an a priori obvious judgement such as logical axioms and all purely deductive propositions.[58] This concept is then transferred over to nature.

The concept of truth is also rooted in the realm of judgement, of course. What is true is manifest directly or indirectly; what is false manifests its opposite directly or indirectly. We can also say: truth (falsehood) is that property of the contents of consciousness, by virtue of which—using objective reasoning—they compel approval (rejection). Everything depends here on the concept of evidence [*Evidenz*], which we could perhaps call Brentano's fundamental concept. We must look for what he means even in such self-evident judgements as $2 \times 2 = 4$; they cannot be reduced or defined further. Evidence and truth are correlative concepts, with evidence being the subjective side of truth, so to speak, which is itself objective in a certain sense, namely independent from individual acts of consciousness, a function of what is conceived, not of the conceiving subject. All positivistic theories of truth, including pragmatism, go in circles. Only as maxims of thought do economics and usefulness remain worthy of consideration.

Actuality or reality means the capability of having an effect. Thus the conditions of our own minds are real for us in the first instance. For here, as noted above, we experience causality directly. If we were not internally active, we would not be conscious of reality. In the second instance, we lay down external things—mental as well as physical—as real provided we observe effects from them on us. Whoever denotes divinity as the 'most real being [*Wesen*] of all' also regards it as the original cause. By contrast, general laws are indeed true, but not real, because they are not capable of effect.

---

[57] The logic of the 'apodictic judgements' combines four concepts that are hardly comprehensive: necessity, security, evidence, exactitude (Brentano). [SN]

[58] Also belonging to the axioms are those expressions that state the connection between premises and conclusions of a compelling system –'deductive axioms'—which one cannot deduce from experience without immediately running into a vicious circle. [SN]

5.2.3.2. The paths of knowledge

We recognize principles of law by pure reason, a priori, from mere concepts and self-evident propositions. Such recognition does not require a determination of fact, which is why this knowledge is most appropriately expressed in hypothetical propositions. In the case of mathematics, which is immediately relevant here, its a priori evidence is to be maintained even today. If there are three geometries, each according to an assumed curvature of space (i.e. relating to spatial forms), each of them is in itself a priori and their applicability to objective space is only a matter of empirical knowledge.

Yet a priori knowledge issues not only from mathematical propositions, but from all mental conceptions, namely from those that may also extend our learning. The mere notion of two notes [*Töne*] infers their relation with respect to pitch, volume, chronological order, duration, etc., which can be asserted of the imagined tonal pairing, and any similar pairing. The mere notion of three notes of different pitches infers a quite definite relationship to one another, according to which one note must lie between the other two. The notion of a succession of pitches, ordered according to pitch, contains the possibility of its infinite continuation, but cannot for one moment be proven by experience (see *Psychology of Tone*).

Such propositions are not strictly synthetic, however, for they are understood not merely by means of concepts, but about them, if relations are to be counted as part of the conceptual material [*Vorstellungsmaterie*]. All the same, we must question how such analytical judgements as extensions of knowledge are possible. For this we need, among other things, to seek out the most general, simplest, and directly perceptible relations as well as a theory of how we apprehend them. The beginnings of this 'general theory of relations' [*allgemeine Verhältnistheorie*] are at hand, but these must still be verified and elaborated. A priori judgements themselves cannot thereby become more convincing, but their epistemological structure and significance can become more comprehensible.

Facts as well as laws are recognized (experienced) a posteriori. Immediately given sensory contents and their executive mental functions are experienced directly; what is developed from this is experienced indirectly. Conclusions drawn from the outside world independent of consciousness, and the laws it reflects, have the form of probable conclusions. The only way in which we can subordinate mental phenomena to definite laws (which enable predictions) is by assuming the existence of an outside world based on causal laws, in which our bodies with their mental and motor organs and other more or less similar psychophysical substances exist as parts [of a whole]. Admittedly, in place of this great hypothesis, which includes an assumption of the validity of causal laws, two others appear to be possible at first glance: that of a single primal power (Berkeley), and that of an unconscious 'productive power of imagination' [*produktive Einbildungskraft*] within us (Fickte). But if one tries to develop these theories seriously, they both blend into the outside world. For, in order to derive explanations and assumptions, we must ascribe to the assumed agency as many parts as are needed—as elementary matter—for the other theory, and must establish the same laws between these parts.

For the naive, unscientific consciousness, the belief in an outside world is of course no hypothesis and no product of reflection, but rather is tied instinctively to sensory phenomena. But *that* external world is poles apart from the scientific universe.

Brentano, again, already recognized the enormous significance of mathematical probability—which differs from 'philosophical' probability only by degree—for the formation of all hypotheses. But since it is often claimed that the application of the concept of probability itself already involves presuppositions about the outside world and causal laws, I devoted a special study to this question and believe I have showed that this is not the case.[59] The so-called a posteriori probability too—as it emerges from the law of large numbers—involves no such precondition, and it is superficial to look for a physical mechanism that forces events to fit this law. The principle of objective 'ranges' [*Spielräume*] as Johannes von Kries puts it, would lead in my view to the same conception if only it were understood more widely (not simply in terms of spatial or temporal play space, but also for the logical kind, i.e. disjunctions).

---

[59] Stumpf, 'Über den Begriff der mathematischen Wahrscheinlichkeit', *Sitzungsberichte der Philosophisch-Philologischen und Historischen Classe der Königlich Bayerischen Akademie der wissenschaften* 20 (1892): 37–120.

The calculation of probability is therefore purely a priori, derived from the mere concept of probability. In logic it has not at all been recognized as such. This is indispensable for the construction of a clear theory of induction. At the same time, however, it demonstrates the total impossibility of popular empiricism, for according to this view, each inductive conclusion rests not on facts alone but also on an a priori foundation. Hence we could agree with Kant, not only in holding on to the concept of absolute necessity, but also in that nature is a creation of reason, even if not in the same sense and according to the same principles of the *Critique of Pure Reason*. Laws based on experience, however, are not confined to causal laws. We must also differentiate empirical structural laws from laws based on matter [*Substanzgesetze*]. In both cases there are abbreviated methods in which particular major premises are assumed to be sufficiently well established. In the former case we presuppose the general law of causality, in the latter such regularities as have been determined particularly in chemistry regarding the coexistence of certain properties.

The following should also be mentioned regarding my position on some of the principles of logic. I had always maintained Brentano's sharp distinction between judgement and mere conception, but later on I did not accept the changing of all judgements or statements into existential judgements and the consequent revolution in the theory of conclusions, principally because I—like Alexius Meinong—could not interpret general affirmative judgements as negations.

The concept of a 'set of facts' [*Sachverhalte*], which has played an increasing role in recent times (Otto Selz, Oswald Külpe, *et al.*), was introduced by Brentano who was fully aware of its import. I have merely replaced his expression 'content of judgement' [*Urteilsinhalt*] with the term used today, indeed I first used it in my lecture on logic at Halle in 1888.

I always devoted some special paragraphs about logic to the importance of fictions[60] for scientific research, but never treated it as more than a kind of framework that must be discarded after use.

---

60 Stumpf's plural 'Fiktionen' implies counterfactual scenarios rather than a sense of the literary imagination.

I discussed the old question of the most appropriate classification of the sciences in an article, not because of the equally valid question of form, but because of the objective investigations into epistemology that are bound up with it.[61] I was particularly concerned to re-establish the importance of the old distinction between the natural sciences and the humanities, which rests on the differences in subject matter. I was happy to see Erich Becher siding with me in his comprehensive book.[62]

5.2.3. On natural philosophy

The amazing development of physics and chemistry, which provide the most general foundations of our natural sciences, has pursued just the path described above. Sensory phenomena were and are their starting point, but their actual subject matter increasingly became the objective world. They approach it using hypotheses, which draw even the objective nature of space and time into their sphere in the most daring ways. That these cannot really be as they appear to us is revealed by even the most obvious analysis. I would define space as that existing in the real world which enables geometric relationships of mass; time, I would define as that which enables changes, and relationships of mass between such changes. Indeed, changes themselves cannot be defined without time; both concepts are simply correlative. The concept of objective time contains nothing of the past, present, and future. This is quite remarkable and allows us to treat time as the fourth dimension of space in mathematical physics, which, incidentally, I regard as a purely arithmetical operation in which the distinctiveness of time is expressed with respect to the three other dimensions.

That the transition from a mechanical to an electromechanical conception of nature lies in the framework just outlined needs no further elaboration. The hypothesis of an outside world has in no way been restricted in its explanatory means. Every assumption is physically

[61] Stumpf, 'Zur Einteilung der Wissenschaften', in *Abhandlungen der Königlich-Preußischen Akademie der Wissenschaften. Philosophish-historische Classe* (Berlin: Verlag der Königliche Akademie der Wissenschaften, 1906), 1–94.

[62] Erich Becher, *Geisteswissenschaften und Naturwissenschaften. Untersuchungen zur Theorie und Einteilung der Realwissenschaften* (Munich: Duncker & Humblot, 1921).

viable, if it is free from contradiction and permits quantitative predictions by means of which it can be tested. The graphic conception of spatial movement had first to be attempted, but holds no particularly privileged position.

But the transition from an effect at a distance to that at close range [*Fern- zur Nahewirkung*] was epistemologically unavoidable. I did not know how else physical causality could be expressed, except as: 'if between two contiguous substances there are definite combinations of conditions, then a change occurs in both whereby the new conditions on each side are connected with the former ones on the other side; every change then depends on the occurrence of such combination of conditions.' (This formula can be applied, with slight elaboration, to psychophysical interaction.) That is to say that every action is interactive, but also that there is no direct interaction of everything with everything, rather only that contiguous substances can effect each other. Atoms or electrons, without which modern physics and chemistry are unthinkable, could also not affect each other through empty space, but only through the mediation of an ether, which I regard as an imperative demand of atomic theory.

The introduction of the concept of gestalt into physics, as Wolfgang Köhler stipulates in his ingenious book on physical forms [*Gestalten*],[63] appears to encounter certain difficulties from this point of view, for the law of interaction always requires physicists to pursue effects from particle to particle, while the psychologist in describing facts of consciousness wants to emphasize the priority of the whole over the parts.

The difference between living organisms and non-living entities seems to me to lie in the enormously complicated structure of even the simplest living beings or germs. Physicochemical forces working under complex mechanical conditions, if thoroughly studied, probably suffice to allow an understanding of the processes of nutrition and reproduction (except for certain mental triggers). Under no circumstances can the natural sciences admit the existence of forces that work one way at one moment, then in another way the next, even counter to themselves,

---

[63] Wolfgang Köhler, *Die physischen Gestalten in Ruhe und im stationaren Zustand: eine naturphilosophische Untersuchung* (Braunschweig: Friedrich Vieweg & Sohn, 1920).

as was the case with the old 'life force', Karl von Hartmann's 'unconsciousness', and August Pauly's psycho-vitalist factors. Terms such as entelechy or dominants can be of no help either. Then again, it seems not out of the question to me, indeed very plausible, that the well-known conscious mental conditions of desire and pain, of emotions and acts of will, function as triggers for neural processes. Even Hermann Lotze, the sharpest adversary of the old theory of life force, certainly did not think to deny such psycho-vitalism in this empirically controllable form. And in evolutionary theory, for example, Erich Becher's very noteworthy 'principle of utilization' [Ausnutzungsprinzip] could rest on some such foundations.

But for philosophers, the problem of vitalism recedes when set against that more general problem of teleology. The innumerable intricately arranged particles exhibited by even a single-celled organism (we must also take its environment into account, for organisms without specific, inorganic surroundings are inconceivable) bring about consistent life-sustaining processes. The problem, as Ferdinando Galiani correctly noted, is one of mathematical probability. Every such complex of particles is an exceptional case among numerous other possible ateleological, senseless arrangements of the same elementary particles, all equally conceivable in themselves. It is a priori highly improbable, therefore, and even though it is empirically given, it calls for a hypothesis to dispel the improbability. Evolutionary theory solves many riddles, but not this one. If the present formations [Gebilde] have proceeded in continuous lawful causality from particular initial conditions, then these initial conditions, however simple, are again singular cases of the same degree, since each of the ateleological arrangements conceivable today corresponds to a different initial condition, out of which it must by necessity have proceeded by virtue of the same natural forces. The problem of purposiveness is therefore only pushed back by the theory of evolution. And this is also true if the world process has gone on for all eternity, because the mathematical ratio of the singular cases to the others remains the same. Some kind of ordering principle is therefore logically necessary. If we label this as all-pervasive reason in the world, we are already using an expression belonging to a specific domain, even though it is the loftiest known to us. If we realize the inadequacy of the concept and the impenetrable mystery of this primordial entity [*Urwesen*], this final question is fully in line with general scientific thinking.

5.2.4. On psychology and philosophy of mind

The separation of the natural sciences from sciences of the mind is rooted in the fundamental difference between sensory phenomena and the mental functions or, respectively, the content of outer (sensory) and inner (psychological) perception. Phenomena and functions are given to us in closest connection, but they are essentially different. Observation of the functions is the foundation of the sciences of mind, but they stick to their point of origin as little as do the natural sciences. Just as the latter proceed to the material outer world, the former seek to understand the workings of mental forces in general, alongside their resultant actions and products, by our inner world, observable to us alone. Psychology occupies a similar position in the sciences of the mind, as physics does in the natural sciences.

The investigation into sensory phenomena as such, which takes up so much room today, is not truly psychology, but simply phenomenology, a sort of pre-science driven collectively by physicists, physiologists, and psychologists. Psychologists in particular have accepted it because they found in it a field scrutable by exact experiment, within which they can pursue the laws governing the mental functions involved. Thus preparatory work in phenomenology captivated me too for a long time; but understanding the functions always remained my goal.

5.2.4.1. On phenomenology

It seems to me a greatly exaggerated claim to say that there are no pure sensations [*Empfindungen*] (phenomena). We cannot observe musical notes without observing them, but this need not necessarily alter them. After all we know of attention, this clarifies its opposite, benefiting our understanding thereof. And so I see no reason for the fruitless scepticism of this beloved objection, just as I cannot concur with talk of the 'relativity' of sensation. Nevertheless I set out in *Psychology of Tone* not from sensation, but from 'sensory judgement' and determined the conditions of reliability in advance because even sensations are only given to us as the contents of apperception, which can be false or unreliable. Experimental psychophysics thus becomes a quantitative science of judgement [*messende Urteilslehre*]. Within sensory judgements I distinguished between direct and indirect, and opposed the obsession everywhere to draw on indirect criteria, on mere accessory impressions [*Nebeneindrücke*]. Furthermore, I distinguished between judgements about sensation and about sensory distances. I also advanced the thesis—which I still maintain—that relations between sensations can be perceived directly in and by themselves. One cannot hear the relation of two notes, admittedly, but one can notice it, and to notice is to perceive.

One of the main questions of phenomenology seemed to me that of the attributes (fundamental characteristics) of sensations. Even in my book on space, the concept of 'psychological parts' [*psychologische Teile*] forms the centre of its line of argument, i.e. the concept of dependent or partial contents, which according to their nature cannot be represented separately, but present independent means of change in the unified sensation.[64] Husserl had further developed the conceptual side of these observations. I drew on this particularly in my text on the attributes of visual sensation, but dropped the term 'psychological part' as inappropriate.[65] In this essay I was anxious to save for visual sensations the attribute of intensity, which is mostly denied to them at present. Quality, brightness, intensity, and extensity appear to be inherent in all sensations, if to very different extents.

In another main question, already pondered by Aristotle, i.e. the unity or plurality of simultaneous and coincident impressions on the same sense, I decided for plurality in the case of tone, for unity in the case of colour; I rejected forced analogies and have insisted on the essential differences of these two senses in respect of their intrinsic laws.

In the realm of tones, we must determine first of all the properties of simple tones, i.e. those produced by sine waves, for these cannot in

---

[64] Stumpf, *Über den psychologischen Ursprung der Raumvorstellung* (Leipzig: Hirzel, 1873).

[65] Stumpf, 'Die Attribute der Gesichtsempfindungen', *Abhandlungen der Königlich-Preußischen Akademie der Wissenschaften, Philosophisch-historische Klasse* 8 (1917): 1–88.

any way be dissected subjectively into a plurality, neither by exercise nor by attention, and thus offer the best promise of constant results. To produce these tones accurately I implemented the cancellation of overtones by interference tubes, demonstrating in this way that a sounding body resonates only with a note of approximately the same pitch, not with a division thereof, as physicists after Charles Wheatstone often taught, and Wilhelm Wundt had wanted to demonstrate in a particular experiment. This apparatus provided a convenient aid for analysing sounds, and it showed that sound sources we had considered simple were still fairly complex. In consequence, Rudolph König's noted series of observations on electromagnetically driven tuning forks and on the wave siren, for example, directed against Helmholtz, lost their edge.

My views on the basic properties of simple tones have changed since *Psychology of Tone* in as much as I now accept the 'musical quality' recurring between octaves as an equally original element in individual development; the 'pitch', by contrast, simply runs parallel with the frequency. I discussed this property at length in *Psychology of Tone*, and believed at the time I could deduce it empirically from the fusion [*Verschmelzung*] of octave pitches, but I have of course always acknowledged it as a fact.

The differences of fusion, which are now generally accepted within psychology, are also an old inheritance. There were already known in part to Greek theorists. I discovered them unwittingly on the piano during my Prague days, and later proved them objectively with statistics relating to unmusical individuals' judgements about unity. The differences that occurred in the number of judgements about unity have been confirmed on every occasion since.

Because of the importance that these differences appear to have for a theory of consonance, I am also interested in cases where they do not occur, namely in the highest registers and in the shortest sonic impressions [*Toneindrücken*]. Hence the studies on the determination of frequencies of very high pitches through their difference tones. This method demonstrated that Anton Appunn's series of tuning forks— then in general use—was designated by quite fantastically high pitches. The shortest sonic impressions showed that, rather than the musical interval, only the distances were being judged.[66] Catherina von Maltzew later obtained similar results for high, supra-musical registers.

I defined the fundamental phenomenon of music, consonance, in terms of fusion and believe at least to have proved the inadequacy of other definitions, including Helmholtz's, as well as the inaccuracy of Hugo Riemann's and Arthur von Öttingen's dualistic theories of consonance. Yet I distinguished consonance from concordance, which is not a purely sensory property of tones, rather it rests on the introduction of consonant triads as the building blocks of our music system. The rational motive for composing with triads lay, I saw, in the search for the largest number of mutually consonant tones within the octave. This yields the separation of chords into concords and discords, and the foundation of the whole of classical harmony.

My views on defining consonance by fusion have changed in the intervening period. I think that we must acknowledge primary relations even in successive notes as such, which can only be explained physiologically, not psychologically. But the fusion and consonance of simultaneous tones strikes me now as a consequence, not a cause, of the relation. The differences of fusion nevertheless maintain their great significance for musical hearing and for the emotional effect of intervals.

'Gauging the Purity of Consonant Intervals' was a study of musical hearing, performed partly on myself, partly on others.[67] The experiments determined certain deviations from physically pure tuning that point neither to tempered nor to Pythagorean tuning, but rather to strongly aesthetic motives, and are most clearly marked in outstandingly musical people. The most conspicuous case was the constant raising of the ascending octave in most simple tones by members of the Hochschule für Musik in Berlin, most of all by Joseph Joachim. In double-stopping on the violin the simultaneous pitches would of course have this pure intonation.

---

[66] Stumpf, 'Über das Erkennen von Intervallen und Akkorden bei sehr kurzer Dauer', *Beiträge zur Akustik und Musikwissenschaft* 4 (1909): 1-39.

[67] Stumpf and M. Meyer, 'Maßbestimmungen über die Reinheit der konsonanter Intervalle', in *Beiträge zur Akustik und Musikwissenschaft* 2 (1898): 84–167.

The article on subjective tones and double hearing combines observations of myself in this field with those entropic phenomena in other fields that have been neglected so far.[68] How subjective tones are to be included in a theory of hearing remains something of a mystery; precisely because of this an accurate description of the circumstances of their occurrence seemed desirable, and I simply had too much opportunity to collect material for it. The rare phenomenon of double hearing came to me as a kind of compensation after an operation in which my left tympanum was pierced.

In the 'tone tables' the formulae for calculating intervals may claim more than immediate interest, since we can also use them to calculate and predict appropriate results, quite apart from the specific ratios, a matter that even has some relevance for metaphysics.[69]

The main features of the purely physical essay on composite wave forms originate from my time in Würzburg when I still doubted the analysis Helmholtz put forward by means of the cochlea, and therefore the properties of compound frequencies appeared important as such.[70] But it is precisely the fact that the natural classes of these forms of vibrations never actually occurred in the sound phenomena themselves that provides further evidence for Helmholtz's supposition. Many questions raised here, such as that of the definition of periods in such wave forms, have also occupied physicists in the meantime.

In my study of combination tones it was up to me to describe as fully as possible the phenomena and laws of this most difficult topic, over which only very experienced observers and fellow observers—not random experimental subjects—were in a position to adjudicate.[71]

[68] Stumpf, 'Beobachtungen über subjective Töne und über Doppelthören', *Beiträge zur Akustik und Musikwissenschaft* 3 (1901): 30–51.

[69] Stumpf and Karl L. Schaefer, 'Tontabellen', *Beiträge zur Akustik und Musikwissenschaft* 3 (1901): 139–146

[70] Stumpf, 'Über zusammengesetzte Wellenformen', *Beiträge zur Akustik und Musikwissenschaft* 4 (1909): 62–89.

[71] Stumpf, 'Differenztöne und Konsonanz', *Zeitschrift für Psychologie und Physiologie der Sinnesorgane* 39 (1905): 269-283; 'Differenztöne und Konsonanz', *Zeitschrift für Psychologie und Physiologie der Sinnesorgane* 59 (1911): 161-175.

The derivation of these tones from the properties of membranous parts of the organ of hearing is now the task of physiology.

Many of my observations had to do with beats (intermediate tones, etc.). That we can potentially silence them by distributing two tuning forks, one to each ear, while the dissonance persists, was the first distinct argument against Helmholtz's theory of consonance for me, around 1875. I have often found the phenomenon of dichotomous hearing (separated ears) instructive, as a rule.

Contrary to the common theory on the non-spatial property of tone sensations, I claimed [spatial localization through] local signs [*Lokalzeichen*] for both ears and differences of volume for low and high tones.[72] That it was possible to locate up to ten notes played strictly simultaneously in random arrangements to both ears over a few minutes without any movement of the head (Baley), is only explicable by such immanent local signs.[73] Recently von Hornbostel and Wertheimer have famously given further, quite surprising, explanations of the spatial behaviour of hearing; the former has now expanded his investigation to the acoustic perception of distance.

The subject of my final experimental work was the analysis of vowels, of speech sounds generally, and the synthesis of vowels based thereon, in which expanded interference tests played an essential role. For the syntheses I established three conditions from the outset: a large number of entirely simple tones; a delicate and constant regulation of the volume of each tone; and validation of the verisimilitude of the vowels produced unwittingly in tests. Several articles have reported

---

[72] Stumpf, 'Zum Begriff der Lokalzeichen', *Zeitschrift für Psychologie und Physiologie der Sinnesorgane* 4 (1909): 70–73.

[73] We recall from Stumpf's earlier discussion of Lotze's *Lokalzeichen* that these perform the task of spatial localization in consciousness whereby non-spatial representations are accompanied by 'a qualitative property of some kind which the impression acquires . . . in virtue of the peculiar nature of that place at which it comes into contact with the body.' Our consciousness, Lotze continues, accepts this accompanying qualitative information, in that 'they act as marks or as local signs, under whose guidance it [consciousness] proceeds in spreading out the impressions into an image occupying space.' See R. H. Lotze, *Microcosmus: An Essay Concerning Man and His Relations to the World* [1856-58, 1858-64], trans. E. Hamilton and E. E. C. Jones (Edinburgh: T. & T. Clark, 1885), 4th ed. (1899), 1: 309.

the preliminary results, and a book summarizing all of them is almost finished.[74] For general phenomenology views that deal with so-called 'complex qualities' [*Komplexqualitäten*] come into consideration, and result from all these observations. This work proved that the hotly debated foundation of Helmholtz's vowel theory was correct. For the majority of consonants, the pitch could be determined and analysed up to a certain point. Eventually, the same methods of analysis and synthesis could be applied to musical instruments. The results relating to speech sounds are recorded in textbooks on physiology, but have also been applied practically—and thereby confirmed— by otologists, as well as by telephone and radio technicians.

The laws governing the relation of sensations to external stimuli, namely the law of specific energies and Fechner's law, also play a part in my work. For me, the conceptual difficulties of Fechner's law seem solvable by its interpretation of sensory *distances* (a view reached independently by Joseph Delboeuf, Ewald Hering, Hermann Ebbinghaus, and myself), and by the fact that, regarding pitch, a striking confirmation of it, or analogy with it, was found in the musical scales of Asia (Siam, Java) with their equal intervals that rest not on tonal relations but on judgements of distance. Of course, this formulation does not aim at an explanation, but rather just at a psychologically correct wording of the law. I also regard the physiological derivation—now the aim everywhere—as correct, at least with regard to intensities.

I also count space among the attributes of phenomena. This view, from which it follows that a colour is just as unlikely without an extension as an extension is without any form of quality, that even the first visual sensations must somehow therefore appear spatial (nativism), has almost entirely permeated the empiricism among psychologists that has dominated since Lotze's time. Muscular sensations that we identify with spatial conception (which we had at least considered as indispensable preconditions for the latter) must be content with a humble role. Only the third dimension—which is obviously poorly provided

---

[74] Stumpf, *Die Sprachlaute; experimentell-phonetische Untersuchungen nebst einem Anhang über Instrumentalklänge* (Berlin: J. Springer, 1926).

for in our (visual) perception—still has to fight. I would no longer approve of the three syllogisms in my book on spatial conception in the form given there; they are actually only supposed to be descriptions of that which we discover in our conception of space, i.e. as necessary deep properties [*Tiefeneigenschaften*].[75] Several other things in this part of the book are out of date. But I should certainly point out that I never considered spatial sensations as direct and dependent on stimuli alone, rather I emphasized the contribution of central factors, as in the case of visual size.

For a conception of time I adhered to Brentano's original formulation, which is based on continued existence with subjective backwards displacement [*Zurückschiebung*] of all mental contents during a short, objective span of time. These continuing contents appear to me to be of a non-eidetic type [*unschaulicher Art*], which is particularly important for the much-debated question of comparing successive data.

Another question in phenomenology is ultimately that of the differences between mere conception [*Vorstellung*] and sensation. The result of my extensive investigations was that mere eidetic conceptions [*anschauliche Vorstellungen*] are phenomena of the second order, which differ from those of the first order principally by their weaker vividness and intensity, as well as by some other additional features.

In so far as causes for association [i.e. eidetic conceptions] exist, the laws of their emergence (reproduction) fall under the formula of 'contiguity' or 'complementation', besides which no special law of similarity is necessary. The question is whether the reproduction ever happens purely mechanically or whether instead it requires functional activities. Moreover, there is a purely physiological reproduction without associative causes, which is hardly a surprise considering the principal similarity of sensations and conceptions. During dreams this [purely physiological] type probably predominates.

---

[75] Stumpf, *Über den psychologischen Ursprung der Raumvorstellung* (Leipzig: Hirzel, 1873).

5.2.4.2. On psychology in the narrower sense

Elementary mental functions or states are characterized by definite fundamental properties: (1) by the quite idiosyncratic relation between action and content (whereby the content may consist of sensory phenomena, but also of non-eidetic elements or of functions themselves); (2) by the lack of spatial properties in self-observation (although they undoubtedly take place in objective space); (3) by specific laws of structure. They possess among them multiple qualitative differences, and it is quite hopeless to refer them back to a single fundamental function, as sensualism and voluntarism do. Above all, intellectual and emotional functions are distinct categories, and within each of these categories there is a hierarchy of function types such that each step subsumes the preceding one: within intellectual functions there is perception (differentiation), aggregation, formulation of concepts, judgement; within emotional functions there are the passive and active emotions. These depend as a whole on intellectual functions, to which they are added, however, as new, not derivative, states [*Zustände*]. All of these relations present a picture of multiple structures, whose properties have barely been described. Among Brentano's merits is not least the fact that he recognized this task clearly and carried it out to a considerable extent. Among his students, Marty, Meinong, and Husserl in particularly made efforts in the same direction. Before Brentano, Lotze placed emphasis on the structural peculiarity of the functions of consciousness, especially 'correlative thinking' [*beziehendes Denken*]. Following Brentano, though surely not at his prompting, Dilthey emphatically entered the field of structural psychology. But his interests and achievements were more orientated towards a sophisticated, sympathetic understanding of mental connections in general, in mental history in individuals and groups, than in the analysis of mental elementary structures—'microscopic psychology', as Brentano occasionally dubbed it.

My paper on the concept of emotion is directed above all against William James and James Lange's sensualistic definition of this, while my studies of the 'sensations of feeling' [*Gefühlsempfindungen*], by contrast, treat sensory feelings as true sense impressions (phenomena).[76] I was forced to defend the latter thesis against misunderstandings. It is not really as subversive as it seemed to some. For, aside from the fact that it simply renews an older theory advocated by English psychologists, I did not deny the close instinctive correlation of this class of sensation with actions of pleasure and displeasure, desire and disgust, but had especially emphasized them, and therefore chose the term 'sensations of feelings' [*Gefühlsempfindungen*]. The occasional claim that expressions such as pain or pleasure (obtained by physical causes) denote nothing more than sensory data went too far. On the contrary, their significance [i.e. of sensations of feelings] in normal life encompasses those instinctive emotions.

A dividing line runs through the whole of man's inner life, separating higher functions from lower ones within each domain. It arises through the appearance of general concepts. Despite the many attempts to reconcile these with individual conceptions, the results do not stand up to critical scrutiny. Of course, it is one thing to describe their capacities to abbreviate thought processes, etc., and another to describe their essence, just as the physiology and anatomy of the lungs are two separate things. Among emotional functions, emotion and the process of volition presuppose certain concepts, just as logical thinking does among intellectual functions. Volition is a desire for something that is somehow deemed valuable as a result of my momentary state of mind. Both concepts, that of causality and that of value, are acquired in their most general and most primitive form by our inner perception of the lower cravings which are prior to volition. Thus, the will cannot be something original, rather just an evolutionary product of individual life.

The animal kingdom appears to show us what mental life can achieve without conceptual thinking, and it is a good deal. But no a priori prejudice would deter me from conceding the beginnings of higher functions if the facts permitted it. Even in that case, however, the first

---

[76] Stumpf, 'Über den Begriff der Gemüthsbewegung', *Zeitschrift für Psychologie und Physiologie der Sinnesorgane* 21 (1899): 47-99; and 'Über Gefühlsempfindungen', in F. Schumann (ed.), *Bericht über den II. Kongreß für experimentelle Psychologie in Würzburg vom 18-21. April 1906* (Leipzig, Barth, 1906), 209–213.

inklings of conceptual thinking would have to have been utilized as something specifically new. Although the physical evolution of the 'new brain' may always proceed smoothly, the mental side cannot manage without some discontinuity. But then nature does occasionally make a leap, probably even in the physical domain (quanta, heterogeneity, mutations), certainly in the psychophysical, where each entry of a new sensory quality undoubtedly constitutes a leap. And does the most miraculous leap not happen every time that mental life arises from the physical processes of procreation and fetal development? The discontinuities are only hidden and moderated, as it were, by the fact that the new sensory qualities always first occur in such tiny beginnings; qualitatively, however, they nevertheless weave a new thread into the fabric. This does no harm to the intrinsically law-governed evolution of the world.

Among the principal questions in general psychology, that of the unconscious is still among the most pressing. Unconscious functions in the strict sense seem never to have been proven by arguments produced so far. Then again, there are of course unconscious dispositions such as all mental activities leave behind. I regard unconscious, real, unnoticed component parts of phenomena as possible and also real. They form the lower boundary of the degrees at which something is observable; often the smallest reinforcement of attention is enough to make them noticeable. As soon as we distinguish between functions and phenomena, no problems of principle remain in this theory whatsoever.

If we admit the existence of unnoticed component parts, then it is not hard to define the nature of our view of gestalt, on which certain of my younger scientific colleagues seem to want to base the whole of psychology, indeed even logic, in order to be able to study its laws.

I draw a distinction between mental functions and the mental formations [Gebilde] that constitute their specific contents. Thus: from summarizing, I distinguish the quintessence; from judging, the set of facts [Sachverhalt]; from conceptual thinking, the conceptual content; from feeling and desire, passive and active value. Of course, these elements have no independent reality like Platonic ideas, but I would not, like Oskar Kraus (who cites the later Brentano), describe them as fictions—an expression that strikes me as risky and given to misunderstanding, for it suggests a sceptical, subjectivist, or relativist interpretation. Formations [*Gebilde*] are the starting point and subject matter of the science I described as eidology [*Eidologie*].

By soul, I understand a unity of mental functions and dispositions, and I concur with Lotze that it seems unnecessary to look behind this unity for something synoptic or sustaining. Since a strong will pulls everything into its sphere, and since those functions and dispositions that are connected to the will, especially to the moral will, play the most decisive role in the life of adults, the will is rightly regarded as the nucleus of personality; I see in this the truth of voluntarism.[77] The will is not the root, but indeed the crown of evolution.

If we wanted to distinguish soul and mind, I should use the latter term for the whole of our higher inner life. The preliminary stages found throughout the animal kingdom attest [humanity's] social phenomena in language, art, formation of communities, etc., which are based on the cooperation of individuals, and form the subject matter of the concrete sciences of the mind [*Geisteswissenschaften*]; but here again the transition is certainly never constant, and in the final analysis the new is rooted in conceptual thinking. In *The Origins of Music* I sought to establish this fact more concretely for this art. The possibility of inwardly reliving something, on which this 'comprehending psychology' [*verstehende Psychologie*] is based, arises only with respect to specifically human development. But the cultural historian will first insist on certain laws, though admittedly these may not have the precise form of natural laws, and I do not want to deny some plausibility even to Hegel's three-stroke [dialectical] rhythm along these lines.

5.2.5. On ethics

I developed my thoughts in this context almost entirely through lectures, and outlined the most fundamental aspects while talking about ethical scepticism. Like Brentano, I see an analogy between the way the intrinsic goodness or value of certain contents is based on apodeictic

---

[77] A school of thought within metaphysics that places the will above both intellect and emotion. The term *Voluntarismus* was used by such German academics as Wilhelm Wundt and Friedrich Paulsen.

feeling [*Gefühlsevidenz*], and the foundation of theoretical knowledge is based on apodeictic judgements [*evidente Urteile*]. The empiricist deduction of altruism from egoism is well and truly wide of the mark. Our fundamental principles [*Grundlegung*] differ from hedonism, even from altruistic hedonism, in that we recognize other values besides desire as primary, and they differ from Kant's ethics in that we repudiate purely formal conditions. Truth, positive emotions (such as aesthetic ones), goodness (attitudes aiming at true worth) are immediately valuable. We can certainly establish a unified, learned formula for these, but only at the expense of certainty, and therefore it is pointless. A string of derivative, but still very general values like power, freedom, honour, etc., make up the 'table of goods' [*Gütertafel*], which is not all that different from the Platonic table. Only such an ethic of goods or values seems to me both capable of being developed in detail and in a position to do justice to the actual transformations of ethical evaluation by changing the coefficients by which abstract (absolute) values must be multiplied under different circumstances and life conditions, in order to obtain concrete (relative) values. This is essentially what must already happen in every individual case of a moral decision. The modification of abstract values in individual cases depends on perspectives that are established, and from which our ethical reflection follows. The highest good or happiness (the ancient's *eudaimonia*) is the totality of intrinsic values *in abstracto*; *in concreto* it is the totality of goods possible under given life conditions for individuals, and for mankind generally, including extrinsic goods. The concept of the transcendental ideal (the Platonic idea of the Good) can of course only be obtained by empirically given true values through a process of augmentation. The question of egoism–altruism is solved by the fact that what is truly good is worth attaining in and of itself, so that in each individual case it is not the perspective of ego and maturity [*Alter*], but only that of the greatest possible intensive and extensive realization that should be decisive. Ethical action is purely objective action, just as scientific cognition is purely objective judgement.

In the question of free will, the interests of ethics—for which the problem exists exclusively—seem to me compatible with a determinism that regards ethical awareness [*Erkenntnis*] itself as a power that can be developed by nurturing and self-nurturing. Freedom becomes indivisible from the possession of ethical awareness [*Erkenntnis*], and is therefore not given once and for all, but originates and grows with the whole ethical personality. Penal law recognizes free will only in this sense.

5.2.6. On metaphysics

Metaphysics can only be fruitfully expanded from the ground up, as a continuation of the sciences whose results it is intended to generalize still further. Aside from that which enters its domain from the sciences discussed above, it is concerned above all with the relation between the physical and the mental, and the ultimate questions about God and immortality, which anyone who calls himself a philosopher must seek to answer in his own way, and should not be detained from the lifelong consideration thereof, even by a critical philosophy that has become dogmatic. In comparison with the parallelistic view of body and soul prevailing over the psychologists and physiologists in the last third of the preceding century (and put forward spiritedly and impressively by Fechner), I struck a blow for the old theory of interaction, which is based purely on reason; recently this has gained some ground again, even among Wundt's and Erdmann's students. Objections derived from the law of energy are easily solvable, while experiments by Max Rubner and Lyman Atwater can readily be inserted into the theory of interaction. On the other hand, parallelism is conceptually unclear; it is not viable in view of the different structures of the physical and the mental, and consequently when elaborated it forces us to accept mental causal series extending forwards and backwards, for which there is not a shred of empirical evidence. I can only regard panpsychism, to which parallelism leads, as science fiction [*eine wissenschaftliche Phantasie*], with a dubious appeal to boot. For nature only becomes poetic if we breathe *human* spirit into it. Otherwise, both standpoints have edged closer to one another, partly as a result of refinements to the concepts of substance and causality, but also under compulsion of the facts. And I dare to hope for a unification of both in a 'monism of interaction and evolution' in the not-too-distant future. The metaphysician may also consider Spinoza's idea that innumerable other ways of expressing the basis of the world exist or are developing beyond the two domains known to us. But admittedly it ends here with the mere spiritual order postulated for the organic world.

The conformity between properties in the elementary particles of matter, and the interaction between all spatially contiguous or interpenetrating parts of the world (like nerve centres and cerebral elements) cannot be accepted as the final facts of our world, if the above research maxims—among them the laws of probability—are to be valid. A unifying principle of the world must account for everything, and from the outset our inclination is to identify it with the principle of a spiritual order postulated for the organic world. The debate between theism and pantheism loses its edge as soon as one asks what causality, substantiality, personality mean anyway, and what they may still mean *here*. There remains an eternal contingency of all individuals on the fundamental essence, and nothing further can be discovered about this kind of contingency and this fundamental essence. Even the concept of spirituality can only be understood in a 'transcendent' sense.

And so the hardest question of all, that of the origin and meaning of evil, remains unanswerable. Whether we, like theists, retreat to the inscrutable will of God as a final bulwark, or side more with pantheists in emphasizing the essential connection between the Holy Spirit and the laws of nature, or conceive of evil, indeed even of wickedness, as part of God's own nature, the evolution of the world as a development inherent in the absolute—all of this is much of a muchness. Many might even find the greatest comfort in the notion that God suffers and struggles in and with us. Certainly the struggle with problems of theodicy led many to pantheism, especially in its more pronounced mystical forms. But in these things, as in ethics, all too learned formulae serve no purpose, except that of concealing our ignorance. Even a pantheist may, in his darkest hour, place his life and fate in God's hands, and at times of greatest happiness thank the creator that this world full of suffering also contains such wonderful things, and that a heart is given to him to grasp them. But it still always comes down to degrees of anthropomorphism, and can only be talked about allegorically. If even applied science apprehends the laws of the outside world with the aid of symbols, why should we want to do without symbols? They are far from mere fiction. It is only necessary to remember their status in case the name of God be misused, and the anthropomorphism be taken too far.

The consciousness that is applied to eternity by our life has never left me. Although spiritual life emanates from material life, and during our existence must constantly be stimulated and nurtured by sensory impressions, it still seems not to be dependent on them. A continuation of our higher inner life—proportionate to the degree to which its nucleus, the moral personality, has developed—remains conceivable, though the form of this existence is indeed entirely unimaginable. Surely it was not petty, egoistic motives that inspired men like Lessing, Kant, and Goethe, no less than Lotze, Fechner, and Brentano to such ideas, but respect and reverence for what is infinite in us and the meaninglessness of a world where the single true value only emerges in order to disappear again, and finally to vanish once and for all.

I surely do not need to say that spiritualistic and occult inclinations have always remained foreign to me. It is a matter of taste whether one wants forever to be taken behind the light, and whether the guitar playing of mediums, their wisdom about the beyond, and their other emanations seem worthwhile for this purpose.

5.2.7. On aesthetics and musicology

Reflections on the effect of art, especially of music, formed the beginning of my scientific thought. I have often treated aesthetic problems in courses and lectures, but only one of these lectures has been published: 'Our Appetite for Tragic Drama'.[78] It seemed to me one could make progress with this old question, not by exclusively promoting some explanatory principle or other, but by calling on the cooperation of all mental qualities, from the mere need for sensation up to the highest moral and metaphysical ideas. A second fundamental idea was that true enjoyment of art does not rest on instinctively being carried away, but first develops alongside an objectively synoptic conception, in which the totality of actions and characters presents itself vividly to us.

---

[78] Stumpf, 'Die Lust am Trauerspiel', *Philosophische Reden und Vorträge* (Leipzig: J. A. Barth, 1910), 1–64.

Empathy is merely a way-station. Even ethical effects are artistic when conveyed by such observation of ethical dispositions. Only within this context can even the downfall of a hero gain its artistic effect. Finally, I emphasized the difference between momentary effect and after-effect, which led to a lengthy explanation.

Similar approaches seem valid for all other arts. It was not granted to me to develop this systematically for music, where the condition of an aesthetic subject matter caused particular difficulties, and gathers together all the central questions of aesthetics. I would distinguish three main factors in musical effect here, which can have very different relations according to each individual: pure sensual euphony [*Wohlklang*] (including the sensory effect of rhythm); pleasure in the construction and technical execution; lastly, enjoyment in the content of a composition. In this third, and most controversial point, my thoughts align most closely with those of Lotze.

But I was mostly occupied with transferring these controversies, which were debated *ad nauseam* within accepted music aesthetics, into the larger discourse of *music psychology*, and subsequently to fit this into a general *systematic musicology*. Musicology, according to its professional practitioners, often just means music history, even today. And yet, for music in particular, the conditions for an objective, causal understanding are extraordinarily favourable. Physics, physiology, psychology, ethnology, general aesthetics, and philosophy can collaborate here with music history. My efforts to promote such collaboration proved popular, but have also met with resistance. In the philosophy faculty at Berlin University, the necessity of such connections has been acknowledged since the time of Helmholtz and Spitta, where tests in systematic domains (acoustics, psychology of tone, music aesthetics) form an indispensable part of the musicological examination for promotion to full professor.

Within systematic musicology, my essay 'Music Psychology in England' and my book *The Origins of Music* belong alongside my experiments on physical and psychological acoustics.[79] In the essay, a

---

[79] One will also find matters concerning music aesthetics in several of my later articles, including in the popular article on the Berlin *Volkskonzerte* as well as in some reviews.

preliminary study for the later volumes of *Psychology of Tone*, I discussed the relation of music to language, and that of human speech to animal utterances [*Animalmusik*] with reference to Herbert Spencer and Charles Darwin; mostly, however, I dealt with the exaggerated nativism of Edmund Gurney (in *The Power of Sound*), who essentially ignored genetic explanations in favour of the erotic feelings of animal ancestors.[80] The path had to be cleared for explanations that hark back to the lasting effects of experiences of individuals, and to the musical thought accompanying such experiences. Gurney, a connoisseur of music incidentally, answered me in print;[81] but I did not want to continue the methodological disputes that Lotze quite rightly compared to sabre-rattling. Later, particularly within Oswald Külpe's group (though also in England and America), the effects of single tonal steps were studied among numerous test subjects, and their statements diligently recorded. But this, I think, leaves us stuck with formalities and happenstances, which have little significance for the essence of real musical feeling. And, above all, we forget that isolated intervals gain their principal effect not from themselves, but from earlier connections, and that only someone equally talented musically and psychologically—who could give rapt attention to the whole musical structure as well as his own experience—can give information on the significance of such building blocks that have been singled out. Even he would not be able to put the deepest thoughts concerning the whole or the details into words, however, and that is just as well.

I have already reported on the development of my studies in musical ethnology or comparative musicology in the earlier part of this chapter. All that had been presented in histories of music hitherto as examples of exotic music had been collected by explorers, and hence was based for the most part on largely unreliable first impressions of melodies, which were then harmonized with a bias for modern European harmony.

[SN]. See 'Musikpsychologie in England', *Vierteljahrsschrift für Musikwissenschaft* 1 (1885): 261–349.

80 Edmund Gurney, *The Power of Sound* (London: Smith, Elder, 1880).

81 Edmund Gurney, *Tertium Quid: Chapters on Various Disputed Questions* (London: K. Paul, Trench, & Co., 1887).

Yet after Alexander Ellis had numerically determined the tuning of scales in exotic instruments, and J. Walter Fewkes used the phonograph to record the songs, the way was open for an exact [*exakte*] comparative musicology. This was then most effectively developed within our Berlin circle, particularly by von Hornbostel. We now know—without appreciating the masterpieces of our age any the less, or advocating progress by a return to primitive forms—that the supposedly universal 'language of feelings' does not merely exhibit enormous changes in the course of time, but simultaneously exhibits equally significant differences throughout the globe. The impressive development of harmonic music led many, even Hugo Riemann, to the prejudgement that all music must emerge from triads, and hidden harmony must underlie even entirely monophonic music, as though neutral thirds and other deviant intervals could only be detunings of the actual intended pure intervals [*Schritte*]. These prejudgements have now been set aside; only occasionally is a false friend of ancient Greek music induced to harmonize in an untoward style. We know a great many forms of music, among them *heterophony*—particularly widespread in Asia—for which I suggested this term after a passage in Plato's laws, which most likely refers to the same musical form. We know that the inestimable expressive capabilities of our harmony are shackled by rhythmic limitations, and that not only the ancient Greeks but also many primitive peoples are superior to us with regard to rhythm. I do not need to emphasize just how much will be achieved, even for the study of art in general, by such broadening of the horizon.

The little book *The Origins of Music*, which emerged from a public lecture, derives the origin of music from signalling practices and the phenomena of tonal fusion [*Tonverschmelzung*], and outlines the general views I had reached through comparative studies with the use of numerous well-authenticated examples, particularly those recorded on the phonograph; I also sought to give an overview of the most important fundamental forms of music-making that have emerged over the course of time.

Two of my musicological studies are purely historical in nature, yet even these are closely connected to music theory: that on the concept of consonance in antiquity, and that on pseudo-Aristotelian problems of music.[82] The latter had always fascinated me over the years, since they present a kind of antique psychology of tone, which is extraordinarily valuable for a deeper understanding of the music of antiquity and for the conceptions of music. How much light does even one sentence—'consonant simultaneous pitches have no ethos'—throw on the whole of ancient music consciousness! I was led to the conclusion, however, that the text as a whole could not have been written by Aristotle or even during his historical period, but belonged for the most part to the first and second centuries AD (at the earliest). I believe I have produced the most persuasive arguments for this that are possible in such matters. Among the few philologists who had studied the text more closely, Charles-Émile Ruelle declared the matter settled (*tranché*), while Adolf Reinach, whose violent intrusion in the text I had disapproved of, attacked my study in such an angry and scathing manner that I could not bring myself to respond. Many passages are only comprehensible here to someone familiar with the subject, such as acoustics, studies in tone, and music psychology, as with meteorological problems, among others. This is particularly the case with problems concerning the peculiarity of the octave, fusion, and antiphony. My interpretation and correction of the text in paragraph 14, which previously had been entirely opaque but is quite comprehensible in light of the facts of fusion, found immediate approval from Hermann Usener and Christian von Jans, later even from Hugo Riemann. Otherwise a short notice appeared in the *Literarischen Zentralblatt* informing me that very few would appreciate the great trouble I had gone to in these two studies. The author counted himself among the few, remarking regretfully, 'Graeca sunt, non leguntur.'[83] This experience discouraged me from continuing with

---

[82] Stumpf, 'Die pseudo-aristotelischen Probleme über Musik', *Abhandlungen der Preussischen Akademie der Wissenschaften: philosophisch-historische Klasse* 3 (1896): 1–85; and 'Geschichte des Consonanzbegriffs. Erster Teil. Die Definition der Consonanz in Altertum', *Abhandlungen der Königlich bayerischen Akademie der Wissenschaften, philosophisch-historische Klasse* 21 (1897): 1–78.

[83] 'They are Greek, and are not read.'

the history of the concept of consonance from the Middle Ages up to recent times. Riemann later gave a sort of continuation.[84]

These are the rough outlines of my scientific views and aspirations, which I was destined to carry out only in part. I would wish to see even those parts I did manage improved upon today, and am well aware of their shortcomings. The *Table for the History of Philosophy* was about the only work of mine to go through a 'revised and extended' edition, and many purchasers probably mistook it for a textbook.[85] Thus there was no opportunity for me to correct every error. Yet I am quite sure that at least the observations and experiments on which I lavished the greatest care will stand the test of time, and this work will not need to be repeated. The general ideas, as enlightening and valuable as they seemed subjectively to me, may succumb to the probing, sifting test of time. Whatever truth they contain will prevail by virtue of its own validity. I have never tried to establish a school in the narrow sense, and found it more agreeable—more interesting at any rate—for students to reach different results than for them simply to corroborate my theorems. I am filled with all the more joy and gratitude by the devotion of young minds, who with the same fundamental scientific convictions, but by their own independent proposals, carry on the work of research.

---

[84] Hugo Riemann, *Geschichte der Musiktheorie im IX.-XIX. Jahnhundert* (Leipzig: M. Hesse, 1898).

[85] Stumpf's *Tafeln zur Geschichte der Philosophie* went through four editions in total: 1896; 1900; 1910; 1928. The first three instantiations were released through the Berlin publisher Speyer & Peters; the fourth edition through J. Springer, also of Berlin.

Carl Stumpf's publications

Prepared by Uwe Wolfradt and
David Trippett

1. Philosophy

2. Psychology

3. Musicology

4. Biographical sketches

5. Collaborative writings

1. Philosophy (epistemology, philosophy of music, mathematics)

1869 *Verhältnis des Platonischen Gottes zur Idee des Guten* (Halle: Pfeffer).

1878 'Aus der Vierten Dimension', *Philosophische Monatshefte* 14: 13–30.

1885 'Sur la Représentation des Mélodies', *Revue Philosophique de la France et de l'Étranger* 20: 617–618.

1886 'Über die Vorstellung von Melodien', *Zeitschrift für Philosophie und Philosophische Kritik. Neue Folge* 89: 45–47.

1891 'Psychologie und Erkenntnistheorie', *Abhandlungen der Philosophisch-Philologischen Classe der Königlich Bayerischen Akademie der Wissenschaften* 19: 465–516.

1892a 'Über den Begriff der Mathematischen Wahrscheinlichkeit', *Sitzungsberichte der Philosophisch-Philologischen und Historischen Classe der Königlich Bayerischen Akademie der Wissenschaften* 20: 37–120.

1892b 'Über die Anwendung des Mathematischen Wahrscheinlichkeitsbegriffes auf Teile Eines Continuums', *Sitzungsberichte der Philosophisch-Philologischen und Historischen Classe der Königlich Bayerischen Akademie der Wissenschaften* 20: 681–691.

1895 'Hermann von Helmholtz und die Neuere Psychologie', *Archiv für Geschichte der Philosophie. Neue Folge* 8: 303–314.

1896 *Tafeln zur Geschichte der Philosophie* (Berlin: Speyer & Peters).

1897a 'Die pseudo-Aristotelischen Probleme über Musik', *Abhandlungen der Königlichen Akademie der Wissenschaften zu Berlin, Philosophisch-historische Abhandlungen* (Berlin: Reimer), 1–85.

1897b 'Geschichte des Consonanzbegriffs. Erster Teil. Die Definition der Consonanz im Altertum', *Abhandlungen der Königlich Bayerischen Akademie der Wissenschaften*, 1. Classe 21, 1. (Abteilung, München: Franz), 1–78.

1899a 'Bemerkung zur Wahrscheinlichkeitslehre', *Jahrbücher für Nationalökonomie und Statistik* 3: 671–672.

1899b *Der Entwicklungsgedanke in der Gegenwärtigen Philosophie: Festrede, Gehalten am Stiftungstage der Kaiser-Wilhelms-Akademie für das Militärärztliche Bildungswesen, 2 Dezember 1899* (Berlin: Lange).

1901 'Geschichte des Consonanzbegriffes', *Abhandlungen der Philosophisch-Philologischen Classe der Königlich Bayerischen Akademie der Wissenschaften* 21: 1–78.

1903 *Leib und Seele. Der Entwicklungsgedanke in der Gegenwärtigen Philosophie: Zwei Reden* (Leipzig: Barth).

1906a 'Erscheinungen und Psychische Funktionen', *Abhandlungen der Königlich Preußischen Akademie der Wissenschaften zu Berlin. Philosophisch-historische Abhandlungen* 4: 3–40.

1906b 'Zur Einteilung der Wissenschaften', *Abhandlungen der Preußischen Akademie der Wissenschaften zu Berlin, Philosophisch-Historische Abhandlungen* 5: 1–94.

1907a *Die Wiedergeburt der Philosophie* (Berlin: Francke).

1907b 'Zur Einteilung der Wissenschaften', *Abhandlungen der Königlich Preußischen Akademie der Wissenschaften zu Berlin. Philosophisch-Historische Abhandlungen* (Berlin: Königliche Akademie der Wissenschaften & Riemer).

1908 'Vom ethischen Skeptizismus', *Internationale Wochenschrift für Wissenschaft, Kunst und Technik* 2: 993–1008.

1910 'Die Lust am Trauerspiel', *Philosophische Reden und Vorträge* (Leipzig: Barth), 1–64.

1919 'Spinozastudien', *Abhandlungen der Preußischen Akademie der Wissenschaften. Philosophisch-Historische Abhandlungen* 4: 1–57.

1921 'Zahl und Maß im Geistigen', *Vossische Zeitung Berlin. Berlinische Zeitung von Staats- und Gelehrten Sachen, Abendausgabe* (27 May): 245.

1938 'Studien zur Wahrscheinlichkeitsrechnung', *Abhandlungen der Preußischen Akademie der Wissenschaften. Physikalisch-Mathematische Klasse* 2: 1–59.

1939 *Erkenntnislehre*. Volume 1 (Leipzig: Barth). Rpt Lengerich: Pabst Science Publishers, 2011.

1940 *Erkenntnislehre*. Volume 2 (Leipzig: Barth). Rpt Lengerich: Pabst Science Publishers, 2011.

2008 *Die Grundsätze der Mathematik* (Würzburg: Königshausen & Neumann). (This is the first edition of a work that was not published during Stumpf's lifetime. The editor was Wolfgang Ewen.)

2. Psychology (theoretical psychology, studies in the psychology of music and tone as well as the psychology of emotions)

1873 *Über den Psychologischen Ursprung der Raumvorstellung* (Leipzig: Hirzel).

1874 'Die Empirische Psychologie der Gegenwart', *Im Neuen Reich* 4: 201–226.

1883 *Tonpsychologie.* Volume 1 (Leipzig: Hirzel).

1890a *Tonpsychologie.* Volume 2 (Leipzig: Hirzel).

1890b 'Tonpsychologie, 2. Band (Selbstanzeige),' *Zeitschrift für Psychologie und Physiologie der Sinnesorgane* 1: 345–351.

1890c 'Über Vergleichungen von Tondistanzen', *Zeitschrift für Psychologie und Physiologie der Sinnesorgane* 1: 419–462.

1891a 'Mein Schlusswort Gegen Wundt,' *Zeitschrift für Psychologie und Physiologie der Sinnesorgane* 2: 438–443.

1891b 'Wundts Antikritik', *Zeitschrift für Psychologie und Physiologie der Sinnesorgane*, 2: 266–293.

1893 'Zum Begriff der Lokalzeichen', *Zeitschrift für Psychologie und Physiologie der Sinnesorgane* 4: 70–73.

1894 'Bemerkungen über Zwei Akustische Apparate', *Zeitschrift für Psychologie und Physiologie der Sinnesorgane* 6: 33–43.

1897 'Das Wunderkind Otto Pöhler', *Vossische Zeitung* (10 January).

1898a 'Die Unmusikalischen und die Tonverschmelzung', *Zeitschrift für Psychologie und Physiologie der Sinnesorgane* 17: 422–435.

1898b 'Erwiderung', *Zeitschrift für Psychologie und Physiologie der Sinnesorgane* 18: 294–302.

1899a 'Beobachtungen über Subjektive Töne und über Doppelhören', *Zeitschrift für Psychologie und Physiologie der Sinnesorgane* 21: 100–121.

1899b 'Ueber den Begriff der Gemüthsbewegung', *Zeitschrift für Psychologie und Physiologie der Sinnesorgane* 21: 47–99.

1900 'Zur Methodik der Kinderpsychologie' (lecture given on 19 January 1900 at the first meeting of the Berlin Society for Child Psychology), *Zeitschrift für Pädagogische Psychologie und Pathologie* 2: 1–21.

1901 'Eigenartige Sprachliche Entwickelung eines Kindes', *Zeitschrift für Pädagogische Psychologie und Pathologie* 3: 419–447.

1902 'Über das Erkennen von Intervallen und Akkorden bei sehr Kurzer Dauer', *Zeitschrift für Psychologie und Physiologie der Sinnesorgane* 27: 148–186.

1904 'Das Pferd des Herrn von Osten', *Der Tag* (3 September).

1905a 'Differenztöne und Konsonanz', *Zeitschrift für Psychologie und Physiologie der Sinnesorgane* 39: 269–283.

1905b 'Über zusammengesetzte Wellenformen', *Zeitschrift für Psychologie und Physiologie der Sinnesorgane* 39: 241–268.

1907a 'Der Rechenunterricht des Herrn v. Osten' (175–180) in O. Pfungst, *Das Pferd des Herrn von Osten. Der Kluge Hans* (Leipzig: Barth).

1907b 'Einleitung' (7–15) in O. Pfungst, *Das Pferd des Herrn von Osten. Der Kluge Hans* (Leipzig: Barth).

1907c 'Richtungen und Gegensätze in der Heutigen Psychologie', *Internationale Wochenschrift für Wissenschaft, Kunst und Technik* 1: 903–913.

1907d 'Über Gefühlsempfindungen', *Zeitschrift für Psychologie und Physiologie der Sinnesorgane* 44: 1–49.

1907e 'Über Gefühlsempfindungen' in F. Schumann (ed.), *Bericht über den II. Kongreß für Experimentelle Psychologie in Würzburg vom 18–21 April 1906* (Leipzig: Barth), 209–213.

1910 'Das Psychologische Institut' in M. Lenz (ed.), *Geschichte der Königlichen Friedrich-Wilhelms-Universität zu Berlin.* 3 (Halle: Waisenhaus), 202–207.

1911a 'Differenztöne und Konsonanz. Zweiter Artikel', *Zeitschrift für Psychologie und Physiologie der Sinnesorgane* 59: 161–175.

1911b 'Konsonanz und Konkordanz. Nebst Bemerkungen über Psychologie und Wohlgefälligkeit Musikalischer Zusammenklänge', *Zeitschrift für Psychologie und Physiologie der Sinnesorgane* 58: 321–355.

1914a 'Über Neuere Untersuchungen zur Tonlehre' (305–348) in F. Schumann (ed.), *Bericht über den VI. Kongreß für Experimentelle Psychologie in Göttingen 1914* (Leipzig: Barth).

1914b 'Ziele und Wege der Neueren Psychologie' (23–32) in W. Krötzsch (ed.), *Das Kind und die Schule, Ausdruck, Entwicklung und Bildung* (Leipzig: Dürr).

1915 'Bemerkungen und Selbstbeobachtungen' (appendix to S. Baley 'Versuch über die Lokalisation beim Dichotischen Hören'), *Zeitschrift für Psychologie und Physiologie der Sinnesorgane* 70: 366–372.

1916a 'Apologie der Gefühlsempfindungen', *Zeitschrift für Psychologie und ` Physiologie der Sinnesorgane* 75: 1–38.

1916b 'Binaurale Tonmischung, Mehrheitsschwelle und Mitteltonbildung', *Zeitschrift für Psychologie und Physiologie der Sinnesorgane* 75: 330–350.

1916c 'Verlust der Gefühlsempfindungen im Tongebiete (Musikalische Anhedonie)', *Zeitschrift für Psychologie und Physiologie der Sinnesorgane* 75: 39–53.

1917 'Die Attribute der Gesichtsempfindungen', *Abhandlungen der Königlich Preußischen Akademie der Wissenschaften. Philosophisch-Historische Klasse* 8: 1–88.

1918a 'Die Struktur der Vokale', *Sitzungsberichte der Königlich Preußischen Akademie der Wissenschaften zu Berlin* 17: 333–358.

1918b 'Empfindung und Vorstellung', *Abhandlungen der Preußischen Akademie der Wissenschaften. Philosophisch-Historische Klasse* 1: 3–116.

1918c 'Über den Entwicklungsgang der Neueren Psychologie und ihre Militärtechnische Verwendung', *Deutsche Militärärztliche Zeitschrift* 47: 273–282.

1921 'Sinnespsychologie und Musikwissenschaft. Helmholtz' Grundlegungen. Helmholtz zum 100. Geburtstag' in *Erinnerungsblatt der Vossischen Zeitung. Berlinische Zeitung von Staats - und Gelehrten Sachen* 404 (28 August).

1924 'Singen und Sprechen', *Zeitschrift für Psychologie und Physiologie der Sinnesorgane* 94: 1–37.

1928 *Gefühl und Gefühlsempfindung* (Leipzig: Barth).

3. Musicology (studies in comparative musicology and acoustics)

1885 'Musikpsychologie in England. Betrachtungen über die Herleitung der Musik aus der Sprache und dem Thierischen Entwickelungsproceß, über Empirismus und Nativismus in der Musiktheorie', *Vierteljahresschrift für Musikwissenschaft* 1: 261–349.

1886a 'Alexander J. Ellis. On the musical scales of various nations. Reprinted with additions and corrections from the *Journal of the Society of Arts* for 27 March 1885, No. 1688, Vol. 33. For private circulation only. April 1885; Appendix, reprinted with additions of the J. of the Soc. of Arts, October 1885', *Vierteljahresschrift für Musikwissenschaft* 2: 511–524.

1886b 'Lieder der Bellakula-Indianer', *Vierteljahresschrift für Musikwissenschaft* 2: 405–426.

1887 'Mongolische Gesänge', *Vierteljahresschrift für Musikwissenschaft* 3: 297–304.

1892 'Phonographierte Indianermelodien', *Vierteljahresschrift für Musikwissenschaft* 8: 127–144.

1896 'Ueber die Ermittelung von Obertönen', *Annalen der Physik und Chemie, Neue Folge* 57: 660–681.

1898a 'Konsonanz und Dissonanz', *Beiträge zur Akustik und Musikwissenschaft* 1: 1–108.

1898b 'Neues über Tonverschmelzung', *Beiträge zur Akustik und Musikwissenschaft* 2: 1–24.

1898c 'Zum Einfluss der Klangfarbe auf die Analyse von Zusammenklängen', *Beiträge zur Akustik und Musikwissenschaft* 2: 168–170.

1899 'Über Bestimmung hoher Schwingungszahlen durch Differenztöne', *Annalen der Physik und Chemie. Neue Folge* 68: 105–116.

1900 'Die Berliner Aufführungen Klassischer Musikwerke für den Arbeiterstand', *Preußische Jahrbücher* 100: 247–265.

1901a 'Beobachtungen über Subjektive Töne und über Doppelhören', *Beiträge zur Akustik und Musikwissenschaft* 3: 30–51.

1901b 'Tonsystem und Musik der Siamesen', *Beiträge zur Akustik und Musikwissenschaft* 3: 69–138.

1903 'Grammophon und Photophonograph. Eine Betrachtung zur Angewandten Logik', *Der Tag* (1 March).

1904 'Die Demonstration in der Aula der Berliner Universität am 6. Februar 1903', *Zeitschrift der Internationalen Musikgesellschaft* 5: 431–443.

1908 'Das Berliner Phonogrammarchiv', *Internationale Wochenschrift für Wissenschaft, Kunst und Technik*. Supplement to the *Münchner Allgemeine Zeitung* (22 February): 225–246.

1909a 'Akustische Versuche mit Pepito Arriola', *Beiträge zur Akustik und Musikwissenschaft* 4: 105–115.

1909b 'Beobachtungen über Kombinationstöne', *Beiträge zur Akustik und Musikwissenschaft* 5: 1–142.

1909c 'Die Anfänge der Musik', *Internationale Wochenschrift für Wissenschaft, Kunst und Technik* 3: 1593–1616.

1910 'Konsonanz und Konkordanz' in *Festschrift zum 90. Geburtstage Rochus Freiherrn von Liliencron* (Leipzig: Breitkopf & Härtel), 329–349.

1911 *Die Anfänge der Musik* (Leipzig: Barth).

1919 'Zur Analyse geflüsterter Vokale', *Beiträge zur Anatomie, Physiologie, Pathologie und Therapie des Ohres, der Nase und des Halses* 12: 234–254.

1921a 'Über die Tonlage der Konsonanten und die für das Sprachverständnis Entscheidende Gegend des Tonreiches', *Sitzungsberichte der Preußischen Akademie der Wissenschaften* 1: 636–640.

1921b 'Veränderungen des Sprachverständnisses bei Abwärts Fortschreitender Vernichtung der Gehörsempfindungen', *Beiträge zur Anatomie, Physiologie, Pathologie und Therapie des Ohres, der Nase und des Halses* 17: 182–190.

1921c 'Zur Analyse der Konsonanten', *Beiträge zur Anatomie, Physiologie, Pathologie und Therapie des Ohres, der Nase und des Halses* 17: 151–181.

1925 'Phonetik und Ohrenheilkunde', *Beiträge zur Anatomie, Physiologie, Pathologie und Therapie des Ohres, der Nase und des Halses* 22: 1–8.

1926 *Die Sprachlaute. Experimentell-Phonetische Untersuchungen Nebst Einem Anhang über Instrumentalklänge* (Berlin: Springer).

1926 'Sprachlaute und Instrumentalklänge', *Zeitschrift für Physik* 38: 745–758.

1927 'Die Sprachlaute', *Forschungen und Fortschritte* 3:106–107.

4. Biographical sketches and speeches

1895 'Antrittsrede [und] Erwiderung von Mommsen', *Sitzungsberichte der Königlich Preußischen Akademie der Wissenschaften zu Berlin., II. Halbband* 33: 735–739.

1897 'Eröffnungsrede des Präsidenten, Prof. Dr. Carl Stumpf (Berlin)' in *Dritter internationaler Congreß für Psychologie in München vom 4. 7 August 1896* (München: Lehmann), 3–16.

1901 'Bericht C. Stumpfs über Lotzes Briefe an ihn, Dritter Anhang der Biographie' in R. Falckenberg (ed.), *Hermann Lotze, Erster Teil: Das Leben und die Entstehung der Schriften nach den Briefen* (Stuttgart: Fromanns), 193–194.

1917 'Zum Gedächtnis Lotzes (geb. 21.Mai 1817)', *Kantstudien* 22: 1–26.

1918 'Trompete und Flöte' in *Festschrift Hermann Kretzschmar zum 70. Geburtstag* (Leipzig: Peters), 155–157.

1919 'Erinnerungen an Franz Brentano' in O. Kraus (ed.), *Franz Brentano. Zur Kenntnis Seines Lebens und Seiner Lehre* (München: Beck), 85–149.

1920 'Franz Brentano, Philosoph', *Deutsches Biographisches Jahrbuch* 2: 54–61.

1921 'Gedächtnisrede auf Benno Erdmann', *Sitzungsberichte der Preußischen Akademie der Wissenschaften* 1: 497–508.

1922 'Brentano, Franz, Professor der Philosophie (1838–1917)' in A. Chroust (ed.), *Lebensläufe aus Franken. Veröffentlichungen der Gesellschaft für Fränkische Geschichte*, 7th Series. *Lebensläufe aus Franken* 2 (München: Kabitzsch & Mönnich), 67–85.

1924 'Carl Stumpf' in R. Schmidt (ed.), *Die Philosophie der Gegenwart in Selbstdarstellungen*, 7 vols. (Leipzig: Meiner), 5: 204–265.

1928 *William James nach Seinen Briefen: Leben, Charakter, Lehre* (Berlin: Pan).

5. Collaborative writings

1897 Stumpf and Max Meyer, 'Schwingungszahlbestimmungen bei sehr Hohen Tönen', *Annalen der Physik und Chemie. Neue Folge* 61: 760–779.

1898 Stumpf and Max Meyer, 'Maßbestimmungen über die Reinheit consonanter Intervalle', *Zeitschrift für Psychologie und Physiologie der Sinnesorgane* 18: 321–404.

1901 Stumpf and Max Meyer, 'Tontabellen', *Beiträge zur Akustik und Musikwissenschaft* 3: 139–146.

1910 Stumpf and Erich von Hornbostel, 'Über die Bedeutung Ethnologischer Untersuchungen für die Psychologie und Ästhetik der Tonkunst' in F. Schumann (ed.), *Bericht über den IV. Kongreß für experimentelle Psychologie in Innsbruck 1910* (Leipzig: Barth), 256–269.

1921 Stumpf and Gustav Johannes von Allesch, 'Über den Einfluss der Röhrenweite auf die Auslösung hoher Töne durch Interferenzröhren', *Beiträge zur Anatomie, Physiologie, Pathologie und Therapie des Ohres, der Nase und des Halses* 17: 143–150.

1928 Stumpf and Paul Menzer, *Tafeln zur Geschichte der Philosophie: Graphische Darstellung der Lebenszeiten seit Thales und Übersicht der Literatur seit 1440.* 4th ed. (Berlin: Speyers & Peters).

Index

Footnotes are indicated by *fn*